Building Windows 8 Apps
with C# and XAML

Building Windows 8 Apps with C# and XAML

Jeremy Likness

Addison-Wesley

Upper Saddle River, NJ • Boston • Indianapolis • San Francisco
New York • Toronto • Montreal • London • Munich • Paris • Madrid
Capetown • Sydney • Tokyo • Singapore • Mexico City

The publisher offers excellent discounts on this book when ordered in quantity for bulk purchases or special sales, which may include electronic versions and/or custom covers and content particular to your business, training goals, marketing focus, and branding interests. For more information, please contact:

U.S. Corporate and Government Sales
(800) 382-3419
corpsales@pearsontechgroup.com

For sales outside the United States, please contact:

International Sales
international@pearsoned.com

Visit us on the Web: informit.com/aw

Library of Congress Cataloging-in-Publication Data is on file and available upon request.

ISBN-13: 978-0-321-82216-1
ISBN-10: 0-321-82216-1

Text printed in the United States on recycled paper at RR Donnelley and Sons, Crawfordsville, Indiana.

First printing, October 2012

To Ma: Your support and encouragement
have always been a blessing to me.
I will miss not being able to share
that I finished this book with you.

Contents at a Glance

Contents

Foreword

THE LIFE OF THE SOFTWARE DEVELOPER ISN'T AN EASY ONE. Every ten years or so, he has to throw away everything he knows and start all over again. Times change, and technologies change even faster. A decade ago, developers had to retool their skill sets for the move from Win32 to .NET and C#. Today, there's a new platform in town. It's called Windows 8, and with it comes a profound shift in the way Windows apps are conceived and executed.

Windows 8 is like no Windows the world has seen before. The new Windows programming model favors simplicity, security, and battery efficiency above all else. Modern Windows apps run full-screen, single-instance, and one at a time. Their UIs can be built in XAML, HTML, or DirectX. They run in a sandbox that stops malicious code in its tracks, and they're inspected before they're published in the Windows Store to make sure they don't violate the sandbox. They prefer touch screens but play equally well with mice and other input devices. Moreover, they install with a single click and uninstall without leaving a trace.

Underneath the new user interface is a new API: The Windows Runtime API, better known as WinRT. WinRT represents a rethinking of what the Windows API would look like if it were redesigned from the ground up. The old Windows API is outdated, overly complex, and tied to a specific language. The WinRT API, by contrast, is thoroughly modern and can be called from a variety of languages. Indeed, one of the most remarkable aspects of Windows 8 is that for the first time in history, a developer versed in HTML and JavaScript enjoys the same ability to write Windows apps as developers who speak XAML and C#.

What it means for the developer is—you guessed it—time to start over again. WinRT *is* the Windows API now, and the new UI layer, formerly known as "Metro," is the new face of Windows apps. Be bold or be left behind.

Becoming a Windows 8 developer means learning WinRT. It means getting comfortable with asynchronous programming. It means understanding that a Windows app that isn't visible to the user is suspended and that an app that's suspended can be unceremoniously terminated by the operating system at any time. It means learning about contracts, which allow apps to integrate with the charms that slide out from the right side of the screen. It means learning about live tiles, push notifications, and other features that make an app a first-class citizen in the Windows 8 environment. It means understanding the Windows 8 design philosophy and how to use XAML to craft compelling, fluid, and responsive Windows UIs.

When you're in the wilderness, it helps to have a guide who has been there before. I can't think of anyone more qualified to lead you on the journey to Windows 8 enlightenment than Jeremy Likness. Jeremy is the only person I know who works 32 hours a day. (He sleeps the other four.) I used to say that I might work with people a lot smarter than me, but none of them can work more hours than me. I've had to reconsider that with Jeremy. Shoot him an e-mail at 3:00 a.m., and you'll have a reply by 3:02. That's why he's a Principal Consultant at Wintellect and why we turn to him to architect and implement Windows 8 solutions for our customers. A teacher can be only so effective if he isn't out there working in the trenches. Jeremy builds real apps for real customers. That's why I can heartily recommend this book and why I'm excited to see how it's received by the community.

Windows 8 is a bold move on Microsoft's part—perhaps the boldest move the company has made since the introduction of Windows itself. But it's the right move at the right time. The action in software development for the next ten years won't revolve around traditional PCs. It'll be in writing apps for tablets, phones, and other mobile devices. Companies will be built and millionaires will be made from apps for devices with portable form factors, including Microsoft's new Surface tablet. To ignore WinRT is to ignore the part of the Microsoft stack that lets you write for these devices.

Learn WinRT. Go out and write some great apps. Help make this platform a success. And keep this book handy. When you run into problems, it's the next best thing to an instant response to a 3:00 a.m. e-mail. From Jeremy's perspective, it's even better.

—*Jeff Prosise*, Co-Founder, Wintellect

Preface

THE FIRST WHISPERS ABOUT WINDOWS 8 SURFACED IN EARLY 2011. Widespread speculation swept the Internet as developers began to question what the new platform would look like. The rumors included a new platform that wouldn't support the .NET Framework, was based solely on C++ or HTML5 and JavaScript, and wouldn't run any existing software. Early builds and screenshots leaked over Twitter but this only fueled speculation. Finally Steven Sinofsky, President of the Windows Division at Microsoft, took the stage on September 13, 2011 and released an early build of Windows 8 to the world.

I was one of the first eager programmers to download the early build, and I installed it in a virtual machine. It didn't take long for me to realize that the .NET Framework was alive and well, I could run my existing Silverlight applications on the new platform, and C# and XAML were tools available to build the new "Metro-style" applications (this name was changed to Windows Store applications with the RTM version of Windows). I didn't make it to the //BUILD conference hosted in California to release Windows 8, but the sessions were made available almost immediately after they were presented, and I watched them every evening, morning, or while I was traveling by plane.

The Windows 8 platform features the Windows Runtime, a new framework for building applications that provides capabilities never before available on a Windows machine. I was building applications within days and was delighted to find that my existing C# and XAML skills from Silverlight and Windows Presentation Foundation (WPF) applied to the runtime, while a new set of components made it easier than ever to developer rich, touch-based applications. It wasn't long before I reached out to the publisher of my book, *Designing Silverlight Business Applications*, and said, "I want to write my next book on Windows 8."

I was fortunate to get involved in an early adoption program with Microsoft. The consulting and training firm I work for, Wintellect, was hired to provide some hands-on labs and workshops specifically targeted to new developers who want to learn how to build applications for Windows 8. This gave me critical access to early builds of the product and enabled me to start writing about the various features that would ultimately become part of the final release. As I built samples that covered manipulating objects on screen with touch, sharing rich content between applications, and providing live interactive tiles on the start menu with at-a-glance content, my excitement quickly grew.

As part of writing this book, I wrote an article that shares what I believe are the top 10 reasons developers will love building Windows 8 applications. You can read the full article online at:

http://www.informit.com/articles/article.aspx?p=1853667

In summary, these are the reasons I think you will enjoy the new platform:

- **Programming language support**—It is possible to write Windows 8 applications with VB, C#, C++, and XAML, or a special stack that includes HTML5 and JavaScript.

- **XAML**—Developers familiar with the power and flexibility of XAML who have written Silverlight and/or WPF applications in the past will be very comfortable with the XAML used to develop Windows 8 applications.

- **HTML5**—The rich support for HTML5 as a markup option will appeal to web developers crossing over to tablet and touch-based development, although this book will deal primarily with the C# and XAML option.

- **Windows Runtime (WinRT)**—The Windows Runtime provides a number of controls, components, classes, and method calls that make performing complex tasks both consistent and easy using just a few lines of code.

- **Contracts**—The new system of "Contracts" enables a new level of sharing and integration between applications and the end user.

- **Asynchronous support**—The introduction of the `await` and `async` keywords makes programming multi-threaded code more straight-forward than it has even been.

- **Touch**—Touch-based input is first-class in Windows 8 applications with out-of-the-box support from all of the available controls and a straightforward API to interface with touch events and manipulations.

- **Settings**—The settings experience (provided via a Contract) provides a very consistent and familiar way for developers to allow end users to configure their application preferences.

- **Roaming profiles**—Building code that synchronizes across Windows 8 machines through the cloud is simple and easy. (You can literally share a data file with a single line of code.)

- **Icons**—Windows 8 features a rich set of pre-existing icons that you can use to provide consistent interfaces for commands within your applications.

To avoid confusion, I refer to the special new programs built specifically for Windows 8 as "Windows 8 applications" throughout this book. The templates to create these new applications in Visual Studio 2012 are grouped under the name "Windows Store." Although these applications can be distributed through the Windows Store, you can also distribute traditional desktop-style applications through the store. Therefore, I will only use "Windows Store" when I refer to the Visual Studio 2012 templates, or when I compare the newer style of application to the traditional desktop style. Everywhere else, you will see them referred to as "Windows 8 applications."

The top 10 items just scratch the surface of the new platform. Windows 8 is definitely different than previous releases of Windows and does require change. You will need to adopt a new interface that elevates touch to a first-class citizen but always provides ways to navigate using the mouse and keyboard. You will have to get used to code that calls native unmanaged components in a way that is almost transparent, and deal with a new set of controls and components that previously did not exist. This book is intended to guide you through the process of learning the new territory quickly so you can begin building amazing new applications using skills you already have with C# and XAML.

What This Book Is About

The purpose of this book is to explain how to write Windows 8 applications using the C# programming language, Extensible Application Markup Language (XAML), the Windows Runtime, and the .NET Framework. For this book, I assume you have some development experience. While I do cover basic topics related to C# and XAML, I try to focus on the areas specific to building Windows 8 applications. Where I introduce more advanced concepts specific to C# or XAML that are not specific to the Windows 8 platform, I reference other books, articles, or online resources so you can further explore those fundamentals.

Whether you're an existing Silverlight of WPF developer looking to migrate an existing application, or a developer who is transitioning the Windows 8 platform for the first time, this book will give you the guidance and resources to quickly learn what you need to go from a new project to a published application in the application store.

How to Use This Book

The goal of this book is to enable you to write Windows 8 applications with C# and XAML. Each chapter is designed to help you move from a fundamental understanding of the target platform to building your first application. Code examples are provided that demonstrate the features and best practices for programming them. Most chapters build on previous content to provide a continuous narrative that walks through all of the components that make up a typical Windows 8 application.

Each chapter is similarly structured. The chapters begin with an introduction to a topic and an inventory of the capabilities that topic provides. This is followed by code samples and walk-throughs to demonstrate the application of the topics. The code samples are explained in detail and the topic is summarized to highlight the specific information that is most important for you to consider.

I suggest you read the book from start to finish, regardless of your existing situation. You will find that your understanding grows as you read each chapter and concepts are introduced, reinforced, and tied together. After you've read the book in its entirety, you will then be able to keep it as a reference guide and refer to specific chapters any time you require clarification about a particular topic.

My Experience with the Microsoft Stack

My first computer program was written in BASIC on a TI-99/4A. From there I programmed assembly language for the Commodore 64, learned C and C++ on Unix-based systems, and later wrote supply chain management software on the midrange AS/400 computer (now known as iSeries). For the past 20 years, my primary focus has been developing scalable, highly concurrent web-based enterprise applications.

I started my work with Silverlight right before the 3.0 release. At the time, I led a team of 12 developers working on an ASP .NET mobile device management platform that relied heavily on AJAX to provide a desktop-like user experience. When it was evident that the team was spending more time learning various web technologies such as CSS and JavaScript and testing the application on multiple browsers and platforms than focusing on core business value, I began researching alternative solutions and determined that Silverlight was the key our team was looking for.

Since that transition, I worked on XAML applications in the enterprise along with large-scale web applications built with the ASP.NET MVC framework. In addition to the mobile device management software, I helped build the health monitoring system for the back-end data centers that provided video streams (live and on demand) during the 2010 Vancouver Winter Olympics. I worked on a major social media analytics project that used Silverlight to present data that was mined from social networks and analyzed to provide brand sentiment. I worked with a team that built a slate-based sales interface for field agents to close sales and integrate with their point of sale system. I was on the team that produced the Silverlight version of a major eBook reading platform designed for accessibility and customized to provide interactive experiences and audio for children.

All of this work has been with the company Wintellect, founded by well-known .NET luminaries Jeffrey Richter, Jeff Prosise, and John Robbins. All three have produced countless books about the Microsoft stack, .NET Framework, and Core Language Runtime (CLR). They have trained thousands of Microsoft employees (some teams at Microsoft are required to take their courses as a prerequisite to working on their projects) and contributed to the runtime itself by writing and designing portions of the framework. The company has provided me with unique access to industry leaders and architects and their best practices and solutions for creating successful enterprise applications.

I am certified in various XAML technologies, including Microsoft Silverlight developer (MCTS) and WPF Developer (MCP). I was recognized as a Microsoft Most Valuable Professional® (MVP) for Silverlight in July of 2010 and was re-awarded the title in 2011 and 2012. This was due mostly to my efforts to blog, tweet, and speak about XAML technologies at various user group meetings and conferences around the country. I have conducted hands-on labs and training for Windows 8, worked on its earliest builds, and continue to blog and write about the platform as it develops. It is my depth of experience working with XAML and understanding how to build server and web-based software that has provided me with valuable insights into how to build Windows 8 applications.

Acknowledgments

I've learned that a technical book like this is written by a team even though the author gets the credit. Joan Murray once again has helped drive this book to completion and provided incredible support and encouragement throughout the process. She works with an amazing team. Special thanks to development editor Ellie Bru for staying on top of every draft, figure, revision, edit, and feedback loop. Thanks to Lori Lyons and Christal White for keeping me consistent and correcting all of my bad grammar habits to help me present like a polished writer.

I have enormous gratitude to my co-workers at Wintellect for their support. Steve Porter and Todd Fine once again helped support my efforts to balance long evenings and early mornings writing with my daily activities. Jeffrey Richter and Jeff Prosise gave me plenty of insights and wisdom based on their years of writing incredible books before me. Jeffrey's code samples and Jeff's labs were priceless tools that helped me learn the new platform and evolve the scenarios I share in this book. John Garland was a companion on this journey of learning a new platform and technology, and served once again as a brilliant technical editor and helped me shape and organize the content.

Special thanks to Telerik for supporting me at many levels. I appreciate Jesse Liberty bringing me onto his podcast, Chris Sells for his assistance on the HTML and JavaScript side, and Michael Crump for not only supporting this book at multiple levels but also taking the time to provide valuable feedback as a technical editor.

Thanks to the Microsoft team who worked with me through multiple iterations of the Windows 8 platform, from Developer Preview to Consumer Preview, onto Release Preview and beyond. Thanks to Jaime Rodriguez, Tim Heuer, Joanna Mason, Jennifer Marsman, and Layla Driscoll for all of your knowledge and insights. David Kean, I appreciate you patiently explaining the portable class library at the MVP summit and all of your patience and support afterward. Daniel Plaisted, you've been a tremendous help along the way.

These acknowledgments wouldn't be complete without a nod to my fellow MVPs and online supporters who have actively promoted and supported this book. Special thanks to Davide Zordan, Shawn Wildermuth, Jeff Albrecht, Roberto Baccari, David J. Kelley, Zubair Ahmed, and Ginny Caughey. Thanks to the Linked In .NET Users Group (LIDNUG), and especially Peter Shawn and Brian H. Madsen for your support and for providing me with a platform to share my excitement about Windows 8. Thanks to Chris Woodruff and Keith Elder for helping me get "deep fried" on their show.

Thanks to everyone who shared my tweets or visited the Facebook page for this book. Thanks to all of the early readers who provided feedback through the rough cuts of this book, and thanks to *you*, kind reader, for being you!

Last but certainly not least, thanks once again to my superstar wife and incredible daughter for understanding why Dad had to lock himself in the office late at night and in the very early hours of the morning. I couldn't have done this without my girls!

About the Author

Jeremy Likness is a principal consultant at Wintellect, LLC. He has worked with enterprise applications for more than 20 years, 15 of those focused on web-based applications using the Microsoft stack. An early adopter of Silverlight 3.0, he worked on countless enterprise Silverlight solutions, including the back-end health monitoring system for the 2010 Vancouver Winter Olympics and Microsoft's own social network monitoring product called "Looking Glass." He is both a consultant and project manager at Wintellect and works closely with Fortune 500 companies, including Microsoft. He is a three-year Microsoft MVP and was declared MVP of the Year in 2010. He has also received Microsoft's Community Contributor award for his work with Silverlight. Jeremy is the author of *Designing Silverlight Business Applications: Best Practices for Using Silverlight Effectively in the Enterprise* (Addison-Wesley). Jeremy regularly speaks, contributes articles, and blogs on topics of interest to the Microsoft developer community. His blog can be found at http://csharperimage.jeremylikness.com.

1

The New Windows Runtime

THE WINDOWS RUNTIME (WINRT) IS AN ENTIRELY NEW framework for Windows that provides developers a multi-language API for creating applications on Windows 8. Windows Store applications are full-screen applications that are tailored for specific devices, touch interactions, and the new Windows 8 user interface. Windows Store applications are also referred to as *tailored* applications because they adapt to the target device. It is also possible to build traditional desktop applications on Windows 8. The term "Windows 8 application" in this book will refer to the non-desktop, Windows Store version of applications that use WinRT. The introduction of WinRT is one of the largest paradigm shifts in the Windows development world since the introduction of .NET in late 2000.

In this chapter, you will look back at prior development frameworks for Windows and learn how the rising popularity of Natural User Interfaces (NUI) prompted Microsoft to respond with the bold new Windows 8 platform. You will learn about Windows 8 applications and the various languages in which they are written. I will also share how existing XAML-based technologies like WPF and Silverlight fit into the new Windows runtime.

Looking Back: Win32 and .NET

"I can change my mind faster than Bill Clinton."

—Jay Leno at the Windows 95 Launch Party, referring to the new Windows task bar

In 1985, the first version of Windows was released without much fanfare. It wasn't a full operating system, but a layer that sat on top of the console-based MS-DOS and was called MS-DOS Executive, as shown in Figure 1.1. A decade later, things changed dramatically with the launch of Windows 95. Bill Gates appeared on a massive stage in front of the now iconic "Start button" for Windows with talk show host Jay Leno and demonstrated the powerful new operating system. It caught on quickly to the tune of the Rolling Stones' song "Start Me Up" and left close competitors like Apple behind in its wake.

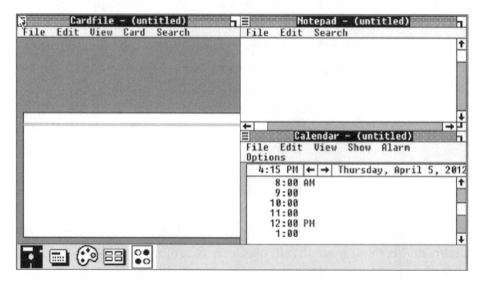

FIGURE 1.1: MS-DOS Executive

To write software for Windows 95, shown in Figure 1.2, developers used an Application Programming Interface (API) that had been developed several years earlier known as *Win32*. At the time, Microsoft was bridging the gap between legacy 16-bit systems and the newer 32-bit machines and conveyed the new support in the name of their API. Win32 exists today (now more appropriately referred to as the Windows API) at the core of all Windows operating systems despite the introduction of newer frameworks and platforms that abstract it away. The API was considered extremely powerful and flexible at the time it was introduced but placed a tremendous burden on the developer to handle many low-level operations required to display a form and interact with the user.

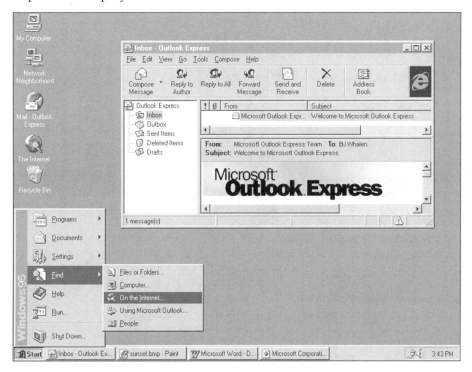

FIGURE 1.2: Windows 95

The following code is all that is required to print the text "Hello, World" using the C++ programming language:

```
#include<iostream.h>
int main()
{
    cout << "Hello World" << endl;
    return 0;
}
```

Compare that with the code in Listing 1.1 required to perform the same task in C++ for the Win32 API (this example uses the Microsoft Foundation Class Library or MFC).

LISTING 1.1: Win32 MFC Version of Hello, World

```
#include <afxwin.h>
class HelloApplication : public CWinApp
{
public:
 virtual BOOL InitInstance();
};

HelloApplication HelloApp;

class HelloWindow : public CFrameWnd
{
 CButton* m_pHelloButton;
public:
 HelloWindow();
};

BOOL HelloApplication::InitInstance()
{
 m_pMainWnd = new HelloWindow();
 m_pMainWnd->ShowWindow(m_nCmdShow);
 m_pMainWnd->UpdateWindow();
 return TRUE;
}

HelloWindow::HelloWindow()
{
 Create(NULL,
  "Hello World!",
  WS_OVERLAPPEDWINDOW|WS_HSCROLL,
  CRect(0,0,140,80));
 m_pHelloButton = new CButton();
 m_pHelloButton->Create("Hello World!",WS_CHILD|WS_VISIBLE,CRect(20,
 20,120,40),this,1);
 }
```

The API was used heavily for decades in software that was written for Windows machines. It demonstrates the trade-off that has always been a part of developing software for Windows machines: The ability to deliver a comprehensive user interface with rich graphics requires a steeper learning curve. For many years, it also meant knowing either C or C++ because although other options existed, both languages dominated the market for what is now referred to as *unmanaged code*. Unmanaged code is compiled directly to native instructions that the target machine can read.

The first version of the Visual Basic programming language (referred to more commonly as VB) was introduced in 1991. VB was based on concepts that date to an older language designed for teaching called BASIC, an acronym for Beginner's All-purpose Symbolic Instruction Code. VB allowed developers to structure their code in logical components that work together. Although VB also generated native, unmanaged code, it did this with the assistance of special runtime libraries that the code would interact with to create the target application.

VB 4.0 was released in 1995 and could create 16-bit and 32-bit Windows programs. The Interactive Development Environment (IDE) packaged with VB made it extremely popular with developers, along with the existing components and the ability to design user interfaces by dragging and dropping controls. VB also integrated well with the Common Object Model (COM), a standard for creating software components that was introduced by Microsoft in 1993.

COM was designed to enable communication between processes and for its ability to dynamically create software components (referred to as objects) that could be accessed from various programming languages. COM allows developers to use components without having to understand how they are internally implemented. This is done through externally exposed interfaces. COM was also an important milestone in the evolution of Windows and, as you will learn later, influences the Windows 8 platform even today.

The typical architecture of a Win32 application is illustrated in Figure 1.3.

Although the Win32 API still exists today, many developers write productive software without even knowing it exists because in the 1990s Microsoft began working on a new framework. It was codenamed Next Generation Windows Services (NGWS). The beta for this new framework was released in late 2000 under its public name: .NET 1.0. It allowed for a new type of software called *managed code*.

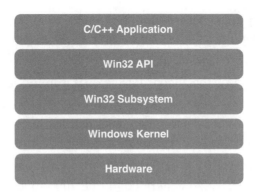

FIGURE 1.3: The component stack of a Win32 application

The traditional approach to building applications is called unmanaged because it compiles directly to native instructions that the target machine can read. Although this has several advantages, it also forces the developer to understand the host machine at a level very close to the underlying kernal. Developers must learn how to allocate memory directly and how to release memory when it is no longer being used. Tasks such as drawing graphics require understanding the display drivers and how to render the pixels into internal buffers that are used to draw the onscreen display.

The .NET Framework introduced managed code to Windows platforms. The code is called managed because a new layer called the Common Language Runtime (CLR) was introduced. The CLR manages memory for the developer, provides a consistent way to interact with various libraries and resources, and also ensures more secure code. The CLR also provides a language-agnostic layer of code, referred to as Microsoft Intermediate Language or MSIL (sometimes simply referred to as IL) that all programs compile to. The runtime interprets this code and translates it to the native operations required to run on a target machine.

The concept of managed code existed well before the .NET Framework. In the 1960s and 1970s when mainframes were prevalent, it was common to write emulators to port code from one system to another. An early game company that wrote what they referred to as "interactive fiction," and is best known for their title "Zork," was founded in 1979 and released titles to various platforms including the Commodore 64 and Apple IIe by creating a "Z-machine" interpreter. Java technology began development in 1991 and featured the Java Virtual Machine (JVM) to manage code written in the Java programming language.

The advantages this model provides include opening the platform to a variety of languages and enabling stronger cross-platform and operating system support. Programs written with unmanaged code often target a specific version of the operating system or have special libraries designed to keep them compatible with multiple flavors (such as Windows XP, Windows Vista, and Windows 7). Managed code can for the most part target a specific version of the .NET Framework, and the framework itself will handle the differences between operating systems it is installed on.

The original version of the .NET Framework supplied an API known as Windows forms (WinForms) for developing graphical user interfaces. The API was based on the Graphics Device Interface (GDI) that provided direct methods for accessing the underlying graphics hardware. The .NET Framework 3.0 was released in 2006 and included the Windows Presentation Foundation (WPF). This new technology was significant because it was based on Extensible Markup Language (XAML) as a declarative way to design user interfaces. XAML enables vector-based graphics and fluid layouts that scale to various display form factors and introduced the concept of data-binding that you will learn about later.

The architecture for an application written with the .NET Framework is illustrated in Figure 1.4. This example uses the WPF framework that is layered on top of the core runtime. The developer is able to use a variety of languages and technologies like Extensible Application Markup Language (XAML) to generate code that takes advantage of the framework and the underlying set of base classes that are part of the Base Class Library (BCL) and provide common services such as file system access and networking capabilities. The languages all generate MSIL that is compiled during execution to native code by the CLR.

Technologies based on the .NET Framework and the Win32 API have dominated software written for Windows machines for the past decade. Although frameworks like WPF revolutionized the user interface of Windows Applications and Silverlight extended the reach of the platform, Windows suffered a major blow from what was once considered an unlikely competitor: a tablet PC. In April of 2010, fifteen years after the

Windows 95 launch party, Apple retaliated by selling almost 15 million units of the iPad in its first year alone. This bold new product embraced a revolution that had began years earlier to give consumers what is known a Natural User Interface (NUI).

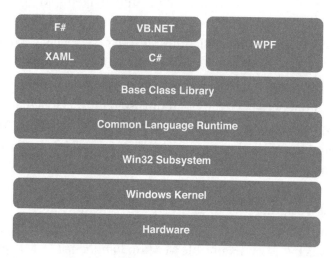

FIGURE 1.4: The component stack of a .NET Framework application

Looking Forward: Rise of the NUI

The typewriter was invented in the early 1800s. The original models featured an alphabetically arranged set of keys that would often jam when the operator typed quickly. Christopher Sholes, a newspaper editor, addressed this issue in the early 1870s by devising a keyboard layout that ensured the most common letter combinations were not located close to each other. A misconception is that this was devised to slow the speed of the typist when in fact the goal was to avoid jams and therefore allow faster typing speeds (Weller, 1918).

The keyboard served a very mechanical function: It connected a letter with a bar that was used to strike the paper and apply the ink to represent the letter. Typewriters have now become a novelty, and the majority of keyboards are electrical. Keyboards exist today that can be rolled into tiny cylinders for easy transport and connect wirelessly to their host machines.

Despite major advances in technology, the keyboard look and feel has remained mostly unchanged for the past century.

The keyboard was first augmented by the invention of the mouse in the late 1960s. Bill English and Douglas Engelbart were working for Xerox at the Palo Alto Research Center (PARC) when they developed the early prototypes of the mouse (Edwards, 2008). The original mouse was so-named because it was connected by a cord that resembled a tail. Today you can purchase wireless mice that use infrared or lasers to track movement instead of a mechanical ball.

The combination of a keyboard and mouse may be the most common way to interact with computers today, but it is hardly intuitive. I'm assuming you are a developer if you are reading this, so there is a good chance you are treated as "support central" by your friends and family. You've probably had to wait patiently while a relative hunted and pecked on her keyboard to type out some text with agonizing slowness, then explain the differences between a click, a double-click, and a right-click as she attempted to navigate.

Research into a different way to interact with computers began nearly the same time the mouse was being perfected in the early 1970s. The idea of a "natural" interface focuses on a method of interaction that is intuitive and therefore easy to learn. If you watched the movie *Minority Report* with Tom Cruise, you probably marveled at the holographic images he could easily manipulate simply by moving and rotating his hands. Manipulating an object with your hands is something natural that you begin to master at a very young age, so it's easier to use those gestures to move a document on a computer screen than it is to learn how to point, click, and drag with mouse.

The Natural User Interface (NUI) began to make its mark shortly after 2000 when the majority of smart phones began to ship with touch screens. This made it easy to simply point, tap, pinch, and swipe your way through various menus and options on the phone. Apple released the touch-only iPhone in 2007 with an interface that was extremely easy to learn and use. I believe this more natural interface is one of the key reasons the iPhone became popular so quickly: It was the first phone non-technical users could get along with.

Around the same time the iPhone was gaining popularity, Nintendo released the Wii console. The console features special remotes that contain sensors so that users can interact with the console by moving their arms and twisting their hands. This interface makes it easy to translate actions you've already learned like tossing a bowling ball or swinging a golf club to video games by incorporating these same movements. The console was an instant hit and broke several records for velocity of sales, including best-selling console in a single month in the United States (http://en.wikipedia.org/wiki/Wii).

In 2009, the public began hearing whispers about a Microsoft initiative codenamed *Project Natal*. In the fall of 2010, Project Natal was released as the Kinect for Xbox 360 and took the Wii concept a step further by eliminating the need for a remote. The Kinect sensor uses special cameras to combine image and depth perception to analyze objects in the room, including players. These cameras allow you to interact through body movements without any type of controller. An array of microphones is also able to pinpoint to sound to a high degree of accuracy and enables you to issue voice commands in a normal voice from across the room.

The popularity of the Kinect led to several open source projects devoted to creating drivers and software to enable its use on computers. After several different competing (and unofficial) products went to market, Microsoft responded by releasing the official Kinect for Windows SDK in June 2012. Version 1.5 includes drivers that are compatible with Windows 8.

The NUI revolution has exploded over the past few years. Sales of slate and tablet PCs have surged. The rapid adoption of these devices has created a phenomenon referred to as the "Consumerization of IT."[1] Employees are refusing to lug around their giant work laptops in lieu of the lighter, easier-to-use touch-based slates that they are willing to purchase with their own cash and bring from home. IT departments are responding by embracing these types of devices in the workplace.

---

[1] Research giant Gartner released a report on the Consumerization of IT in April of 2007. You can read the summary online at http://www.gartner.com/DisplayDocument?id=503272.

The Windows 7 operating system (shown in Figure 1.5) contains a touch API that allows developers to write software that responds to touch-based interactions and gestures. The problem is that the majority of software written for the platform is still based on the old combination of keyboard and mouse. Many of these programs respond to touch simply by replacing a finger tap with a mouse click. This makes it unwieldy to interact with programs because they don't provide the right surface to manipulate content. Users with "fat fingers" (compared to the size of a stylus or touchpad pen) find it nearly impossible to select text or check radio buttons crammed into tight spaces on the screen.

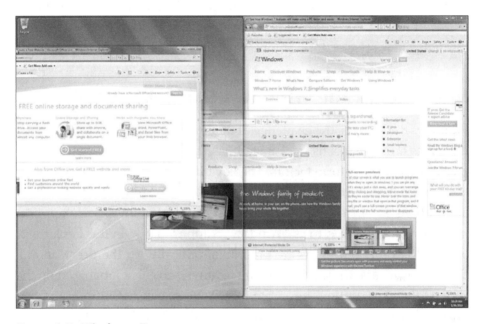

FIGURE 1.5: Windows 7

I believe when consumers realized how easy it is to interact with a NUI, they began to push away from the more traditional models of mouse and keyboard. Microsoft responded in the entertainment space with Kinect and the smartphone space with the release of the new Windows Phone. They realized they needed a better story in the computer space for Windows machines that didn't simply include a touch interface. What was needed was a touch-optimized operating system designed to make it easy for non-technical users to pick up a slate and become productive immediately. Unlike Apple and Android, they also had to tackle this without the benefit of building a fresh platform. There are 1.25 billion Windows machines worldwide (500 million with Windows 7) running software written over the past several decades that can't be forgotten and left behind when the new version is released (http://articles.businessinsider.com/2011-12-06/tech/30481049_1_android-apps-ios).

Microsoft responded to the challenge with Windows 8. A revolutionary operating system, Windows 8 is built on the familiar Windows architecture that enables it to run the same software you are used to operating on your Windows 7, Windows Vista, and Windows XP machines. The platform has been reimagined to provide a first-class touch-based NUI experience through a new style of application—the tailored Windows Store app.

Introducing the Windows Store Application

Windows 8 addresses the challenge of maintaining backwards compatibility across a massive consumer install base while embracing natural user interfaces and tablet form factors. The key to Windows 8 is a special type of application that is written for the new Windows Runtime (WinRT). These applications are most commonly referred to as Windows Store applications, hereafter referred to as "Windows 8 applications" in this book.

Windows 8 applications are tailored specifically for the user running them. They leverage special hardware features and can adapt based on the context they are run in. They scale to various screen resolutions and orientations and adapt easily to the mouse and keyboard when touch is not available. They can tap into various sensors to determine the user's location and respond to the motion of the device they are running on.

The goal for these applications is to keep them alive, fast, and fluid. Applications built for the platform should easily interface with other applications, social networks, and the cloud. They should be easy to learn and intuitive to use because they take advantage of natural gestures and interactions. The Windows 8 application experience extends to the development lifecycle. With the tools provided, it should be fast and easy to build quality applications using the language of your choice.

The Windows 8 application platform runs with help from a special layer called the Windows Runtime or WinRT. Using a technique called *projection*, WinRT maps operating system APIs to objects in your chosen programming language. In C# the interaction looks and feels like interaction between classes. This technique makes it easy to interface without compromising performance because the compiled code invokes the APIs directly as if you are writing raw unmanaged C/C++. There is no intermediary translation or mapping, and the APIs are compiled directly into the Windows 8 OS to access the operating system directly. Unlike the Win32 API, the Windows Runtime is an object-oriented API.

The WinRT APIs are exposed using the same technique as the .NET framework. The Common Language Infrastructure (CLI) is used to provide metadata about the APIs that the compiler can use to project the signature to your language of choice and compile it to native code. The metadata follows the ECMA-335 standard and is stored in files with the .winmd extension for *Windows Metadata*. You can learn more about the standard online on the ECMA website at http://www.ecma-international.org/publications/standards/Ecma-335.htm.

Figure 1.6 illustrates the architecture you will use when you build Windows 8 applications. There are a large number of APIs provided "out of the box" by Windows 8 to perform actions related to graphics, devices, security, networking, interacting with the operating system, and communicating with other applications. There are currently four languages supported by the Windows Store development platform with two different graphics markup engines, one that is XAML-based (both via unmanaged code and the CLR) and another that is based on HTML5 (using the internal "Trident" engine for rendering and "Chakra" engine for interpreting JavaScript that is built into Internet Explorer 10).

It is important to familiarize yourself with the specific traits of Windows 8 applications. The primary graphics interface for these applications is DirectX, and there is no direct access to the older Graphics Device Interface (GDI). Windows 8 applications have no overlapped windows. They execute in a special "Application container" that features various states. Windows 8 applications can be suspended when they are not active and may be terminated when system resources such as memory become scarce.

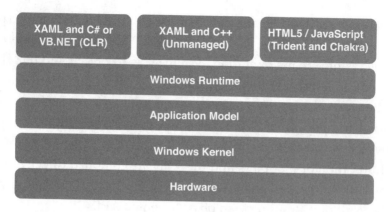

FIGURE 1.6: The component stack for a Windows 8 application

WinRT APIs come in two flavors: direct calls to the underlying kernel and brokered API calls. Brokered API calls are special calls that may impact data integrity, user integrity, or security concerns. To use these special APIs, the Windows 8 application must "declare intent" by flagging the proposed calls in an application manifest. The user is often prompted to give permission (opt-in) for the calls to be made before the application is allowed to run.

Jensen Harris, the Director of Program Management for Windows User Experience at Microsoft, presented a session at Microsoft's Build conference that covered eight specific traits of well-written Windows 8 applications.[2] Microsoft was very secretive with the details of Windows 8 until the Build conference, when they formally announced the operating system and released the developer preview to the general public. It was at that event in a keynote session that Jensen shared the following traits as guidelines to follow when writing software for the Windows 8 platform.

Windows 8 Design

Windows 8 applications have a consistent look and feel. To make it easy for the user to intuitively learn how to interact with your application, you should follow the design guidelines for Windows 8 applications as closely

---

[2] You can view his excellent presentation online at http://channel9.msdn.com/ Events/BUILD/BUILD2011/BPS-1004.

as possible. Several templates are provided with the development environment to make this easy for you. You will learn about various practices and guidelines throughout this book.

You can read Microsoft's guidelines for Windows 8 applications online at http://msdn.microsoft.com/en-us/library/windows/apps/hh465427.

Fast and Fluid

All Windows 8 applications should be fast and fluid. The framework helps manage the responsiveness of the application by only allowing asynchronous access to APIs that may run slowly. For Windows 8 applications, the definition of "slow" is any operation that may take longer than 50 milliseconds to complete. Examples of potentially slow operations include file system and network access. Asynchronous operations avoid blocking the UI while the operation completes in the background of your application. Several enhancements to the C# language and underlying framework make it easier to manage, wait for, and respond to the result of asynchronous calls in your code.

The Visual Studio 2012 templates and IDE contain built-in animations to provide a fluid user interface. Most displays easily pan from side to side and provide the user with the ability to zoom in when they require further detail. You will learn how the different templates provide fluid transitions in Chapter 2, *Getting Started*, and how to apply more advanced transitions in Chapter 3, *Extensible Application Markup Language (XAML)*.

Snap and Scale

Windows 8 applications can easily snap to a region on the display to run side-by-side with another application if the display resolution is great enough (this requires a minimum width of 1344 pixels). This is a built-in gesture users can invoke to manage their running Windows 8 applications. The applications also easily scale to the space that is provided, changing their configuration when the available space becomes larger or smaller or when the user rotates the tablet between landscape and portrait orientations. Once again the templates in Visual Studio 2012 provide built-in capabilities to accommodate these features that you can build upon for your own applications.

Use of Right Contracts

Windows 8 applications and WinRT introduce a new concept called *contracts*. Think of **Contracts** as a language-agnostic way to express assumptions about capabilities in code. The **Share** contract, for example, is like a clipboard on steroids because it manages multiple types including HTML content and bitmap images. Contracts allow the developer to expose services that interact with the operating system directly or can be invoked by the user through charms. Charms are a UI feature and part of the Windows 8 platform that allows the user to invoke contracts through a consistent user interface. An example contract and corresponding charm is **Search**.

When the user selects the **Search** charm from a Windows 8 application, he is presented with an operating system dialog with a text box that he can use to enter search terms. Beneath the search box, the operating system will display all of the programs that support the **Search** contract. The operation system will pass the search terms to whatever program is selected, so that it can process the term in the appropriate context. A movie application can apply the search term to movie titles, and a Windows 8 application that aggregates RSS feeds can search the content of recent news items. This process is illustrated in Figure 1.7.

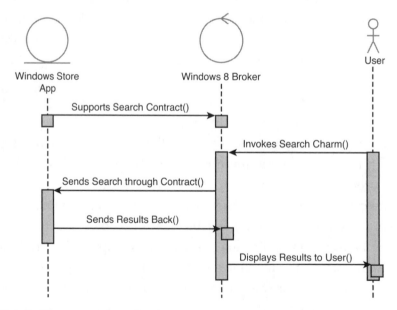

FIGURE 1.7: **Charms and contracts**

Other charms include Settings, Devices, and the **Share** charm for sending data between applications. You will learn more about charms and contracts in Chapter 8, *Giving Your Application Charm*.

Great Tiles

Microsoft introduced the concept of tiles with Windows Phone 7. Unlike application icons that take up space on the start screen solely to provide something to click to launch the application, tiles are live, interactive spaces that can provide dynamic information and context to the user. A weather tile will summarize the current temperature and forecast. A Twitter tile may animate between the most recent tweets that mentioned you. An email tile will display your current count of unread messages.

The use of live tiles transforms the start menu into an executive dashboard that provides rich "at a glance" information. Often you can get the information you need without even launching the application the tile is connected to. This is similar to the experience provided by earlier versions of Windows through the Active Desktop (http://en.wikipedia.org/wiki/Active_Desktop) and Desktop Gadgets (http://msdn.microsoft.com/en-us/library/windows/desktop/dd834142.aspx). Tiles, however, are an integral part of the Windows 8 platform and directly connected with your application.

You can see an example of an old, static desktop in Figure 1.8. About the only "active" information is the date and time in the lower left. Everything else is static, and the icons only serve as placeholders to launch applications. Notice the massive amount of unused "white space" on the right side of the desktop.

Now take a look at Figure 1.9. This is the Windows 8 Start screen. Notice how all of the space is used. In addition, each tile provides relevant content and information. The weather application shows the current weather at a glance (yes, it is a beautiful day here in Woodstock, Georgia). The photo application rotates through the latest images. All of this gives me quick information at a glance. On the right side, I've opted to use smaller tiles or turn off the live updates. Almost everything about the Windows 8 experience is configurable.

FIGURE 1.8: A static desktop

FIGURE 1.9: The Windows 8 Start screen

The infrastructure for updating tiles is designed to conserve resources such as network usage and the battery life of your host device. You'll learn more about tiles in Chapter 7, *Tiles and Toasts.*

Connected and Alive

Windows 8 applications should remain connected and alive. This means they are constantly providing the latest information through tiles, notifications, and content. Through the use of contracts and charms, they can connect seamlessly to social networks, cloud storage, and local devices. In addition to charms and contracts, this is achieved through the integration of data from multiple sources (learn more about options for data in Chapter 6, *Data*) and through syndication of rich network-based content.

Embrace Windows 8 Design Principles

The final trait of a great Windows 8 application is that it embraces the Windows 8 design principles. This trait really encompasses everything. When you design your application, make it fast and responsive. Do more with less. Focus on the key tasks and don't add distractions. Remove anything that is not necessary and always focus on the ease of the end user. How quickly and easily can they complete tasks? How fast can they get to the information they need?

This book will focus on these principles throughout. Fortunately, Microsoft has clearly defined what makes a good Windows 8 application and has integrated these principles into their various development tools and templates. You will learn more about these tools in the next section.

Windows 8 Tools of the Trade

The new runtime requires new tools to build Windows 8 applications. Windows 8 was released to manufacturing on August 15th, 2012 and will be available to the general public at the end of October 2012. Visual Studio 2012 was released to production in August 2012. The next version of Microsoft's flagship development environment is capable of building and deploying the new Windows Store applications. Traditional desktop applications allow you to execute the program immediately after it is compiled.

Like Windows Phone applications, Windows 8 applications must be packaged and then deployed before you can run or debug them.

Visual Studio 2012 is the main tool you will use for building Windows 8 applications. You can download the tool online from http://dev.windows.com/.

When you have Visual Studio 2012 installed, you can create new Windows 8 projects directly from the IDE. Figure 1.10 shows the various options you have to choose from when you start a new project. The templates are grouped by language, followed by a subsection for the Windows Store environment. Several templates exist for Windows 8 applications to help jumpstart your UI.

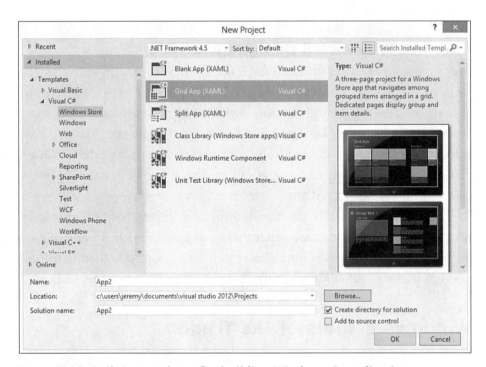

FIGURE 1.10: Built-in templates for building Windows 8 applications

Blend for Visual Studio

Blend is another tool for building Windows 8 applications. It will work for both HTML and XAML-based applications. Visual Studio 2012 focuses on the developer-centric elements of the application. Blend focuses on the more designer-centric elements. Unlike previous versions of Visual Studio that used a separate rendering engine codenamed "Cider" for the designer, the core engine for Blend is embedded within the Visual Studio 2012. The majority of design-related actions can be performed without leaving the IDE.

The specific designer-centric activities that exist in Blend include a UI for designing animations and manipulating visual states. You will learn about animations in Chapter 3 and visual states in Chapter 4, *Windows 8 Applications*. Figure 1.11 shows the start screen for the Blend application.

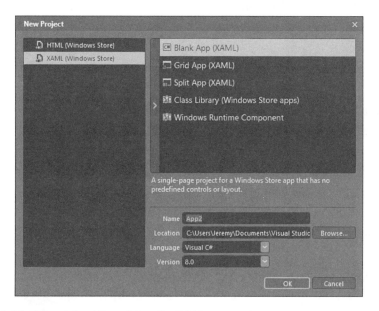

FIGURE 1.11: Blend for Visual Studio 2012

Although the focus of this book is the combination of C# and XAML for building Windows 8 applications, a brief overview of the other language options and an introduction to C# follows.

HTML5 and JavaScript

The JavaScript option is unique because it also includes a different graphics markup engine than the other options. With JavaScript for Windows 8 applications, you create applications using HTML5 for markup (including

CSS support) and JavaScript for programming. The HTML5 uses the same rendering engine as Internet Explorer, code-named "Trident." The advantage to this method is that it makes it easy for you to pull in HTML-based content from the Web to parse and render. It allows you to leverage existing knowledge of HTML, CSS, and JavaScript. You can take advantage of existing tools like jQuery (http://www.jquery.com/) to select and modify elements on the page.

The WinRT APIs are projected to the JavaScript runtime as JavaScript objects. With these classes you can interface directly with devices, receive input from the built-in camera, and react to the various sensors on the host device directly from JavaScript. Asynchronous calls are handled using JavaScript "promises." You can learn more about promises online at http://msdn.microsoft.com/en-us/library/windows/apps/Hh700339. aspx.

The HTML5/JavaScript stack integrates directly with a powerful tool for building your Windows 8 applications: Microsoft Expression Blend. This tool was traditionally used by Silverlight and WPF developers and designers to manipulate the XAML-based user interface. With Visual Studio 2012 the tool has been enhanced to allow designers to also work with HTML5 and CSS.

When should you use this option?

- You are an experienced web developer with HTML5, CSS, and JavaScript skills you wish to leverage for your Windows 8 applications.
- You are working with a design team that prefers to use HTML5 and CSS.
- You are building an application that interacts heavily with HTML content.

The markup for a JavaScript "Hello, World" application requires only a few lines of code, as shown in Listing 1.2.

LISTING 1.2: Windows 8 "Hello, World" in JavaScript

```
<!DOCTYPE html>
<html>
<head>
    <meta charset="utf-8" />
    <title>HelloWorldJavaScript</title>

    <!-- WinJS references -->
    <link href="//Microsoft.WinJS.1.0.RC/css/ui-dark.css"
        rel="stylesheet" />
    <script src="//Microsoft.WinJS.1.0.RC/js/base.js"></script>
    <script src="//Microsoft.WinJS.1.0.RC/js/ui.js"></script>

    <!-- HelloWorldJavaScript references -->
    <link href="/css/default.css" rel="stylesheet" />
    <script src="/js/default.js"></script>
</head>
<body>
    <div id="helloText" />
</body>
</html>
```

To update the contents of the helloText element, you can reference the identifier and set the innerText attribute from JavaScript in **default.js** like this:

```
helloText.innerText = 'Hello, World.';
```

The JavaScript templates provide an almost identical application experience to the other options. You will find it very hard to identify what language was used to produce an application based on the look and feel it provides.

C++ and XAML

The C++ option is exciting for many developers who have traditionally worked with unmanaged code. It allows you to build Windows 8 applications using C++ in conjunction with XAML. The UI elements declared in XAML are projected to the applications as C++ objects and can be accessed and manipulated directly from the code.

The XAML for the C++ "Hello, World" application simply declares a TextBlock element to populate:

```
<Grid Background="{StaticResource ApplicationPageBackgroundThemeBrush}">
    <TextBlock x:Name="HelloText"/>
</Grid>
```

The code-behind simply sets the Text property of the element:

```
MainPage::MainPage()
{
    InitializeComponent();
    HelloText->Text = "Hello, World.";
}
```

You can use the native C++ option to build Windows 8 games that interface directly to DirectX. Take full advantage of the graphics hardware by using High Level Shading Language (HLSL), a feature that is needed by many image processing applications as well as games. This option also allows you to reference existing projects and libraries written in C++ to use with your Windows 8 applications.

When should you use this option?

- You are an experienced C++ developer and you want to leverage this skill for your Windows 8 applications.
- You are working with a design team that is familiar with XAML.
- You don't want to take on the additional overhead of the web browser engine (HTML5/JavaScript) or the CLR (C#/XAML).
- You are interested in writing native C++ code and/or using high performance features like the HLSL engine.

VB/C# and XAML

The final available option is to use the managed VB and C# languages. The unique WinRT framework allows these applications to access APIs directly through projections that appear as native CLR entities. This book will focus on the C# option, but the API calls and templates are almost identical for the VB.NET version; only the language option itself is different.

The XAML for the "Hello, World" application is the same for C# as it was in the C++ example. The code-behind looks like this in C#:

```
public MainPage()
{
    InitializeComponent();
    HelloText.Text = "Hello, World.";
}
```

When should you use this option?

- You are an experienced C# developer and want to continue to leverage your skills for building Windows 8 applications.
- You are a Silverlight and/or WPF developer and wish to continue your investment in XAML knowledge.
- You are working with a design team that is familiar with XAML.

The examples in this book will focus on C# with XAML. You can download the sample "Hello, World" applications online at http://windows8applications.codeplex.com/.

There are two ways you can obtain the source code through CodePlex. The first is by clicking the big **Download** button in the upper right. This will download a compressed package containing all of the latest source files. The second is by navigating to the **Source Code** tab where you can browse code online or download a specific version by clicking the **Download** link. Finally, you can follow the project by clicking a link in the upper right of the home page to be notified of any changes or corrections as they are made.

Behind the Scenes of WinRT

WinRT components are COM objects. They adhere to an Application Binary Interface (ABI) that is a low-level interface between the component and the operating system and other components. The components also implement a special interface called IInspectable that in turn implements IUnknown.

The JavaScript interpreter will use the IInspectable interface to generate the dynamic language bindings. The interpreter grabs the class name, requests the metadata for the component from Windows, and then projects the appropriate interfaces. The end result is that your JavaScript can access the WinRT projections and the interpreter will marshal requests to the underlying components. The interpreter has its own garbage collector responsible for cleaning up instances as they go out of scope.

In the .NET versions, the projected classes actually implement COM Interopability. The .NET application interacts with a CLR class that interfaces to the underlying WinRT (COM) component using a runtime callable wrapper (RCW). The calls are simply marshaled using the project layer to the underlying component. The projection manages the component along with the projected type, so again the native garbage collection in the .NET Framework will take care of objects that are out of scope.

What's important to note for the C# and XAML combination is that the full .NET Framework is being used. There is a special profile for .NET Windows Store applications that restricts usage to a small set of core Base Class Libraries (BCL) and the projection layers. Applications written using the managed language set will take a dependency on the .NET Framework runtime. The overhead for projection is minimal so there should not be concerns about major performance hits when choosing this option.

The C++ option interfaces with WinRT through a set of language extensions. This enables the compiler to map the WinRT components to familiar language patterns with constructors, destructors, methods, and exceptions. Memory management in C++ is usually done through something called "reference counting," but for WinRT components this is generated behind the scenes, so references are managed automatically.

WPF, Silverlight, and the Blue Stack

Silverlight 5 was released in December of 2011, several months after Windows 8 was officially announced at the inaugural //Build conference in 2011. Before //Build, many developers speculated on the future of Silverlight, and it was rumored that both Silverlight and even .NET in general would be not be supported in the new operating system. This was not the case, and Windows 8 machines can run the full .NET framework along with Silverlight applications, both in browser and out-of-browser (OOB).

Is there a place for these applications on the new platform? The answer I believe is definitely, "Yes." There is a substantial amount of time and resources invested in existing applications that run in Silverlight and on the .NET framework using WPF. Many of these applications can run "as is" on Windows 8 machines, especially if they have already been built to integrate touch features. Windows 8 provides two distinct environments that can run side-by-side: Windows Store and Desktop. These are sometimes referred to as "green stack" for Windows 8 applications and "blue stack" for desktop applications because of the colors that were used in the initial diagrams presented by Microsoft to illustrate the Windows 8 platform.

Windows Store, or the green stack, is the focus of this book. (Whenever you see "Windows 8 application," I am referring to this special non-desktop application type.) The Desktop environment, or the blue stack, is the one many developers are already familiar with. It supports the .NET Framework along with various frameworks including WPF and Silverlight. You can continue to write software targeting that environment using the languages and tools of your choice. The decisions developers face is whether to build or migrate to Windows 8 or to continue to support the desktop.

Some applications probably don't make sense in the Windows Store environment. Though a Windows Store version of Outlook would be very welcome, I can't imagine editing a large and complex Excel spreadsheet using the same user interface. I also can't imagine developing software using the Windows Store environment, which is why Visual Studio 2012 runs in the Desktop environment. For those scenarios, it's better to attach the mouse and keyboard and pound out code because building enterprise applications using gestures and touch probably isn't something that will happen in the near future.

Many applications may benefit from versions that support both modes. The main application may run in the Desktop environment while a streamlined version that provides an executive dashboard of information with alerts and news feed is built for the Windows Store environment. For example, Internet Explorer 10 runs as a Windows Store application within the Windows Store environment. From the desktop, you can launch a different version that uses the traditional desktop interface and supports plug-ins. There is no reason to restrict your efforts to one target, and the fact that Windows 8 applications support languages like C# provides an opportunity to share key libraries of code among your various targets.

One special version of Windows 8 that doesn't support the blue stack is referred to as Windows RT. This version runs exclusively on devices with ARM-based chipsets. ARM devices use a special chip that is optimized for low power and to generate little heat. Slates, tablets, and smart phones built using ARM chips can have smaller form factors because they don't require fans to cool the main microprocessor. The chip uses a different native instruction set than traditional Intel machines, and therefore the special version of Windows written for ARM devices will only support Windows 8 applications.

Summary

This chapter covered a brief history of Microsoft and the Windows operating systems along with the various APIs and platforms used to build software. You learned about the new Windows Store platform and related tools for building touch-friendly applications that run on Windows 8. I covered a few different ways to build the applications and reviewed the selection of languages and graphics markup engines that are available.

Windows 8 applications share common traits that are intended to provide a consistent, elegant, and compelling user experience. They are seamlessly integrated, tailor themselves to fit target devices, and are built using the same languages and tools C# and XAML developers are used to. If you can't wait to get started building applications for this amazing new platform, all you need to do is turn the page!

Works Cited

Edwards, B. The Computer Mouse Turns 40. *Macworld*: December 9, 2008.

Weller, C.E. *The Early History of the Typewriter.* La Porte: Chase & Shepard, 1918.

2
Getting Started

"HELLO, WORLD" IS A POPULAR APPLICATION BECAUSE IT IS usually the first program developers write to learn a new language or platform. You learned how to write "Hello, World" using three different approaches in the previous chapter. In this chapter, you learn how to set up your environment to develop Windows 8 applications. There are many options, and it is important to choose the one that makes the most sense for you.

When the environment is set up, I cover the various templates that are provided out of the box in Visual Studio 2012. These templates are designed to help you get up and running with your Windows 8 applications as quickly as possible. They have built-in code and mark-up to handle things like orientation switching or scaling (resizing) the application. You learn how to decide which template to start with based on the goals of your application.

In this chapter, I walk through a simple example of building a Windows 8 application. This example integrates a few advanced features so you can see how easy they are to integrate in the new platform. Finally, we look at the result of building the application. You learn how it was deployed with the system and the structure it takes. I think you'll be surprised to learn just where some of the information about your new application is stored in Windows 8.

Setting Up Your Environment

There are a number of options available to set up your environment for authoring Windows 8 applications. You must be running Windows 8 to develop and test Windows 8 applications. If you don't already have a machine running Windows 8, there are a few different options for setting it up in your development environment. When Windows 8 is installed, you can then install and configure Visual Studio 2012, the primary tool for building Windows 8 applications, and Blend, a tool for designing the user interface by manipulating the Extensible Markup Language (XAML) in your application.

Windows 8

The first step to developing Windows 8 applications is to set up the operating system. This may seem obvious, but you cannot develop Windows 8 Windows Store applications on other machines—you must be using Visual Studio 2012 from a Windows 8 machine. You can obtain the installation media several different ways, including an Internet download from the main website at http://dev.windows.com/.

You will also need to prepare your media for installation. Most OS downloads are distributed as ISO images (ISO stands for International Organization for Standardization) that can be used to create installation CDs and/or DVDs. When you have the image, you can mount it using a tool such as Virtual CloneDrive (http://www.slysoft.com/en/virtual-clonedrive.html). Another option when considering an upgrade is to use the Windows 7 USB/DVD Download (compatible with Windows 8) tool to prepare a DVD or external USB drive (http://wudt.codeplex.com/).

After you have your media ready to install the Windows 8 image, you need to decide which configuration to use for your install. There are three common options available:

- **Full Install**—Choose this option to overwrite your existing operating system and replace it with Windows 8. Be sure to back up any important data on the existing system because it might be overwritten by the upgrade.

- **Dual Boot**—Use this option to allow Windows 7 and Windows 8 to boot side-by-side. When you turn on your computer, you will be prompted to choose which operating system you would like to boot. You have the option of installing the dual-boot either using a partition on your disk drive or by creating a Virtual Hard Disk (VHD) image.
- **Virtual Machine**—Use this option to create a virtual hard drive and load the operating system in a virtual machine. There are many virtual machine products available. I demonstrate this option using Oracle's VirtualBox because it is a free virtual machine host.

The option that you choose will depend on the environment you have. For writing this book, I chose to dedicate a machine to Windows 8 and used the full installation option. The virtual machine option is not the best choice because Windows 8 is a new operating system, and therefore not all of the tools and features have been implemented in the virtual machines yet. For example, I found the mouse support to be very sporadic, and there was no option to use touch even though I have a fully functional touch monitor.

■ WINDOWS 8 ON A STICK

Windows 8 provides a unique new feature called Windows to Go that allows you to install the entire operating system on an external USB drive. This allows you to share the image between various devices, for example your work desktop and home laptop. The first time it boots on a new device, it will automatically scan the hardware and download the appropriate drivers and then load the appropriate drivers on subsequent boots. Although there are some restrictions and differences between this version of Windows 8 and a full install (this is not supported on Windows 8 for ARM, called Windows RT), it is an option you may wish to consider for convenience and portability. Learn more at: http://technet.microsoft.com/en-us/library/hh831833.aspx.

To begin your installation, skip ahead to the section that covers the choice you made for your configuration. Already set up and ready to go? Skip ahead to the "Hello, Windows 8" section of this chapter.

Full Install

The Windows 8 installation is fast and easy. Simply insert the installation media and follow the prompts. When it's installed, you will be directed through several steps to configure your Windows 8 installation. You can personalize the machine name, choose settings for online updates, and specify a user login. Be sure to explore the option to use a Windows Account (also known as Windows Live) for your login. This provides additional features such as synchronization to the cloud and seamless integration to SkyDrive.

When you've completed the personalization steps—that's it! You're done. Windows 8 is ready to go.

Dual Boot

A dual boot installation will allow you to install Windows 8 and retain your existing OS installation. These instructions will assume you are starting from Windows 7. The first step is to create space on your hard disk.

■ WARNING

The following steps require advanced knowledge of your Windows system. They will involve re-partitioning and formatting sections of your hard drive. You should create a full backup prior to continuing. If you are not familiar with or comfortable working with Windows Disk Management, I strongly recommend you choose a different option or work with someone more knowledgeable. You've been warned!

If do not have an available partition or hard drive to install Windows 8 to, you can shrink your existing hard drive to make room. From the **Start Menu**, right-click **Computer** and choose **Manage**. This will launch the **Computer Management** application. In the left navigation, select

Storage→**Disk Management**. This will open **Windows Disk Management**. You will see something similar to Figure 2.1. Right-click the partition you wish to shrink and choose the option **Shrink Volume**.

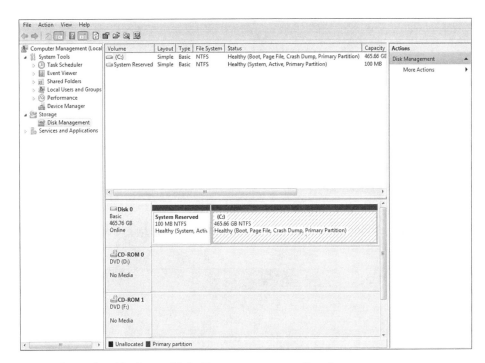

FIGURE 2.1: **The Windows Disk Management application**

The disk manager will scan the volume to find available space. This may take several minutes depending on the size of your hard drive and amount of fragmentation it has. When it is finished, you can specify a size for the new volume. The minimum recommended space for Windows 8 is 20GB. Figure 2.2 shows the dialog with the minimum amount entered in megabytes.

You'll see your favorite spinning icon for several minutes. When completed, a new section called **Unallocated** will appear that should be the size you specified. Right-click the new section and choose **New Simple Volume**. The **New Simple Volume Wizard** will appear. Click the **Next** button. Leave the default space for the new volume and click the **Next** button. Again, keep the defaults (unless you wish to assign a different drive letter).

On the last dialog, select the option to format the volume as NTFS and give it a meaningful label. Your dialog should look like what's shown in Figure 2.3.

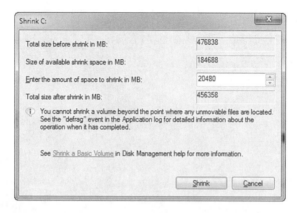

FIGURE 2.2: Specifying the amount of space to free for a new partition

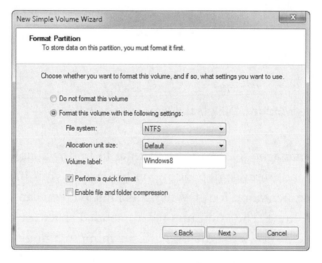

FIGURE 2.3: Formatting the partition for dual boot

Click the **Next** button. The final dialog will show you the various settings you've selected. When you've confirmed they are correct, click **Finish**, and the new volume will be formatted, mounted, and ready for a Windows 8 installation.

Insert your Windows 8 DVD or USB drive and reboot (the instructions to do this are in the "Full Install" section). Choose the **Custom** option for installation. When prompted, select the volume you created. You will recognize the volume because it should show the size you specified and be flagged as a Primary partition. Be sure to select the correct volume; a mistake here could result in overwriting your existing system.

Walk through the install process as specified in the "Full Install" section. When the system reboots, you will be presented with a new menu. Unlike the text-based menu you might be used to in Windows 7, the boot menu for Windows 8 is graphical; has a Windows 8 user interface; and is mouse, keyboard, and touch-friendly. You will be presented with the option to boot into either the old Windows 7 operating system or your new Windows 8 one. Obviously you'll pick the new OS—Windows 8—and after experiencing the incredibly fast boot, you'll be ready to set up your development and jump into your first application.

Virtual Machine Install

You may also wish to install Windows 8 on a virtual machine. The steps you will use vary depending on the virtual machine you decide to use. There are several options available. One popular, open source solution that is free is called VirtualBox. You can download VirtualBox from the website at http://www.virtualbox.org/. You will need the installation media available to install on the virtual machine. Some solutions are able to mount ISO images directly to make the process easier.

Visual Studio 2012

Visual Studio is Microsoft's development environment for building software and is the tool you will use to design Windows 8 applications. It is possible to develop Windows 8 applications for free by downloading the Express version of Visual Studio that comes packaged with the Express version of Blend. Other versions provide additional features ranging from testing modules to architecture design tools. This book will focus mostly on the features that are available with the free edition. Some features covered may require a paid edition. The following is a brief list of differences between the various levels:

- **Test Professional**—This version is designed for business analysts and testers and contains team collaboration features, a number of test features, and lab management.
- **Professional**—This is the entry-level version for developers and includes debugging, code analysis, unit testing, development platform support, and integrated development tools.
- **Premium**—The premium level combines the features of the **Test Professional** and **Professional** versions and then adds code metrics, code coverage, coded UI testing, UML diagrams, sprint planning and backlog management, code review, and storyboarding.
- **Ultimate**—This is the most comprehensive version and includes all of the features of the other versions and adds IntelliTrace (historical debugging), load testing, Microsoft Fakes (a framework for stubbing and mocking unit tests), advanced architecture tools, and feature packs.

Blend

Expression Blend is a design tool that was previously available for Silverlight, WPF, and Windows Phone applications. It has been extended to support Windows 8 applications that are based on both XAML and HTML. Blend is a powerful tool that provides sophisticated previews for content, supports design-time data to visualize pages without running the application, and a drag-and-drop approach to placing both controls and UI behaviors on the design surface.

Many features of Blend have been integrated into the designer for Visual Studio 2012. The previous version of Visual Studio 2010 used a different XAML design tool codenamed "Cider" that did not provide the same rich features found in Blend. The Blend engine provides much more functionality and developers familiar with the previous versions will feel at home within the designer. This book will focus mostly on the features of Blend that are integrated into the XAML designer for Visual Studio 2012.

Hello, Windows 8

In this section, you build your first Windows Store application. The goal for this application is to show you how easy it is to build some fairly advanced features with minimal code. The application supports using your webcam to take a picture and then save it to your picture library, a social networking site, or cloud storage. It also supports receiving images from other applications to preview and save.

After you build and run the application, you explore what happened in the Windows 8 operating system to support the application. You learn about the three phases for a Windows 8 application that include installing or deploying, tapping to launch, and running the application. Finally, I demonstrate using a tool called ILDASM (a code disassembler) to show how WinRT uses the same metadata standards as .NET to expose information about your application.

Creating Your First Windows 8 Application

The process all starts in Visual Studio 2012. There you can choose what language you will be working with (in our case, Visual C#) as well as the type of application. Depending on the version of Visual Studio you have installed, you may have access to develop Windows desktop applications, Web-based applications, reporting solutions, SharePoint integration, or an application that targets the tailored Windows 8 platform. You can see an example of the available templates in Figure 2.4.

To open a new project, simply select **File→New→Project**. Choose the option **Windows Store**, and you will be presented with several template options.

Templates

The project templates in Visual Studio provide different starting points for your application based on common patterns for development. Depending on your needs, you may want to start with a project template that supports interacting with groups of collections and individual items. The advantage of using these project templates is that the code they generate automatically provides support for drilling between the category and detail level, responding to orientation switches between portrait and landscape modes, and resizing when the application is snapped in a split screen. Following is a breakdown of specific features by template.

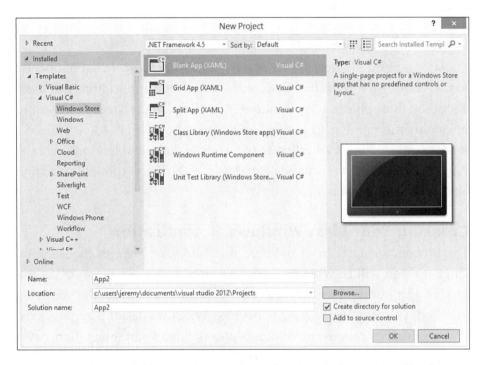

FIGURE 2.4: The available project templates for C# Windows 8 applications

Blank Application

The blank application provides a single page project. There are no predefined controls or layout. This is the simplest starting point and wires up some basic infrastructure so that you can hit the ground running.

Grid Application

The grid application provides you with a multi-page project. The application supports data that is grouped into categories. For example, a feed-reader application could implement a group for each feed and each group could contain a collection of items or individual posts for the feed. The template provides a way to navigate across groups or drill into specific group and item details. The default page for an application generated from this template is shown in Figure 2.5.

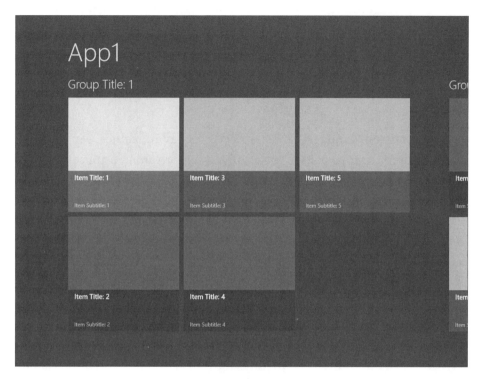

FIGURE 2.5: The grid application template

The project template provides you with several helper classes that will come in handy as you build more complex applications, including

- **BindableBase**—The base class for view models that follow the MVVM pattern. It makes it easier to provide objects that participate in the data-binding system. You will learn more about data-binding in Chapter 3, *Extensible Application Markup Language (XAML)*.
- **BooleanNegationConverter**—Provides an easy way to invert the value of a Boolean data element.
- **BooleanToVisibilityConverter**—Allows you to easily set the appearance of a UI element based on the value of a Boolean data element.

- **LayoutAwarePage**—A base class for a `Page` that tracks both the orientation of the page and the view mode (that is, whether it is full-screen or snapped next to another application).
- **RichTextColumns**—Specifies a custom panel that allows you to bind any number of data elements and have them automatically align into uniform columns.
- **StandardStyles**—A useful dictionary of styles that help define the look and feel of your application. You will learn more about styles in Chapter 3.
- **SuspensionManager**—A helper class for saving values, especially useful for restoring state (you will learn more about application state in Chapter 5, *Application Lifecycle*).

In later chapters, you will learn more about the various elements that make up an application. You will also discover some useful ways to share code between applications. This will allow you to create classes and share them without having to depend on the template to provide them for you.

Split Application

The split application is similar to the grid application but is optimized for navigating the individual items in the group list. It starts with a display that provides an overview of the available groups. When you drill down into a specific group, it provides a split view with the list of available items on one side and the details for a particular selected item on the other side. The split view for an application generated with this template is shown in Figure 2.6.

This template also contains the helper classes and dictionaries listed for the grid application.

Class Library

A class library is used when you want to create libraries that can be shared within applications. The project template provides the minimum profile you need to generate an assembly that can be linked to one of the application templates to provide services such as utilities, reusable code, data models, and other code that is important for your application.

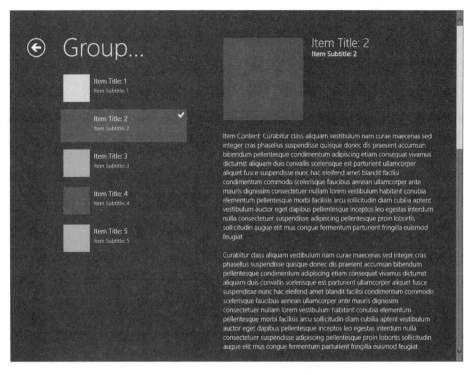

FIGURE 2.6: The split view

Windows Runtime Component

You use the **Windows Runtime Component** template to create reusable WinRT components. These are specialized class libraries that can be accessed from Windows 8 applications built using any of the supported Windows 8 languages. You will learn more about how to create WinRT components in Chapter 4, *Windows 8 Applications*.

Unit Test Library

The unit test library contains special classes that define unit tests for your system. These classes contain methods that are called by the test system. Testing is an important part of building applications. You will learn all about testing in Chapter 9, *MVVM and Testing*.

The ImageHelper Application

Now you are ready to build your first Windows 8 application. For this application, I started with the Blank Application template. You can choose to build the application yourself by following along or download the final product from the book website at http://windows8applications.codeplex. com/. The name of the project and solution is **ImageHelper**.

The first step is to create a meaningful user interface (UI). This is done using a special technology called XAML. You will learn all about XAML in Chapter 3. XAML is a declarative language that supports the creation of various objects and allows you to define their attributes and child elements using Extensible Markup Language (XML). The most common use of XAML is to define the UI elements that make up your application.

The template already generated a default Grid element in the **MainPage. xaml** file. The next step is to define two rows in the grid by placing the following code in between the start and end Grid tags:

```
<Grid.RowDefinitions>
  <RowDefinition Height="*"/>
  <RowDefinition Height="Auto"/>
</Grid.RowDefinitions>
```

The definitions instruct the display engine to create a bottom row that automatically provides enough space for its child elements and give all of the remaining space to the top row. This is because Auto refers to automatic sizing based on the contents, and * indicates "take all of the remaining space."

Next, insert a place holder to show an image after the closing </Grid.RowDefinition> tag but before the closing </Grid> tag. It should be centered in the top row. If it has to be resized or stretched, it should maintain its aspect ratio. The image is centered using the alignment properties. The Stretch property indicates how the runtime should handle resizing the image when needed to fit the available space. The Uniform value specifies that the aspect ratio should be maintained:

```
<Image x:Name="ImageTarget" Grid.Row="0"
    HorizontalAlignment="Center" VerticalAlignment="Center"
    Stretch="Uniform"/>
```

Finally, include a `StackPanel` to show two buttons right after the `Image` you just inserted. The element works as its name implies: It stacks the elements next to each other. In this case, the first button will be used to capture a new image and the second button to save it. The margin attribute simply specifies some padding so the buttons are not next to each other:

```
<StackPanel Grid.Row="1" Margin="10"
    HorizontalAlignment="Center" Orientation="Horizontal">
    <Button x:Name="CaptureButton" Content="Capture New Image"
        Click="CaptureButton_Click_1"/>
    <Button x:Name="SaveButton" Content="Save Image"
        Click="SaveButton_Click_1" Margin="20 0 0 0"/>
</StackPanel>
```

If you are writing the application instead of following along with the existing sample, you should notice a drop-down menu appears after you specify the `Click` attribute (thanks to IntelliSense). Choose the option for **<New Event Handler>** to have the event handler code automatically generated for you. If you pasted the code, delete the value after the click attribute and start over to see the drop-down.

Before you test this new UI, you should set some parameters for your application. These will give it a friendly name to display on the **Start** screen as well as provide some behaviors and capabilities you will need in order to complete the application. First, double-click the file called **Package.appxmanifest** in your **Solution Explorer.** You should see a dialog similar to the one shown in Figure 2.7.

The application manifest is important and contains four sections. The dialog allows you to modify the sections and saves it to the underlying XML format. You can few the source XML file by right-clicking the manifest file and selecting **View Code**. The sections are as follows:

- **Application UI**—Information about how the application appears to the end user. This is where you can specify a friendly name like Image Helper and give the application a short description. You can restrict your orientations and manage tiles and notifications (you will learn more about those in Chapter 7, *Tiles and Toasts*).

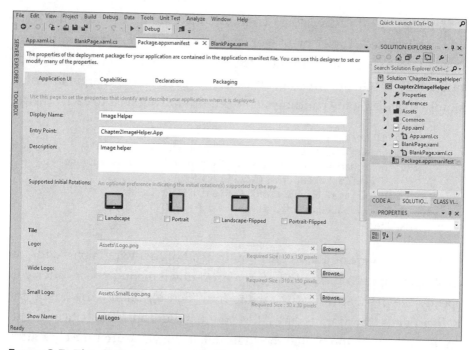

FIGURE 2.7: **The dialog for your application manifest**

- **Capabilities**—The Windows 8 platform restricts the features and devices that your application can use by default. If you wish to interact with those items, you must declare the capability—otherwise, the user will receive an error when attempting to use the capabilities while running the application. Even when you specify a capability, the user may be prompted to "opt-in" to using it. The following capabilities should be selected for this application: **Internet (Client)**, **Pictures Library Access**, and **Webcam**. You can click any capability to read a description about it and get help.

- **Declarations**—Windows 8 applications can integrate with each other using a powerful new platform that includes charms and contracts. You will learn more about declarations in Chapter 8, *Giving Your Application Charm*. For this application, choose the **Share Target** declaration and click the **Add** button. Next, click the **Add New** button under **Data formats** and type **Bitmap**. The dialog should appear similar to what's shown in Figure 2.8.

- **Packaging**—Allows you to edit all of the unique attributes that describe a package when it is deployed. You can provide a unique name to refer to the package as, a display name to show when enumerating packages on the system, and information about the publisher. I left the package name as is and gave it the display name Image Helper.

Be sure to save the package manifest after you are done editing the various properties.

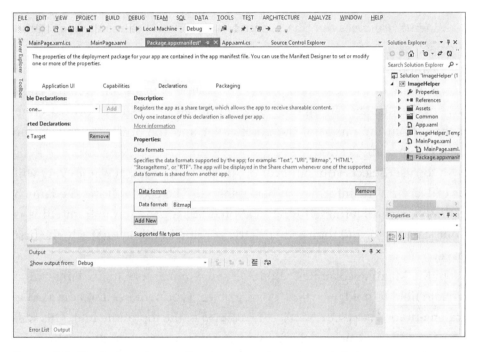

FIGURE 2.8: **Declaring the application as a share target that can accept bitmaps**

Now you can write some code for the application. Don't worry if this is confusing at first—you will start by implementing some specific features and then learn more about what those features do in subsequent chapters. First, because the application was declared as a **Share Target**, you need to implement the right event to handle sharing. In the **App. xaml.cs** file (the code-behind file for the application), add an override to the

App class with the following code (note that it copies the code generated by the template for launching the application—the only difference is that the page is passed a parameter):

```
protected override void
    OnShareTargetActivated(ShareTargetActivatedEventArgs args)
{
    var rootFrame = new Frame();
    rootFrame.Navigate(typeof(MainPage), args);
    Window.Current.Content = rootFrame;
    Window.Current.Activate();
}
```

When a user uses the **Share** charm, a list of applications that declared themselves as a **Share Target** is provided. To see this in action, open an application that shares images (such as the **Photos** application) and hold down the **Windows Key** and press **C** (or swipe your finger from the right side of the display). In Figure 2.9, you can see the result of my selecting a share from the image of the book cover and the option to choose the ImageHelper application.

If the user selects your application, the OnShareTargetActivated event will be called with the information being shared. The code follows the launch code that creates a frame for navigation, adds a page to the frame (this is your start page), and then activates the windows and navigates to the first page.

In the MainPage.xaml.cs, you have some more work to do. First, add a private field to hold a WriteableBitmap object (you will need to add a using statement for Windows.UI.Xaml.Media.Imaging to the top of the file). This will be used to keep track of the camera capture or the shared item that the application is working with:

```
private WriteableBitmap _writeableBitmap;
```

Next, add code to capture an image from the camera. You might be surprised at how easy this is. Add two more using statements:

```
using Windows.Media.Capture;
using Windows.Storage.Streams;
```

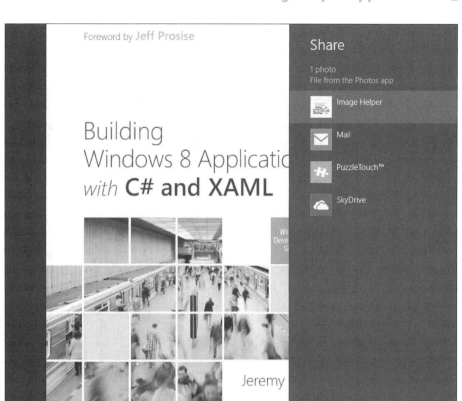

FIGURE 2.9: The Share charm from the Photos application

The code to capture an image from your computer's web camera is shown in Listing 2.1. This will replace the empty method that was generated for the click event from XAML. Enter the code if you are building the application from scratch and then compile, deploy, and run the application by pressing **F5**. You will be prompted for permission to use your webcam the first time it is run, as shown in Figure 2.10.

In just a few lines of code, you were able to activate the user's webcam, allow him to capture a picture, and bring it into the application. If a webcam does not exist, you'll get a page that indicates you should connect a camera. Otherwise, simply tap the image you see to take a photo.

FIGURE 2.10: **Obtaining permission to use the camera**

LISTING 2.1: **Code to Capture an Image from the Built-in Web Camera**

```
private async Task LoadBitmap(IRandomAccessStream stream)
{
    _writeableBitmap = new WriteableBitmap(1, 1);
    _writeableBitmap.SetSource(stream);
    _writeableBitmap.Invalidate();
    await Dispatcher.RunAsync(
        Windows.UI.Core.CoreDispatcherPriority.Normal,
        () => ImageTarget.Source = _writeableBitmap);
}

public async void CaptureButton_Click_1(object sender,
    RoutedEventArgs e)
{
    var camera = new CameraCaptureUI();
    var result = await camera.CaptureFileAsync(
        CameraCaptureUIMode.Photo);
    if (result != null)
```

```
    {
        await LoadBitmap(await result.OpenAsync(
            Windows.Storage.FileAccessMode.Read));
    }
}
```

To stop the application, you can either swipe from the top edge of the application to the bottom, or you can press **Alt+F4.** This will terminate the application but will not stop the debugger. To do that, click the **Stop** icon in Visual Studio 2012 or press **Shift+F5**.

▪ TIP

Most gestures in Windows 8 have keyboard and mouse equivalents. For example, if you swipe from the right edge of the screen, you will see the **Charm Bar**. You can move your mouse pointer over the right edge of the **Task Bar** to accomplish the same thing. With the keyboard, hold down the **Windows Key** and press the letter **C** at the same time. When you are debugging the application and want to return to the desktop, hold down the **Windows Key** and press **D**. If you are using more than one monitor and wish to switch which monitor the start menu appears on, hold down the **Windows Key** and press **Page Up** or **Page Down**.

The code starts by referencing the system-supplied object to manage camera captures. The async and await keywords are used together to asynchronously send a request for the user to grab a photograph (you will gain a much better understanding of asynchronous programming in Chapter 6, *Data*). Control will be passed back when the user selects a photo or cancels from the UI. If the user selected a photo, the remaining code reads in the bits and stores them in a special WriteableBitmap object so that the pixels can be referenced later (when the user saves them to disk) while also being referenced onscreen to show the image. The bitmap logic is in its own method called LoadBitmap so that it can be used with various sources.

The code that will save the image is in Listing 2.2 to replace the other click method. It will require the following using statements to be added:

```
using Windows.Storage;
using Windows.Storage.Pickers;
using Windows.Graphics.Imaging;
using System.Runtime.InteropServices.WindowsRuntime;
```

This code is a bit more involved but still far easier than what you may be used to. The user is prompted for a location to save the file and even given a specific file format to save to—this is all done through the WinRT **Picker** component. When the user selects their destination for the file, the image is encoded using the *Portable Network Graphics (PNG)* format and saved to the destination that the user specified. You can run the application, save the image, and preview it by using the file explorer to navigate to the folder you saved it in. You can learn more about the graphics and imaging libraries in Windows 8 here at http://msdn.microsoft.com/en-us/library/windows/apps/br226400.aspx.

LISTING 2.2: **Code to Save the Image**

```
public async void SaveButton_Click_1(object sender,
    RoutedEventArgs e)
{
    if (_writeableBitmap != null)
    {
        var picker = new FileSavePicker();
        picker.SuggestedStartLocation =
                PickerLocationId.PicturesLibrary;
        picker.FileTypeChoices.Add("Image", new List<string>()
                { ".png" });
        picker.DefaultFileExtension = ".png";
        picker.SuggestedFileName = "photo";
        var savedFile = await picker.PickSaveFileAsync();

        try
        {
            if (savedFile != null)
            {
                IRandomAccessStream output = await
                    savedFile.OpenAsync(FileAccessMode.ReadWrite);
                BitmapEncoder encoder =
                    await BitmapEncoder.CreateAsync(
                    BitmapEncoder.PngEncoderId, output);
                encoder.SetPixelData(BitmapPixelFormat.Rgba8,
                    BitmapAlphaMode.Straight,
                    (uint)_writeableBitmap.PixelWidth,
                    (uint)_writeableBitmap.PixelHeight,
```

```
                    96.0, 96.0,
                    _writeableBitmap.PixelBuffer.ToArray());
                await encoder.FlushAsync();
                await output.GetOutputStreamAt(0).FlushAsync();
            }
        }
        catch (Exception ex)
        {
            var s = ex.ToString();
        }
    }
}
```

The error handling is there just to allow you to set a breakpoint if there is an issue. I purposefully kept this example simple for the first program so you can focus on some of the fast and easy features. In the next few sections, you learn how Windows 8 stores information about your application and enables integration between applications in the Windows 8 platform. First, there is one last step to perform.

When you created the application, you declared a capability for sharing and wrote some code to pass the sharing information to the main page of the application. To receive that information, implement the code in Listing 2.3. This code simply grabs the bitmap data that was shared, loads it to the WriteableBitmap, and displays it the same way as if it had been captured from the web camera. The code goes into MainPage.xaml.cs and replaces the empty OnNavigatedTo method that was generated from the template. You will need to add using statements for both Windows.ApplicationModel. Activation and Windows.ApplicationModel.DataTransfer as well as add a declaration for the _shareOperation field.

LISTING 2.3: The Code to Receive a Shared Bitmap

```
protected async override void OnNavigatedTo(NavigationEventArgs e)
{
    var args = e.Parameter as ShareTargetActivatedEventArgs;
    if (args != null)
    {
        _shareOperation = args.ShareOperation;

        if (_shareOperation.Data.Contains(
            StandardDataFormats.Bitmap))
        {
            _bitmap = await _shareOperation.Data.GetBitmapAsync();
```

```
            await ProcessBitmap();
        }
        else if (_shareOperation.Data.Contains(
            StandardDataFormats.StorageItems))
        {
            _items = await _shareOperation.Data
                .GetStorageItemsAsync();
            await ProcessStorageItems();
        }
        else _shareOperation.ReportError(
            "Image Helper was unable to find a valid bitmap.");
    }
}
```

Notice there are two formats that the application supports. One is a raw bitmap format. When a bitmap is passed in, a stream reference to the contents of the bitmap is saved, and then the bitmap is loaded like this:

```
private async Task ProcessBitmap()
{
    if (_bitmap != null)
    {
        await LoadBitmap(await _bitmap.OpenReadAsync());
    }
}
```

Some applications may reference photos stored on the local device. Instead of packing the contents of the photo in a stream to send over to the share target, the applications will create a list of storage items instead. The storage items refer to files in storage, and some of those files could be images. The code in Listing 2.4 iterates each storage item and loads the first one it finds that is an image format.

LISTING 2.4: **Iterating Storage Items**

```
private async Task ProcessStorageItems()
{
    foreach (var item in _items)
    {
        if (item.IsOfType(StorageItemTypes.File))
        {
            var file = item as StorageFile;
            if (file.ContentType.StartsWith(
                "image",
                StringComparison.CurrentCultureIgnoreCase))
            {
```

```
                    await LoadBitmap(await file.OpenReadAsync());
                    break;
                }
            }
        }
    }
}
```

Compile and then run the application the same way you did before (by pressing **Ctrl+F5**). It should behave the same way it did the last time you ran it. Now exit the application (**Alt+F4** or swipe from top to bottom).

Navigate to an application with images (the easiest is probably the **Photos** application) and show the **Charm Bar**. This is done one of two ways. With your thumb, you can simply swipe from the right side of the touch screen to show the bar. If you are using a mouse, simply hover in the bottom right corner of the screen. You should be presented with a list that includes the image application.

Select the ImageHelper application. The application will slide in from the side. This effect is known as a *fly-out* because it comes in from the side to overlay the existing application. This application reuses the main page to keep it simple; in most cases, you will design a special page for the fly-out that accommodates a narrower screen width. The resulting view will contain a thumbnail of the desktop, with the same buttons to either capture a new image or save the snapshot to disk as you did with the web camera capture.

This example is simplified to show the results of the sharing. When you click the buttons, the application are dismissed. You will not be able to save the file because the file picker tries to overlay the application, which is not allowed in the fly-out. This is part of the share behavior. You will learn more about sharing and how to handle these scenarios appropriately in Chapter 8.

Under the Covers

This first application did quite a lot! Not only were you able to capture an image from the web camera and save it, you were also able to take images shared from other applications and view those from within the application. If your login is connected to a SkyDrive account, you can save your images to the cloud (it will appear as an option in the save file dialog) without changing any code in the application. How does Windows 8 manage these interactions between applications? The answer lies in the details of WinRT.

Applications Are WinRT Components

You learned about the WinRT architecture in the previous chapter. You also used some WinRT components in your first application. The `CameraCaptureUI` is an example of one component, and the `FileSavePicker` was another. What you may be surprised to learn is that the ImageHelper application you created is also a WinRT component! Applications are special WinRT components that can be launched either from the start menu or through contracts.

The lifecycle of a Windows 8 application can be summarized in three simple steps: install, tap, and run. The installation step involves the deployment of your component to the operating system. It is registered with the system (including any capabilities and declarations). When the user taps the icon on the **Start** menu, Windows 8 locates your component and launches it. That is when the application is actually run.

Extensions and Classes

It might surprise you to learn about the way Windows 8 keeps track of your applications. It uses the Windows Registry. The Registry is a hierarchical database that Windows uses to store configuration settings and preferences. The Registry was introduced with Windows 3.1, which makes it over 20 years old! It is this same database that drives the Windows 8 experience, including the contracts that integrate applications with each other.

When you deploy your application, the entry into it is stored as a class in the registry. Classes are the unique identifiers for WinRT components, including applications. Extensions represent contracts. There are numerous contracts in the system, and they all contain a collection of classes that can interface with the contract.

To see how this works, open a command line (the easiest way is to press the **Windows Button** to access the **Start** screen, and then type **cmd** and click the resulting **Command Prompt** icon). Type **regedit** and press **Enter**. When prompted for security, click **Yes**. This will open the classic registry editor that has existed for several versions of Windows. You can also launch it from the application search by pressing the Windows Key and typing **regedit**.

Expand **HKEY_CURRENT_USER**→**Software**→**Classes**→**Activatable Classes**→**Package**. Under package, you will see an entry that starts with the package name (this is the long string that appears by **Package name** on the **Packing** tab of the manifest). This is the registry entry for the application you just built and deployed. You can see the entry is a combination of the package name, the version, the culture, and a generated code. This entry provides information to Windows 8 about how your application should be launched (for example, HTML-based applications must be launched using a host that contains the web browser engine) and what class and method to call to kick things off.

Now expand **HKEY_CURRENT_USER**→**Software**→**Classes**→**Extensions**→**ContractId**. Extensions represent the system contracts. You may recognize some of the contracts such as **Windows.ShareTarget** and **Windows.File**. There is another contract called **Windows.Launch** that represents the contract for WinRT components that can be launched from the start menu. If you expand that node, you will see several items listed, including the ImageHelper application. The same application is also listed under the **Windows.ShareTarget** node.

The application you created was a special WinRT component that Windows 8 stored in the registry. When a user chooses the **Share** charm, Windows 8 will open the registry to find applications listed as a share target and display them as options to the user. When the user taps an option, the class is referenced in the registry where Windows 8 can determine what components to create and what methods to call. The same thing happens when the user launches your application. The application tile is really a special type of **Launch** charm that uses the same technique to look up the class and launch the component.

Using *ILDASM*

In addition to registering information about your application to the operating system, Windows 8 applications also publish metadata. This metadata details the interfaces, classes, methods, and properties exposed by the WinRT components and applications. Whether your application is written in HTML5, C++, or C#, the same type of metadata information is published. This makes it easy for other programs to inspect your component to determine how to use it. It also makes the features of the component available for projection so they can be mapped as local objects in your preferred language.

You can use the ILDASM tool to inspect the metadata for components. To see this in action, open a developer command prompt. Start by bringing up the charm overlay; this is shown in Figure 2.11.

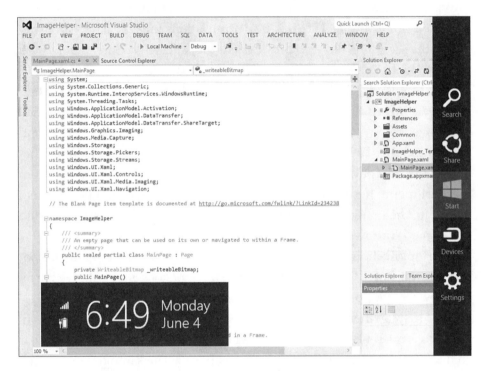

FIGURE 2.11: Bringing up the charm overlay from the Desktop

When the overlay appears, click the **Search** icon and type **Command**. This should provide a list of options. To make it easier to use the command prompt, right-click the **Developer Command Prompt** icon to show the application bar; then click the icon with the text **Pin to taskbar**. Finally, left-click or tap the **Developer Command Prompt** menu item to open the command prompt. Type the following and press **Enter**:

```
ildasm.exe
```

This will launch the .NET Framework IL Disassembler. It is typically used to inspect .NET assemblies and view the associated IL. For Windows 8, it can also inspect WinRT applications and components. This is because the metadata for Windows 8 applications follows the ECMA-335 standard. This is the open standard Microsoft published for the Common Language Infrastructure. You can read the standard online at http://www.ecma-international.org/publications/standards/Ecma-335.htm.

From within Visual Studio 2012, right-click the project name **ImageHelper** in the **Solution Explorer** to open the solution context menu. Choose the option **Open Folder in Windows Explorer**. This will open the folder that the application resides in. Drill down into the **bin→Debug** folder to see the output from compiling the application. The contents of the folder should look similar to what you see in Figure 2.12.

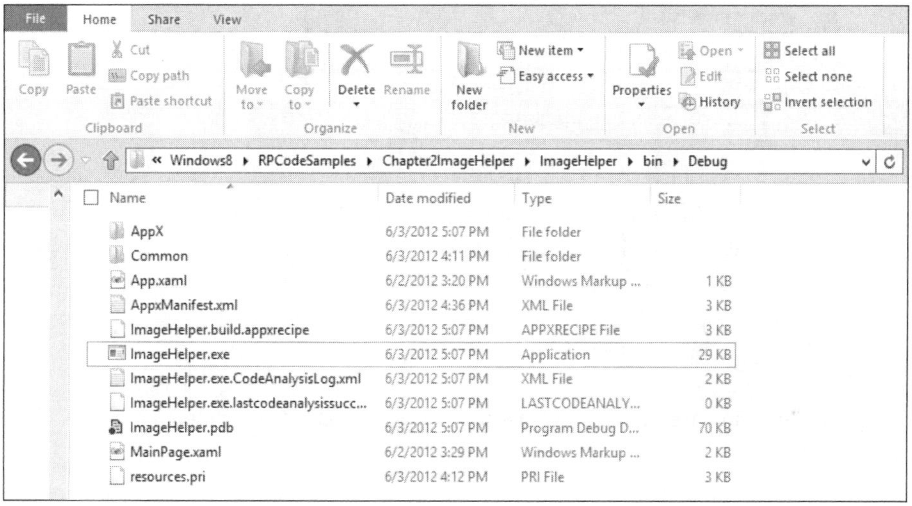

FIGURE 2.12: The output files for the Windows 8 application

Click the ImageHelper file (in the example figure, file extensions are shown—this is a preference setting; they might not display on your system, so choose the file with the type **Application**) and drag it onto the ILDASM dialog. You should see a tree appear as the program parses the metadata for the executable. You can expand the nodes on the tree to see the classes, methods, properties, and events that were generated for the application.

This is shown in Figure 2.13. As you can see, the C# application actually generated IL code and runs with the .NET Framework. The WinRT components for the operating system are projected to the application and appear like native classes.

FIGURE 2.13: **The internal metadata and code for the ImageHelper application**

The application uses several core WinRT components. Even when the components are part of the operating system, it is possible to inspect their signature using the ILDASM tool. For example, to capture an image from the web camera, you included a reference to Windows.Media.Capture and used the component CameraCaptureUI. You can inspect this component if you know where to look.

From the ILDASM tool, either navigate to **File→Open** or press **Ctrl+O**. In the file picker dialog, navigate to the Windows 8 metadata folder:

```
C:\windows\system32\WinMetadata
```

There you will see a list of files that end with the .winmd extension. These files contain the metadata information about the WinRT components they are named for regardless of what language they were built with. Scroll down and select the **Windows.Media.winmd** file (the extension will not appear if you do not have Explorer configured to show file extensions, but the dialog should display the type as **WINMD File**). Click or tap the **Open** button. Figure 2.14 shows the result of expanding several nodes for the component. You can clearly see the class definition and method you used to capture the image.

FIGURE 2.14: Metadata for a WinRT component

You can get a good idea of how comprehensive the Windows 8 platform is by inspecting the number of files available in the metadata folder. Those are just the built-in WinRT components; many more are available through your own code and other applications that are installed on the system. As you can clearly see, the Windows 8 platform is built on decades of legacy technology that many developers are familiar with. It is how it stitches the best parts together that make it so powerful and easy to use.

Summary

In this chapter, you learned several ways to set up an environment to begin developing Windows 8 applications. You learned about the various tools available to create applications and the various templates provided by Visual Studio 2012. You built a sample application that was able to capture images from the camera, receive images shared from other applications, and save the images to your local file system or the cloud with only a few dozen lines of code.

After building and deploying the application, you learned how Windows 8 uses the registry to store information about the application and the contracts it implements. You also learned about the open standards Windows 8 applications used to provide metadata about components and how to inspect the metadata using the ILDASM tool. In the next chapter, you will learn more about XAML technology and how it will help you build the UI for your Windows 8 applications.

3

Extensible Application Markup Language (XAML)

IN THE PREVIOUS CHAPTER, YOU DEVELOPED AN APPLICATION with a simple user interface that was defined using a file that ended with a .xaml extension. XAML is the acronym for Extensible Application Markup Language. It was popularized through its use in Windows Presentation Foundation (WPF) and Silverlight applications. Using XAML for Windows 8 applications should feel very familiar for developers who have used it with other technologies in the past.

XAML is an XML-based declarative markup language that was developed by Microsoft. It is often mistakenly referred to as a user interface language and is compared to HTML. Although XAML is the key technology that drives the visual interface for Windows 8 applications, it is not limited to creating UI elements for platforms like Silverlight and WPF. In fact, XAML drives other technologies including Windows Workflow Foundation (WF).

XAML is defined as a system for representing structured information. XAML contains three distinct nodes: objects, members, and text. The objects in XAML reference either CLR types that are instanced by the XAML parser or WinRT component calls, whereas members reference properties on the types, and text is used to set values. The best way to think about XAML is as a rich object graph that is defined declaratively using XML. In the next section, you learn how XAML allows for declarative instantiation of objects.

The examples in this book are available online at the book source code website at http://windows8applications.codeplex.com/.

Declaring the UI

When using C#, VB, or C++ for your Windows 8 applications, you define the user interface using XAML. The XAML is really a set of declarations for objects that the Windows 8 application will parse and create to make the UI behave the way you want it to. Take a look at Listing 3.1. This is the XAML for the complete UI for the ImageHelper application.

LISTING 3.1: Using XAML to Declare the UI

```
<Page
    x:Class="ImageHelper.MainPage"
    IsTabStop="false"
    xmlns="http://schemas.microsoft.com/winfx/2006/xaml/presentation"
    xmlns:x="http://schemas.microsoft.com/winfx/2006/xaml"
    xmlns:local="using:ImageHelper"
    xmlns:d="http://schemas.microsoft.com/expression/blend/2008"
    xmlns:mc="http://schemas.openxmlformats.org/
➥markup-compatibility/2006"
    mc:Ignorable="d">
    <Grid Background="{StaticResource
➥ApplicationPageBackgroundThemeBrush}">
        <Grid.RowDefinitions>
            <RowDefinition Height="*"/>
            <RowDefinition Height="Auto"/>
        </Grid.RowDefinitions>
        <Image x:Name="ImageTarget" Grid.Row="0"
            HorizontalAlignment="Center" VerticalAlignment="Center"
            Stretch="Uniform"/>
        <StackPanel Grid.Row="1" Margin="10"
            HorizontalAlignment="Center" Orientation="Horizontal">
            <Button x:Name="CaptureButton"
          Content="Capture New Image"
          Click="CaptureButton_Click_1"/>
            <Button x:Name="SaveButton" Content="Save Image"
          Click="SaveButton_Click_1" Margin="20 0 0 0"/>
        </StackPanel>
    </Grid>
</Page>
```

The XAML instructs the parser to create a `Page` object. That object has certain properties. For example, it references the `MainPage` class to specify where the code for the page exists. The page has a child `Grid` object that defines how the elements will appear on the screen. The grid references a resource for the background color. Resources are introduced and explained later in this chapter. An `Image` object is used to host the snapshot or shared bitmap. The `Button` elements not only render buttons on the screen, but also specify how to connect the buttons to application code when they are clicked.

All of the items in the example in Listing 3.1 could have been created programmatically. You can create a new instance of a `Page` object, create a new `Grid` object and assign it to the page, and so forth. Using XAML makes it easy to declare the layout as well as provide a design-time view so you can see what the resulting user interface will look like.

The top of the declaration contains some important *namespace* declarations. In XAML and XML, namespaces are used to provide uniquely named elements and attributes by providing a scope. The `x:Class` attribute is a special attribute in the XAML namespace (defined by the `x:` portion of the attribute) that defines the declaration as a partial class so it can map to the code-behind file. The `xmlns:` namespace is the default XML namespace, and can be used to define your own scopes. The same way you provide a using statement at the top of a C# file to include a namespace, you can use `xmlns:` to define a scope for using other namespaces in XAML. To assign the `MyApp.MyNamespace` namespace to the `local` prefix, you simply add this to the declarations:

```
xmlns:local="using:MyApp.MyNamespace"
```

Then you can address a type called `MyType` in the `MyApp.MyNamespace` namespace like this:

```
<local:MyType/>
```

An assembly that contains the target namespace must be referenced to declare a scope for that namespace, and the assembly that contains the target type must be referenced by the project in order to successfully resolve that type from XAML.

You may notice that the elements after the XAML namespace declarations form a sort of hierarchy. There is a parent object with children, and each child may have their own children. Some elements may be disabled or set so they do not display. The elements that do display make up a special hierarchy. This hierarchy is referred to as the *visual tree*.

The Visual Tree

The visual tree describes the UI elements that are visible on the screen. The diagram in Figure 3.1 represents the visual tree for the very simple ImageHelper application.

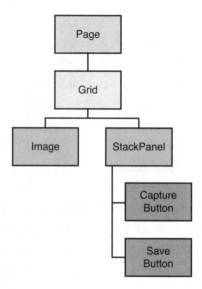

FIGURE 3.1: The visual tree

It is important to understand the visual tree because UI elements can raise special events called *routed events*. To understand why routed events are necessary, consider the act of a user touching a section of the screen. That area happens to be where one of the buttons is rendered. Which UI element should be responsible for the event? Technically, the button is part of the StackPanel, and the StackPanel is a child of the Grid. The user is really touching all three elements at the same time.

When this happens, an event is raised that *bubbles* up the visual tree. It fires in the inner-most (or lower-most) element of the tree. To see this in action, download the **ImageHelper2** example from the book website for Chapter 3. This example adds a `PointerPressed` event to the `Grid` and `StackPanel` elements. It also adds a red `Rectangle` element between the two buttons:

```
<Rectangle Width="30" Height="30" Fill="Red"
    Margin="20 0 0 0"
    PointerPressed="Rectangle_PointerPressed_1"/>
```

When you add an event to a XAML element in the designer, you can simply press the **Tab** key to automatically generate the *code-behind event handler* for that event. The event "listens" for something to happen. When that event happens, it calls the handler for the event. The handler can then do something, such as open the web camera to capture a photo or open the dialog to save a file. The `PointerPressed` event is a special event that fires whether the user taps the screen with her finger or a stylus or left-clicks with a mouse. It is one of the ways Windows 8 simplifies your work as a developer by providing a way to easily handle multiple input devices.

The code that is called for the events simply writes some text to the debug window and appends it to a text block on the page:

```
private void ShowPointerPressed(string source)
{
    var text = string.Format("Pointer pressed from {0}", source);
    Events.Text = string.Format("{0} // {1}", Events.Text, text);
    Debug.WriteLine(text);
}
```

Compile and run the application from the debugger (press **F5**). Click or tap the red rectangle. What happens? You should see three events appear on the screen and in the debug window (if you can't see the debug window, press the following keys at the same time: **Ctrl+Alt+O**):

```
Pointer pressed from Rectangle // Pointer pressed from StackPanel
➥// Pointer pressed from Grid
```

This is what is referred to as bubbling. The event traveled up the visual tree, traveling from the `Rectangle` to the host `StackPanel` and finally to the parent `Grid`. Next, click the space between the rectangle and one of the adjacent buttons. Do the results surprise you? You might expect to see the StackPanel fire the event, followed by the Grid, but only the Grid event appears in the debug window. Why is that?

The XAML engine is smart enough to recognize "empty space" and not fire an event. It assumes you don't want the empty space in the StackPanel to respond to touch events. The StackPanel doesn't specify a background, so it is transparent, and any empty spaces that are pressed will simply "pass through" to the parent element. The Grid element specifies a background, so it is able to process touch events. Update the StackPanel to have a gray background by adding the highlighted code:

```
<StackPanel Grid.Row="1" Margin="10"
            Background="Gray"
            PointerPressed="StackPanel_PointerPressed_1"
            HorizontalAlignment="Center" Orientation="Horizontal">
```

If you would like the "empty space" to process events, you can set the background to Transparent. This has the same visual effect of not specifying a background, but with one key difference. The background will "exist" with a transparent surface that is available to process events, so that the empty space can register taps, holds, and other gestures.

Run the application again and tap on any of the gray space that is not part of a button or the rectangle. You should see that the StackPanel is now picking up the event. Now tap the **Save Image** button. What happens? Are you surprised again? (No event is generated.) One feature of bubbling is the ability to stop the event from bubbling further up the tree (yes, you can literally burst the bubble). The Click event on the button is really an alias for the PointerPressed event, and because it handles the event, it cancels the event to prevent it from bubbling further.

■ NOTE

On Windows 8 slates and tablets, you have a variety of options to interact with Windows 8 applications. A button can be "pressed" by clicking it, tapping it with a finger, or touching it with a stylus. In this book, any time you read the word "click" or "tap," assume you can achieve the same effect by using the left-button on your mouse, your finger, or your stylus. If I am expecting you to perform a specific gesture using a certain form of input, I'll explicitly call that out in the text. Where possible, I will also include the relevant keyboard shortcuts and mouse gestures you can use that are equivalent to their touch-based counterparts.

In the code-behind file **MainPage.xaml.cs**, add the highlighted code to the event handler for the `PointerPressed` event in the `StackPanel`:

```
private void StackPanel_PointerPressed_1(object sender,
    Windows.UI.Xaml.Input.PointerRoutedEventArgs e)
{
    ShowPointerPressed("StackPanel");
    e.Handled = true;
}
```

Compile and run the application again. Click either the rectangle itself or in the space around the rectangle. This time you should see the `StackPanel` event but no `Grid` event. This is because the `StackPanel` indicated it handled the event to prevent the event from bubbling further up the visual tree.

Dependency Properties

Most XAML objects derive from the base `DependencyObject` class. This is a special class that enables objects to participate in the *dependency property system*. The system enhances traditional properties and enables them to be inherited, to affect other classes, and to be manipulated in specified ways.

A dependency property is exposed internally as a static field that is registered with the dependency property system. By convention, the name of the field should end with `Property`. To register the property, you call the static `Register` method of the `DependencyProperty` type. To see this in action, open the **DependencyProperties** project. Take a look at the class called `MyDependencyObject` that inherits from `DependencyObject`:

```
public class MyDependencyObject : DependencyObject
```

The dependency property simply holds an integer. It is hosted using the static, read-only DependencyProperty like this:

```
public static readonly DependencyProperty
    MyNumberProperty = DependencyProperty.Register(
        "MyNumber",
        typeof (int),
        typeof (MyDependencyObject),
        new PropertyMetadata(2, OnMyNumberPropertyChange));
```

The property is named by the property system convention of ending with Property. The first parameter is the name of the property itself (without the suffix). The next parameter is the type of the property, which for this example is an integer. The third parameter is the type of the owner—the class that the dependency property depends on. The last parameter is optional and can provide a default value for the property and/or a method to call whenever the property changes.

The property specifies a method that is called when the property changes. The implementation of this method simply writes the new value to the debug console:

```
private static void OnMyNumberPropertyChange(DependencyObject d,
    DependencyPropertyChangedEventArgs e)
{
    Debug.WriteLine("Property changed: {0}", e.NewValue);
}
```

The **MainPage.xaml** file references this new dependency object. The XAML contains a Slider control. The Slider is used to manipulate values on the dependency object. The dependency object is defined in data context of the grid:

```
<Grid.DataContext>
    <local:MyDependencyObject/>
</Grid.DataContext>
```

Beneath the DataContext for the Grid is the definition for the Slider control. It is bound to the MyNumber property of the dependency object. This binding means that the Slider will get an initial value from the referenced object. When the Slider is moved, the binding will update the target property because the binding is specified as a two-way binding:

```
<Slider Minimum="1" Maximum="100" Height="20"
        HorizontalAlignment="Stretch"
        Value="{Binding Path=MyNumber,Mode=TwoWay}"
        x:Name="Slider"/>
```

You learn more about data-binding later in this chapter.

▪ NOTE

The DataContext is a special dependency property you learn more about in the Data-Binding section of this chapter. The property can be any object but is most often a class that derives from DependencyObject or implements INotifyPropertyChanged. Both of these options provide property change notification that the data-binding system uses to know when to update values. The DataContext is unique not only because it specifies the base object for data-binding instructions, but also because it is inherited. When you set the DataContext at the root Grid level, all child controls will also use the same DataContext unless they specifically override the value.

Although the dependency property system is used to register the dependency properties, they must be exposed to the runtime as common CLR properties. This is referred to as "backing" the properties. The value can be exposed as an ordinary property, but the getter and setter methods will reach out to the dependency property system to determine and/or set their value. Here is the backing code:

```
public int MyNumber
{
    get { return (int) GetValue(MyNumberProperty); }
    set { SetValue(MyNumberProperty, value);}
}
```

The GetValue and SetValue methods are provided by the base DependencyObject class. They are used to query the active values to expose to or update from the backing CLR property. Run the program in debug mode and move the Slider. You should see the new values appear in the debug output window as the result of the property-changed callback you defined.

Dependency properties offer several benefits over regular CLR properties. These include the following

- **Property change notification**—Dependency properties automatically inform the data-binding system when an underlying value changes.
- **Property change callbacks**—Developers can specify a delegate to receive callbacks when dependency properties change and therefore can react to changes outside of the data-binding system.
- **Default values**—Dependency properties can be defined with a default value that can be primitive or complex based on the type of property.
- **Value precedence**—There are multiple ways to influence the actual value of a dependency property including data-binding, styles definitions, XAML literals, and animations.
- **Inheritance**—Child elements can inherit the values of dependency properties from their parent elements.

All of these attributes make dependency properties ideal for the data-binding system that is built into XAML.

Attached Properties

Attached properties are special types of dependency properties that do not belong to a specific dependency object. Instead, they are attached to existing objects. There are two main reasons you would want to use an attached property. First, attached properties are useful for providing additional attributes that are not specific to an element but are useful in the context of other elements. An example of this is the `Grid.Row` attached property. By itself, a `TextBlock` isn't aware of the concept of a "row" because it may exist in any number of panels. When it is positioned within a `Grid`, it is useful to designate where the element should be placed. The attached property provides this additional information, and the parent `Grid` can query the attached property to lay out its children.

Querying an attached property is done through the special `GetValue` method. You must pass the class name that owns the attached property as well as the property name. For example, to query what row a `TextBlock` named `ValueText` is in, you can execute the following code:

```
var row = ValueText.GetValue(Grid.RowProperty);
```

The second common use for attached properties is for a reusable behavior. Attached properties are passed the element they attach to, allowing you to manipulate the element in code. As an example, assume you wanted to make certain buttons automatically open the sharing dialog to make it easy for the user to send data to other applications on their system. Instead of adding code to every page, you want to make it easy by providing a simple attribute. When the attribute is set to `True`, the button will automatically open the dialog for sharing when clicked.

In the **DependencyProperties** project, the `MagicButton` class makes this happen. Note that the class itself does not have to derive from `DependencyObject`. The attached property is defined almost the same way as the dependency property through a different method:

```
public static readonly DependencyProperty IsShareButtonProperty =
    DependencyProperty.RegisterAttached(
    "IsShareButton",
    typeof(Boolean),
    typeof(MagicButton),
    new PropertyMetadata(false,
        new PropertyChangedCallback(Changed)));
```

When the property is changed, the host object is first checked to ensure it is a `Button`. If it is, the `Click` event is intercepted and used to show the sharing dialog:

```
static void button_Click(object sender, RoutedEventArgs e)
{
    DataTransferManager.ShowShareUI();
}
```

Finally, the attached property must provide a projection so that it can be used in XAML. The format is slightly different from a dependency property because the context is from a static reference rather than an instance of a dependency object. Instead of exposing a property, two static methods are provided. These are automatically parsed from XAML and modified to look like "natural" properties in the designer:

```
public static void SetIsShareButton(UIElement element, Boolean value)
{
    element.SetValue(IsShareButtonProperty, value);
}
public static Boolean GetIsShareButton(UIElement element)
{
    return (Boolean)element.GetValue(IsShareButtonProperty);
}
```

The verbs for Get and Set are not shown in the designer, so you can attach the property like this:

```
<Button Content="No Magic"/>
<Button Content="Magic"
        local:MagicButton.IsShareButton="True"
        Margin="20 0 0 0"/>
```

When you run the project, the first button does nothing. Clicking the second button will open the sharing dialog. This will have no effect because the application does not contain the code to satisfy the share contract. You'll learn more about that in Chapter 8, *Giving Your Applications Charm*.

Although this example was simple and contrived, it should be obvious how flexible and powerful attached properties can be. Whenever you find yourself building a complex behavior that may be repeated for several controls in the system, consider refactoring it as a reusable attached property instead. Another benefit of attached properties is that their values can be enumerated by the designer, making it easy for users to understand how to use them from XAML.

To recap, the DependencyObject class is the base class for the dependency property system. This system provides the ability to compute the values of special extended properties and provide notifications when values have changed. This is the base class for most of the controls that exist in the framework. This allows the controls to expose their properties to allow data-binding and animations through storyboards (these are covered later in this chapter).

Data-Binding

Data-binding uses an object to synchronize information between a source and a target. The source is the underlying data element and is any type of CLR object, from Plain Old CLR Objects (POCOs) to dependency properties or other complex types. It can also be a WinRT object that has a `BindableAttribute` or implements `ICustomPropertyProvider` (the focus of this book is C#, but if you are building components using C++, you will need to understand these two approaches to expose your objects if you wish for them to participate in data-binding). The target must be the `DependencyProperty` of a `FrameworkElement` that the value is being synchronized with, such as the `TextProperty` of a `TextBox` or `TextBlock`. The data-binding object often references a type that implements `IValueConverter` to help transform the data from the source to the target and back again (you'll learn about value converters later in this chapter). Figure 3.2 illustrates how the data-binding object brokers interactions between the source and the target.

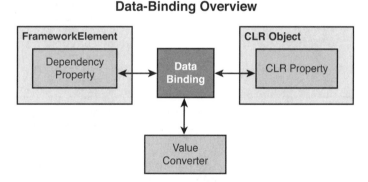

Data-Binding Overview

FIGURE 3.2: The data-binding system

Data-binding is specified declaratively by using the extension syntax with `{Binding}` as the keyword. The following example from **DependencyProperties** illustrates a simple binding:

```
<TextBlock Text="{Binding MyNumber}"/>
```

Unless overridden, the binding will always attach to the current object that is set to the DataContext. The next parameter by default is a path to a property on that object–in this case, the MyNumber property. You can pass a variety of parameters to the Binding object. Table 3.1 lists these parameters and their purpose.

TABLE 3.1: Binding Parameters

Parameter Name	Possible Values	Description
Converter	Any keyed resource that implements IValueConverter.	Allows conversion between types.
ConverterLanguage	A language value.	By default, a converter is passed the language based on the application context. When this parameter is set, it will override the default value and pass the speci- fied value instead.
ConverterParameter	Any type of object or reference to an already existing object.	The object specified for this parameter will be passed to the converter. It is typically used to modify the conversion somehow; for example, by passing a flag to invert the result of a Boolean operation.
ElementName	The name property of an element in the cur- rent XAML name scope (or the name scope of the template parent if the binding target is inside of a template).	Allows you to bind to another element. This property is mutually exclusive to Source and RelativeSource.

Mode	OneWay to update the target property at the time of binding or when the source changes. OneTime to only update the target property at the time of binding. TwoWay to update the target property at the time of binding and then update either the target or source whenever the other changes.	Mode determines the direction of the data-binding. A good way to think of it is whether your binding is "read-only" or "edit" when you want to capture values from the user and update them back to the source from the target UI element.
Path	A valid path to a property on the source object. Can be a property name (including dot notation for nested properties) or an indexer (that is, [3].Name for the name property of the third element in a list and [Foo] for the value of the "Foo" entry in a dictionary).	The path points to the property on the source object that is used for the data-binding.
RelativeSource	TemplatedParent for the control where a ControlTemplate is applied. Self to bind the target element to itself.	This property is used to provide a relative binding to either a template or to bind an element to itself (for example, to allow one property to update another). It is mutually exclusive to ElementName and Source.
Source	The source object to use for the data-binding, usually a static resource defined in the resource dictionary (leaving this property empty will default the binding to the current DataContext).	Use this property to specify a certain object other than the current DataContext for the source object in the data-binding. It is most often either a property on the current DataContext or a static resource declared in the resource dictionary.

You can see some examples of different types of bindings in the **DependencyProperties** project. The second value that is shown uses ElementName binding to bind directly to the Slider control:

```
<TextBlock Text="{Binding ElementName=Slider, Path=Value}"/>
```

There is also a binding that shows the size of the font of the text field by binding to itself:

```
<TextBlock  Text="{Binding RelativeSource={RelativeSource Self},
➥Path=FontSize}"/>
```

For data-binding to work correctly, the host object must inform the data-binding system when any of the properties change. Without this notification, data-binding will never reflect the most recent value. There are two ways to raise this notification in C# code. The first is to use a dependency property. Dependency properties automatically participate in the data-binding system and provide the necessary property change notifications.

The second way is to implement INotifyPropertyChanged. The interface defines a single event called PropertyChanged. For anything but OneTime bindings, the Binding object will register to this event when present and listen for properties to change. Using this approach, you are responsible for raising the event whenever the values of properties change. Open the **DataBinding** project and view the DataBindingHost class, as shown in Listing 3.2. Notice that the class tracks the value of the IsOn property using a private field. The public property updates the field and raises the PropertyChanged event when a property is set. The helper method RaisePropertyChanged is used for this. Although it is not necessary for this simple example, on a larger object it will come in handy to manage notifications for several different properties.

LISTING 3.2: Property Change Notification

```
public class DataBindingHost : INotifyPropertyChanged
{
    private bool _isOn;

    public bool IsOn
    {
```

```
    get
    {
        return _isOn;
    }

    set
    {
        _isOn = value;
        RaisePropertyChanged();
    }
}

protected void RaisePropertyChanged([CallerMemberName]
    string caller = "")
{
    PropertyChanged(this, new PropertyChangedEventArgs(caller));
}

public event PropertyChangedEventHandler PropertyChanged =
    delegate { };
}
```

The helper method uses a special trick to raise the PropertyChanged event. If you are a Silverlight or WPF developer, you probably recall the various tricks developers had to use to call the event. These ranged from passing a hard-coded string to the method (a technique that can cause issues when the developer mistakenly misspells a property name) to passing a lambda expression and then walking the expression tree to extract the property name (this approach was strong-typed but resulted in an awkward syntax). With C# 5 you can simply tag a string parameter with the CallerMemberName attribute, and it will be set at compile-time to the calling method. In the case of a property, it is set to the property name, which makes it convenient to use for property change notification.

One thing you may ask is, "Why implement this interface when dependency objects do the same thing?" The answer is straightforward. The DependencyObject class is part of the presentation framework for XAML. It lives in Windows.UI.Xaml and makes the most sense to use when creating custom controls or objects that expose properties that need to be animated. The INotifyPropertyChanged interface is part of the core framework and does not require a dependency on XAML or the UI. It allows you to create lightweight objects that are referred to as Plain Old CLR Objects (POCO for short) that you can extend, test, and even share with code written for other systems that don't use XAML. The interface can be used to provide property change notification anywhere, but a DependencyObject must work within the dependency property system.

In Listing 3.2, you may have noticed the practice of setting the event handler to an empty delegate. This helps simplify the code. In the rare case that an event is unregistered before calling the handler, the code could throw an exception. Typically, you would check for null before calling the handler. Setting an empty delegate ensures there will always be at least one event registered, even if it's the "do nothing" default handler.

The main advantage for using data-binding is a clean separation between the UI concerns and the underlying data. A simple example is a Boolean value you would like to show as green for "true" and red for "false." The data model should not have to be manipulated to generate the colors because those are a function of the UI. Instead, you can use data-binding to pull the value and a value converter to transform it.

Value Converters

Open the project **DataBinding** and take a look inside the **Converters** folder. There are three examples of value converters. Value converters all implement the IValueConverter interface, which defines two methods: Convert and ConvertBack. The first is almost always implemented and converts a source type on the data-binding object to a target type on the element it is bound to. The second method is used when you want to use the converter on a two-way binding. It is used to convert back from the type on the target element to the type on the source—for example, you might want to convert the text in a TextBox control to a number or color or other value on your binding source.

The visibility converter transforms a Boolean value to the enumeration used by XAML to show or hide a UI element:

```
return visible ? Visibility.Visible : Visibility.Collapsed;
```

If you bind the value directly to a text property, the data-binding system will call the ToString() method on the value and fallback to the type name. Using a converter, you can transform the value to more meaningful text:

```
return truth ?
    "The truth will set you free." :
    "Is falsehood so established?";
```

Finally, you can convert the value into more complex objects including a brush with a specific color:

```
return truth ? new SolidColorBrush(Colors.Green)
    : new SolidColorBrush(Colors.Red);
```

Converters are stored as resources that can be reused in your XAML pages. You learn more about resources later in this chapter. The converters in this example are declared with a key to reference them by in the **MainPage.xaml** file, for example:

```
<converters:VisibilityConverter x:Key="CvtVisibility"/>
```

This creates what is known as a *static resource* because it is fixed and cannot be changed, although it can be referenced multiple times throughout XAML. The convention for referencing a static resource is obvious in the data-binding command (note the highlighted key):

```
Visibility="{Binding IsOn,Converter={StaticResource CvtVisibility}}"
```

Listing 3.3 shows the full set of bindings from the **MainPage.xaml** file.

LISTING 3.3: Various Bindings

```
<CheckBox IsChecked="{Binding IsOn, Mode=TwoWay}"/>
<TextBlock Text="Is On?" Grid.Column="1"/>
<TextBlock
    Text="Now You See Me."
    Visibility="{Binding IsOn,
➡Converter={StaticResource CvtVisibility}}"
    Grid.Row="1"/>
<TextBlock
    Text="Now You Don't."
    Visibility="{Binding IsOn,Converter=
➡{StaticResource CvtVisibility},ConverterParameter=True}"
    Grid.Row="1" Grid.Column="1"/>
<TextBlock Text="{Binding IsOn}" Grid.Row="2"/>
<TextBlock Text="{Binding IsOn, Converter=
➡{StaticResource CvtText}}" Grid.Row="2" Grid.Column="1"/>
<Ellipse Grid.Row="3" Grid.ColumnSpan="2" Height="100" Width="100"
    Fill="{Binding IsOn,Converter={StaticResource CvtColor}}"/>
```

You can run the example to see for yourself the variety of ways a single piece of data can be transformed into interactive information in your UI. Notice that the source DataBindingHost simply defines a single Boolean property and is completely decoupled from the UI. The two different states are shown in Figure 3.3.

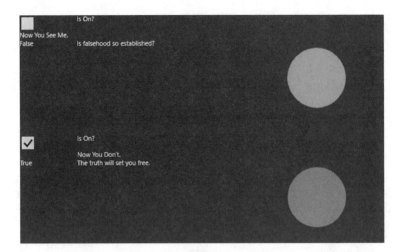

FIGURE 3.3: **How data-binding and converters can change visuals**

Using data-binding and value converters, you are able to transform that data into text and color and even use it to turn off elements on the display.

Storyboards

Storyboards affect dependency objects by updating their properties and impact the target values over a period of time. The most common application of this behavior is animations used for transitions between states and to emphasize certain actions to the user. Storyboards inherit from the Timeline object. Table 3.2 lists the various properties on the timeline and what they do.

TABLE 3.2: Properties of the Timeline Class

Property	Description
AutoReverse	When this property is set to true, the timeline will play backward (in reverse) when it reaches the end.
BeginTime	The begin time determines the delay between starting the animation and the first property change taking effect. A begin time of 2 seconds, for example, will delay the timeline from starting until 2 seconds after the Begin method is called.
Duration	Determines how long the timeline lasts.
SpeedRatio	This is the ratio of the timeline's speed relative to its parent. A ratio of 0.5 will cause a timeline to play at half the rate of speed as its parent timeline.
FillBehavior	Fill behavior is important because it determines what happens when a timeline stops. If the property is set to Stop (default), the timeline will no longer affect the target property when it completes. If the property is set to HoldEnd, the timeline will continue to affect the value of the target property even when the timeline completes (but only until it is explicitly stopped).
RepeatBehavior	This property can be set to several different values. An integer count will determine how many times the timeline is played (including the reverse if AutoReverse is set). A duration will determine the total time the timeline will play (for example, a timeline with a duration of 30 seconds and a RepeatBehavior value of 2 minutes will repeat four times). The special value Forever will cause the timeline to repeat indefinitely.
Completed	This event is fired when the timeline completes.

Take a moment to review the **Storyboards** project.

The project illustrates various uses of the timelines. Here is a sample storyboard definition from the project:

```
<Storyboard x:Name="FirstOneAnimation"
            Storyboard.TargetName="FirstOne">
    <DoubleAnimation Duration="0:0:5"
                        Storyboard.TargetProperty=
         "(Rectangle.RenderTransform).(ScaleTransform.X)"
                        From="-300" To="300"/>
</Storyboard>
```

The target is a rectangle defined later in the XAML that is colored red due to an implicit style setting. You'll learn more about styles in the next section. The storyboard can use the TargetName property to point to an element with that name or the Target property to point to a specific object such as a resource.

The target property can be the name of the property, or it can use what is called path notation. Path notation involves taking each object in the XAML hierarchy and enclosing it in parentheses, followed by a period and then the next property.

The pattern looks like this:

```
(object.property).(object.property)
```

In the example, the target is a rectangle, so the first portion of the property path indicates that it is the RenderTransform property of the Rectangle that is being targeted. This will contain a matrix transformation that can be used to manipulate the element. In this example, the transformation is a translation that will move the Rectangle along the X axis. The period indicates that the path should continue to the value assigned to the transformation, which in this case is a TranslateTransform class. Ultimately, it is the X property on the transformation class that is targeted for animation.

There are additional storyboards included in the example to show you a variety. The second example automatically repeats and reverses itself, so it will run until it is explicitly told to stop. It also contains an easing function that modifies the computations for the animation. Animations are frame-based. When a range is provided, the number frames the graphics card is capable of displaying for the duration is computed and used to derive how much offset should be applied per frame. You don't have to worry about how fast the graphics display is rendering because the animation will handle that for you. You only need to specify the start and end values and the duration.

It is also possible to create discrete animations that abruptly change values. The third storyboard changes colors. Instead of fading between the colors over time, it will immediately switch the new color when the *key time* is reached—that is, the time within the duration the discrete value should change. The last animation also uses a discrete value but demonstrates the use of an object animation to hide the animation by applying a value of `Visibility.Collapsed`.

Every storyboard defines a "base timeline" that the children of the storyboard operate against. In addition to the base timeline, the storyboard can contain a collection of other timelines (or other storyboards and animations). Like all dependency objects, storyboards follow rules of inheritance. If you set the duration at the storyboard level, all child timelines will inherit that duration. If a child specifies the duration, this will override the parent setting.

Four animations are built into the framework. You can build your own, but the following will address most of your needs:

- **ColorAnimation**—This animates the color property of a dependency property and transitions between the "from color" and the "to color."
- **DoubleAnimation**—This animates a double value across a range. Most properties in the runtime are doubles, so this animation addresses most use cases.
- **PointAnimation**—This animates between two points and is most often used to position geometry objects.
- **ObjectAnimationUsingKeyFrames**—This allows you to set discrete values at specific times.

The first three animations can also be specified as discrete animations using key frames. The basic animations move through a range of values over the specified duration. Discrete animations switch abruptly from one value to the next at a specified time or key frame in the animation. As an example, you might start an animation by setting the element to visible, move it across the screen, fade its opacity, and then end on a key frame that sets it to the collapsed state to remove it from the visual tree.

In addition to the methods and events described in Table 3.2, storyboards add the ability to begin, pause, resume, stop, and seek animations, as detailed here:

- Begin kicks off the animation.
- Stop ends the animation.
- Pause keeps the animation from playing further but maintains the current position in the timeline.
- Resume starts the animation from the paused position rather than starting over from the beginning.
- Seek allows you to skip ahead into the animation.

The storyboard example illustrates some simple animations. Animations become far more interesting when they are used with transformations, which can cause the elements to slide, rotate, expand, contract, and even appear to rotate away from the user in three dimensions using projections.

Animations may also be impacted by easing functions. By default, a timeline is linear, and the values change along the same velocity. An easing function changes the velocity to provide a more organic effect. There are many easy functions built into the framework. Two examples include

- A bounce ease can cause an element to oscillate between values faster and faster to give the same effect as a basketball settling on the court.
- A circle ease rapidly accelerates or decelerates to create the effect of an element sliding in quickly and then slowing down abruptly when it reaches its destination.

The ability to separate the behavior of the UI using storyboards from the functionality of the application is very important. Design is an important aspect of applications but is not the central focus of this book. Fortunately, as a developer, I can abstract the UI from the code. When a user selects a menu item, I can program the impact of that selection while the designer handles the UI event of the click and creates animations and other effects as needed. This abstraction will be explained in more detail later in this book. Storyboards are a powerful way to add subtle cues to the application that help the user understand when items are in focus, when actions need to be taken, and even to present toast notifications for the user to acknowledge. The Visual State Manager (VSM) works with storyboards to provide some valuable services that are visited in detail later in this chapter.

Styles and Resources

In the previous example, you might have noticed that the Grid element contained a Resources collection, and in that collection was a Style. Styles are a special type of dependency object. The content of a Style is a list of Setter elements. Setter elements provide a value for a property. What makes Style instances unique is that they can be defined once and then applied multiple times. They can implicitly affect any element of a given type and can be based on other styles to provide a hierarchy.

Style definitions are a key to success in Windows 8 applications because they provide a decoupled way to describe the look and feel. The developer doesn't have to worry about nuances such as font sizes and complex color gradients when they can be defined separately by styles. The property for Style is defined on the FrameworkElement class and allows styles to be applied to any element that is a descendant of the framework element.

If you recall, DependencyObject is the base class for the dependency property system. This is extended by UIElement, a base class for objects that have a visual appearance and can process input. Events for keyboard, pointers, touch, manipulations, and focus are declared on the UIElement class. The UIElement class is extended by the FrameworkElement class. This class adds layout capabilities, object lifetime events (such as the Loaded and Unloaded events), support for data-binding, and support for Style instances.

Style instances are most often declared in resources. In XAML, UI elements can contain a collection of resources used by that UI element and its children. Resources are simply dictionaries that can contain reusable values. Each value is provided with a key that is used to reference the value. Examples of resources include storyboards, styles, and value converters. The main restriction for resources is that they cannot be items that exist in the visual tree. The reason for this is that any element may only exist exactly once in the visual tree. Resources can be reused, so this would potentially result in an element being reference more than once. This will result in an error that the element is already the child of another element.

Resources are scoped to the UI element and follow the inheritance you are probably used to now in XAML. A resource declared at the Page level will be available to all items in the page, while a resource declared for a specific Grid element is only available for the children of that Grid. You can also group resources together in easily referenced collections called *resource dictionaries*. In the **StoryboardExamples** project, open up **App.xaml**. Notice that there is a ResourceDictionary tag. Inside the dictionary, a file is referenced:

```
<ResourceDictionary Source="Common/StandardStyles.xaml"/>
```

The reference is at the highest level for the application, so it makes the resources available everywhere. This is why the button and text already had a distinct Windows 8 style even though you didn't specify any special attributes. If you open the file that is referenced called **StandardStyles. xaml**, you will see the standard styles used within Windows 8 applications. Use this as a guide and reference it often because this will be important for keeping your applications fluid and consistent. You'll find definitions for buttons, common icons, and even animations and transitions that are often used.

Resources can be accessed through code. The resource collection is a dictionary. In the example, the main grid for the application hosts the storyboards. You can access them through code like this:

```
var firstOne = (Storyboard)MainGrid.Resources["FirstOneAnimation"];
```

When you click the button for the application, the event handler filters the list of resources in the main grid down to any resources that are of type Storyboard and then calls the Begin method. This automatically starts all of the storyboards. If you add an additional storyboard to the collection, it will be automatically grabbed by the logic for the button click:

```
foreach (var storyboard in
    MainGrid.Resources.Values.OfType<Storyboard>())
{
    storyboard.Begin();
}
```

Although they are defined as resources, some styles will affect your controls even if they are not directly referenced because they are implicit styles. An implicit style is automatically applied to any instance of a type within the current scope automatically. Instead of having a key to reference the style explicitly, it targets a type and is applied implicitly. The `Rectangle` elements were colored using an implicit style:

```
<Style TargetType="Rectangle">
    <Setter Property="Fill" Value="Red"/>
</Style>
```

An explicit style has a key associated with it and must be explicitly declared on the element that will use it. The background for the Windows 8 application is set using an explicit `Style`:

```
<Grid
    x:Name="MainGrid"
    Background="{StaticResource ApplicationPageBackgroundThemeBrush}">
```

`Style` instances can also handle complex, nested objects and attached properties. They can target attributes, nested properties, and define complex objects such as brushes. Any time you find yourself applying a margin or formatting, you should stop and reconsider applying the formatting through a `Style`. This moves it to a central location that keeps it consistent across your application and makes it easy to change when necessary. Many examples in this book provide inline formatting to keep the examples simple; later examples will use styles more often to define look and feel.

`Style` instances affect the theme of the application. This example demonstrated `Style` definitions embedded directly in a resources section on a control. It will be more common for your applications to define a separate dictionary of Style instances and reference it. The templates for C# and XAML automatically generate a place to define your common Style definitions..

Layout

Windows 8 applications must provide a fluid, responsive layout that works well in all form factors your application may be forced into. These include both portrait and landscape orientations with multiple dimensions as well as snapped views. XAML provides a number of UI elements to facilitate the layout for your application.

The standard application consists of a *root visual* or "master" UI element that represents the full surface area of the application. This is typically set to be a Frame element. This is a special container that supports navigation. The container is capable of swapping out Page elements that represent a logical page within your application. You will learn more about the navigation framework in Chapter 5, *Application Lifecycle*.

Inside of each logical page is a set of controls that provide formatting and layout for all of the elements you wish to display on that page. Layout elements range from simple surface areas used to place other elements on to lists and a special new set of controls that support grouping of data. You learn about these later. First you review a few simple panels that have been carried forward from Silverlight and WPF. You can see examples for most of these panels in the **Layout** project for Chapter 4.

Canvas

The canvas best accommodates a fixed surface. It is used when you need specific precision over the layout of your containers and are not building a fluid layout. The Canvas hosts other controls on a simple matrix, and you position children by specifying the offset from the top-left corner of the Canvas to the top-left corner of the element. The Canvas allows you to specify a ZIndex to control how elements are rendered relative to each other. Higher values cause the controls to render closer to the viewer or the top of the stack of controls.

The Canvas always provides a fixed layout. It does not respond to resize events and therefore will not flow children to fit smaller or larger screen sizes. It is the least flexible of all the built-in panel types.

Example code for the Canvas:

```
<Canvas Width="400" Height="400" Background="White">
    <Rectangle Fill="Red" Width="200" Height="150"/>
    <Rectangle Fill="Green" Width="150" Height="75"/>
    <Ellipse Fill="Blue" Width="250" Height="250"
    Canvas.Left="75" Canvas.Top="75" Canvas.ZIndex="-1"/>
</Canvas>
```

This will result in the layout shown in Figure 3.4.

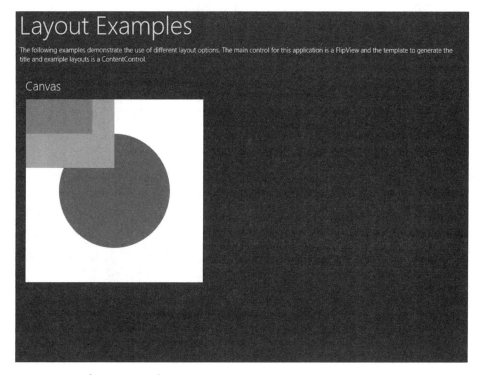

FIGURE 3.4: The **Canvas** layout

Grid

The Grid is by far the most common—and the most powerful—layout control. It is also the default layout control in the Visual Studio templates. The Grid is often compared to an HTML table because it allows specification of rows and columns. The layout system in XAML is very flexible. You can specify the size of cells based on pixels, based on automatically sizing to the cell contents, based on points, or based on a ratio relative to other cells. You may also nest controls inside of other controls. A common layout practice is to define an automatic or fixed height or width for the navigation or ribbon bar and then allow the remaining cells to expand to fit the available width.

One important feature of the Grid is that it participates well in fluid layouts. It is capable of stretching to fill the available space within the parent container as well as accommodating the varying size requirements of its contents. There are three ways to specify the GridLength property that determines the width of a column or the height of a row:

- Using points
- Using Auto to determine the size based on the dimensions of the child elements contained within the cell
- Using star notation, which represents a fraction of the remaining available space

The star notation is probably the trickiest to understand. The star modifier simply indicates the remaining space. The star modifier by itself represents one unit of the remaining available space. When you specify a different value, the proportion will change by that value. Table 3.3 illustrates how the star values are computed given a grid that is exactly 400 pixels wide.

TABLE 3.3: Grid Sizes Using the Star Notation for a 400-Pixel-Wide Grid

Column 1	Column 2	Column 3	Formula
* 133.33	* 133.33	* 133.34	1 + 1 + 1 = 3. Each column is 1/3 of 400.
* 200	0.5* 100	0.5* 100	1 + 0.5 + 0.5 = 2. The first column is 1/2 of 400. The remaining columns are 1/4 of 400 (0.5/2).

1*	2*	3*	1 + 2 + 3 = 6. The first column is 1/6 of 400, the second is 1/3, and the third is 1/2.
66.666	133.334	200	
100	0.5*	2*	0.5 + 2 = 2.5. The first column takes 100, so the remaining columns have 300. 0.5 / 2.5 = 1/5 of 300, 2 / 2.5 = 4/5 of 300.
100	60	240	

The way the grid handles arranging and measuring is important because it can impact how you design custom controls. Listing 3.4 shows a sample Grid layout.

LISTING 3.4: XAML for the **Grid** Layout

```
<Grid Background="White" Width="400" Height="400">
    <Grid.RowDefinitions>
        <RowDefinition Height="1*"/>
        <RowDefinition Height="2*"/>
    </Grid.RowDefinitions>
    <Grid.ColumnDefinitions>
        <ColumnDefinition Width="1*"/>
        <ColumnDefinition Width="2*"/>
    </Grid.ColumnDefinitions>
    <Rectangle Fill="Red" Width="250" Height="125"/>
    <Rectangle Fill="Green" Width="150" Height="75"
        Grid.Row="1"/>
    <Ellipse Fill="Blue" Width="250" Height="250"
        Grid.Row="1" Grid.Column="2"/>
</Grid>
```

This will result in the layout shown in Figure 3.5.

StackPanel

The StackPanel is a special panel that stacks children either horizontally or vertically, depending on its orientation. It is a good choice when you don't have the requirement to align columns or rows or have a dynamic list of items that you want to add without having to compute rows and columns beforehand. Based on the orientation, the StackPanel will automatically compute the height or width of the element and place it either to the right or bottom of the previous control.

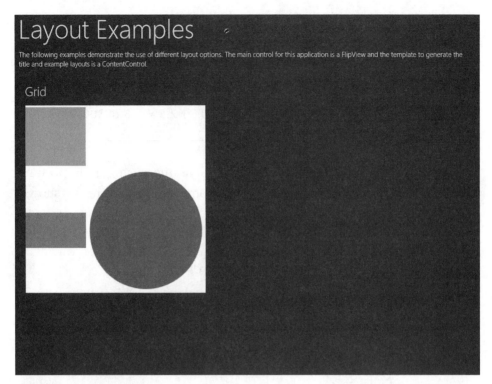

FIGURE 3.5: The **Grid** layout

The caveat to using the StackPanel is that it always provides infinite space in the orientation direction for its children. To view all items that are placed within a StackPanel, you will need to use a ScrollViewer to scroll the virtual pane. If you require a control to size based on available space, you'll need to use a WrapGrid that will be described later. The stack panel is best suited to smaller lists of data that you know can size and fit within the available space.

Example code for the StackPanel:

```
<StackPanel Background="White" Width="400" Height="400">
    <Rectangle Fill="Red" Width="250" Height="125"/>
    <Rectangle Fill="Green" Width="150" Height="75"/>
    <Ellipse Fill="Blue" Width="250" Height="250"/>
</StackPanel>
```

This will result in the layout shown in Figure 3.6.

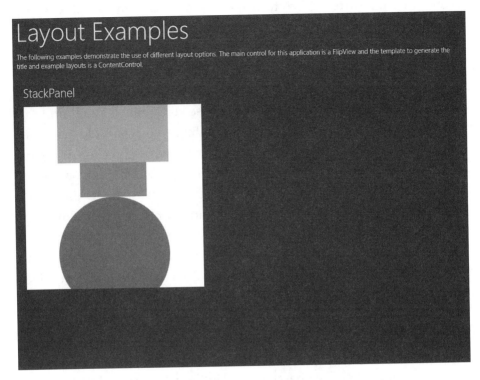

FIGURE 3.6: The **StackPanel** layout

VirtualizingPanel and VirtualizingStackPanel

A specialized panel, referred to as a *virtualizing panel*, helps you deal with large amounts of data. The ListBox control uses the virtualizing stack panel for the default container to lay out content. This can be overridden, but there is a good reason for using it.

The ordinary stack panel will take on an infinite number of items because it provides an infinite length for the orientation. If you provide 5,000 items, the stack panel will generate 5,000 items even if the display will only fit 10 of them. This can obviously lead to tremendous overhead when dealing with large datasets.

The virtualizing stack panel, on the other hand, will compute the required size for only the subset of data that is available to render on the display. If only ten items can fit, the virtualizing stack panel will only instantiate ten controls. When the user scrolls through the list, it will keep the same fixed number of controls but swap the content of the data. You will learn more about how data templates work in the next chapter.

The drawback to using a virtualizing stack panel is that the scrolling is not smooth. In the example for the layout engine, two list boxes are rendered, and one is overridden to use the base stack panel. You'll find that the base stack panel allows for smooth scrolling—you can slide the thumb a few pixels and reveal only part of the control that is off the top or bottom of the scroll window. In the virtualized stack panel, you can only scroll one item at a time—there is not a partial scroll because the entire item is swapped into or out of view. This is the tradeoff between handling large amounts of data without degrading performance and providing a smooth UI. You can also build a custom control that provides the benefits of both, which is what many third-party control vendors have done and provided as part of their control suite.

WrapGrid

This control is a special type of grid that automatically handles rows and columns based on the data passed to it. Unlike a Grid control that requires you to specify a specific row or column, the WrapGrid does this for you. It will position the child elements sequentially from left to right or top to bottom based on an orientation and then wrap to the next row or column.

This is a powerful control you'll see demonstrated in the Chapter3Panels application. It allows the data to flow and fill the available screen size by taking up as many rows and columns are available. The user can still swipe to view more items as needed. This keeps you from having to compute how much available space there is as the grid will resize based on the current resolution.

The WrapGrid is always defined as part of a template for a list control, as shown in Listing 3.5.

LISTING 3.5: XAML for the **WrapGrid** Layout

```
<ItemsControl>
 <ItemsControl.ItemsPanel>
    <ItemsPanelTemplate>
        <WrapGrid
            ItemHeight="200"
            ItemWidth="200"
            MaximumRowsOrColumns="2"
            Width="400"
            Height="400"
            Background="White"/>
    </ItemsPanelTemplate>
 </ItemsControl.ItemsPanel>
 <ItemsControl.Items>
    <Rectangle Fill="Red" Width="250" Height="125"/>
    <Rectangle Fill="Green" Width="150" Height="75"/>
    <Ellipse Fill="Blue" Width="250" Height="250"/>
 </ItemsControl.Items>
</ItemsControl>
```

This will result in the layout shown in Figure 3.7.

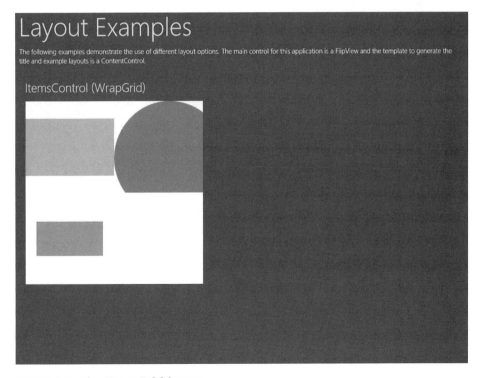

FIGURE 3.7: The **WrapGrid** layout

VariableSizedWrapGrid

The Windows 8 Start Menu is a great example of what the VariableSized WrapGrid can do. You'll notice that some tiles are longer than others, so elements in the grid take up different amounts of space. This is common when you want to display different types of elements in the grid, and some may have different orientations or dimensions.

There are two ways you can specify how many cells an item takes up in this grid. The first is to use the VariableSizedWrapGrid.ColumnSpan and the VariableSizedWrapGrid.RowSpan attached properties on a child element. This will instruct the host grid to span the required cells for that item.

If you are binding to a list of items, you will need to subclass the host object (typically a GridView) and override the PrepareContainerForItemsOverride method. You will learn more about this technique later in this chapter when you walk through the **Panels** example.

Listing 3.6 shows an example layout.

LISTING 3.6: XAML for the **VariableSizedWrapGrid** Layout

```
<ItemsControl>
  <ItemsControl.ItemsPanel>
    <ItemsPanelTemplate>
      <VariableSizedWrapGrid
        MaximumRowsOrColumns="2"
        ItemWidth="200"
        ItemHeight="200"
        Width="400"
        Height="400"
        Background="White"/>
    </ItemsPanelTemplate>
  </ItemsControl.ItemsPanel>
  <ItemsControl.Items>
    <Rectangle Fill="Red" Width="250" Height="125"
      VariableSizedWrapGrid.ColumnSpan="2"/>
    <Rectangle Fill="Green" Width="150" Height="75"/>
    <Ellipse Fill="Blue" Width="250" Height="250"/>
  </ItemsControl.Items>
</ItemsControl>
```

You can see the result of this layout in Figure 3.8. Note the variable size and spans allow the initial rectangle to display in its entirety. The circle is only cut off because the surface size is limited to 400 pixels by 400 pixels in this example.

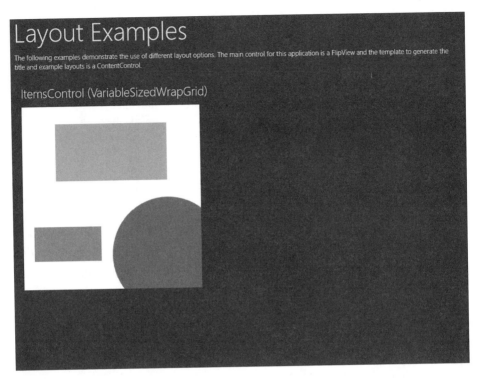

FIGURE 3.8: The VariableSizedWrapGrid **layout**

ContentControl

The ContentControl is the most basic container. It is simply a control with a single child element. It does not, by itself, specify any form of layout. The ContentControl is often used to mark a spot where a control (or controls) may render later or for controls that can have one content item to inherit from. It's important to note that the default behavior of the ContentControl is to provide a best fit for the child control.

To see this behavior, you can create a grid with two evenly sized columns. Provide a default style for rectangles that will stretch to fill the space and are colored green with a blue stroke, as shown in Listing 3.7.

LISTING 3.7: The Definition for a **Grid** to Hold Instances of the **ContentControl**

```
<Grid.Resources>
    <Style TargetType="Rectangle">
        <Setter Property="Fill" Value="Green"/>
        <Setter Property="HorizontalAlignment" Value="Stretch"/>
        <Setter Property="VerticalAlignment" Value="Stretch"/>
        <Setter Property="Stroke" Value="Blue"/>
        <Setter Property="StrokeThickness" Value="3"/>
        <Setter Property="Margin" Value="2"/>
    </Style>
</Grid.Resources>
```

Now add two ContentControls. Have both controls stretch to fill the available space. On the second control, add the special attached properties for HorizontalContentAlignment and VerticalContentAlignment. Set them both to "Stretch". The full code is shown in Listing 3.8.

LISTING 3.8: The Instances of the **ContentControl** for the **Grid**

```
<ContentControl HorizontalAlignment="Stretch"
                VerticalAlignment="Stretch">
    <ContentControl.Content>
        <Rectangle/>
    </ContentControl.Content>
</ContentControl>
<ContentControl Grid.Column="1"
                HorizontalAlignment="Stretch"
                VerticalAlignment="Stretch"
                HorizontalContentAlignment="Stretch"
                VerticalContentAlignment="Stretch">
    <ContentControl.Content>
        <Rectangle/>
    </ContentControl.Content>
</ContentControl>
```

You will notice that only the rightmost control actually renders. This is due to the behavior of the ContentControl. Even though the container has stretched to fill the available space, it does not provide that space to the child. Unless the child has a fixed height and width, the child will not be given any size to expand into, so Stretch ends up sizing the control to 0. When a HorizontalContentAlignment and/or VerticalContentAlignment is specified, the child can position itself relative to the parent container, and if the specification is Stretch, it will be given the entire space to expand into.

ItemsControl

The ItemsControl is a special container that allows for a collection of children. It is most often used with controls that require lists of data, such as list boxes and combo boxes. In addition to a panel that determines how to arrange the content, the items control provides an ItemsSource property. This property can be assigned any enumerable list (one that supports IEnumerable) that is used to generate the content for the control.

ScrollViewer

The ScrollViewer wraps a scrollable list of other UI elements. The ScrollViewer contains an extent that is a virtual surface as large as is needed to render all of the content. It contains only a single element that in turn can be anything from a control to a panel that has its own children. If the child item is a list that contains 1,000 items and each are 20 units high, the extent of the ScrollViewer will be 20,000 units high. The "view port" is the visible portion of the ScrollViewer and represents the subset of the full display that is scrolled into view. ScrollViewers can scroll horizontally, vertically, or both.

A major advantage of using the ScrollViewer control is the built-in support for touch and zoom. Touch is supported automatically by the control. In cases where you may be able to scroll in more than one direction, the control can implement the concept of "rails" or zones where the scroll is locked into a specific direction. This prevents the screen from wobbling due to slight variations in direction introduced by the user's finger as they scroll. Pinch and zoom is also supported within the viewable area, and all of these settings are configurable through properties on the control.

Here is an example of the XAML used to define a ScrollViewer:

```
<ScrollViewer Width="400" Height="400" Background="White">
    <StackPanel Background="White" Width="400" Height="500">
        <Rectangle Fill="Red" Width="250" Height="125"/>
        <Rectangle Fill="Green" Width="150" Height="75"/>
        <Ellipse Fill="Blue" Width="250" Height="250"/>
    </StackPanel>
</ScrollViewer>
```

The resulting scrollable layout is shown in Figure 3.9.

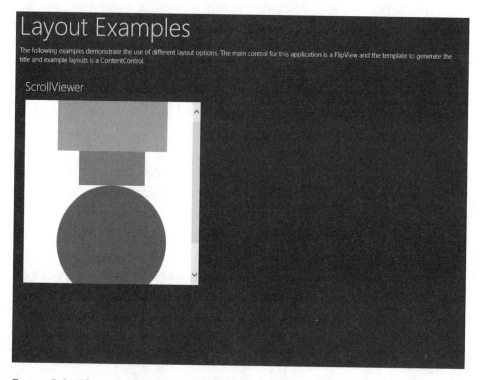

FIGURE 3.9: **The scrollbar shown for a StackPanel inside a ScrollViewer**

ViewBox

The ViewBox is a unique container. The sole purpose of the ViewBox is to resize content. You can create content that is a virtual size and then shape it to fit the visible screen. The ViewBox allows you to determine the method it uses to stretch the content to fill the available space. The different modes are as follows:

- **None**—The content is not resized and is simply clipped to fill the view box.
- **Fill**—The content is distorted to fill the space, and the aspect ratio is changed as needed.
- **Uniform**—The content is sized to fill the space as best as possible without changing the aspect ratio ("banding" may occur with additional white space to the top and bottom or sides of the content).

- **UniformToFill**—The content is sized to fill the maximum space possible while preserving the aspect ratio (the content will be clipped if the aspect ratios don't match).

Listing 3.9 shows the full XAML for a grid that demonstrates the various options to stretch. Although many other containers and controls are available, these are the key ones to understand because they are the base classes and templates that the other controls derive from or use.

LISTING 3.9: A Grid Set Up to Demonstrate the **ViewBox** Control

```
<Grid HorizontalAlignment="Right" VerticalAlignment="Top"
      Margin="10" Width="400">
    <Grid.Resources>
        <Style TargetType="TextBlock">
            <Setter Property="Text" Value="Viewbox"/>
            <Setter Property="FontSize" Value="72"/>
            <Setter Property="FontWeight" Value="Bold"/>
        </Style>
        <Style TargetType="Viewbox">
            <Setter Property="Height" Value="50"/>
            <Setter Property="Margin" Value="5"/>
        </Style>
    </Grid.Resources>
    <Grid.ColumnDefinitions>
        <ColumnDefinition Width="100"/>
        <ColumnDefinition Width="100"/>
        <ColumnDefinition Width="100"/>
        <ColumnDefinition Width="100"/>
    </Grid.ColumnDefinitions>
    <Viewbox Stretch="None">
        <TextBlock/>
    </Viewbox>
    <Viewbox Stretch="Fill" Grid.Column="1">
        <TextBlock/>
    </Viewbox>
    <Viewbox Stretch="Uniform" Grid.Column="2">
        <TextBlock/>
    </Viewbox>
    <Viewbox Stretch="UniformToFill" Grid.Column="3">
        <TextBlock/>
    </Viewbox>
</Grid>
```

When you finish the grid, you will see consistent results in both the designer and the application when you run it. The result looks like what's shown in Figure 3.10.

FIGURE 3.10: **The various stretch formats available**

You can see the example for the Viewbox yourself by flipping to the last page of the **Layout** example. You can also open the **ViewboxExample.xaml** file in the designer in the **Panels** solution. When you run the solution for the **Panels** application, you will see a set of options for various layouts that manage lists of objects. The first example is the GridView control.

GridView

The GridView control is a powerful control that allows you to display a list of data in a format that is easy for the user to navigate. An important feature of the control is that it is able to handle grouped data. This means you can categorize long lists and provide subheaders to logically organize the data.

In the **Panels** project, a simple class is defined that describes a type of shape. The class includes definitions for red, green, and blue components to enable different colors. A second class called SimpleItemList provides a collection of SimpleItem instances. The **ItemDisplay.xaml** file defines a user control to represent the data. Think of a user control as a reusable collection of UI elements. In this case, it enables you to define the look and feel for an item once and then reuse that look and feel in other areas of the application.

The user control takes advantage of a ContentControl to render the actual shape represented by the data item. The container uses a Converter to transform the SimpleItem from the current DataContext into an actual filled shape. Instead of taking a single parameter, the converter takes the entire SimpleItem class. First, it defines a solid brush based on the color values:

```
var color = Color.FromArgb(0xff, (byte)item.Red,
    (byte)item.Green, (byte)item.Blue);
var brush = new SolidColorBrush(color);
```

Next, it renders a shape based on the type of the item. For example, a circle is an ellipse with equal Height and Width properties:

```
case ItemType.Circle:
                    var circle = new Ellipse();
                    circle.Width = 200;
                    circle.Height = 200;
                    circle.Fill = brush;
                    retVal = circle;
                    break;
```

On the main page, a special element called a CollectionViewSource is declared. This is a simple proxy to collections that makes it easy to provide support for grouping and selection. The first collection supports grouping and is declared like this:

```
<CollectionViewSource x:Name="CVSGrouped"
    IsSourceGrouped="True"/>
```

Setting up the collection is simple. The source is assigned to a query that groups the items by the shape they represent:

```
CVSGrouped.Source = from item in list
                    group item by item.Type into g
                    orderby g.Key
                    select g;
```

The query is formatted using Language Integrated Query or LINQ. This is a special feature that adds a standard method for querying data regardless of the data type—in this case, a simple list. If you are not familiar with LINQ, I recommend learning more. You can start with the book *Essential LINQ* available at http://www.informit.com/store/product. aspx?isbn=0321564162.

The GridView control is bound to the source list. The control itself has several parts that are completely customizable. For example, you can specify how to show a heading for each group:

```
<GroupStyle.HeaderTemplate>
    <DataTemplate>
        <TextBlock Text="{Binding Key}"/>
    </DataTemplate>
</GroupStyle.HeaderTemplate>
```

Templates are reusable parts of XAML. A **DataTemplate** is a special template that provides a look and feel based on an underlying data source. In this example, the header is defined by a **DataTemplate** that contains a simple text element bound to the key for the group. From the query you saw earlier, that key is really the type of the shape so the heading will display a category like "Circle" or "Rectangle."

Another template defines how the individual items in the group are arranged:

```
<GroupStyle.Panel>
    <ItemsPanelTemplate>
        <VariableSizedWrapGrid Orientation="Vertical"/>
    </ItemsPanelTemplate>
</GroupStyle.Panel>
</GroupStyle>
```

You learned about the VariableSizedWrapGrid control earlier. You may recall that there is a special way to determine when an element needs to take up more space. In this example, rectangles and ellipses will span two columns, and circles and squares only span one. A new class called ShapeView is derived from the base GridView control:

```
public class ShapeView : GridView
```

Next, the PrepareContainerForItemOverride method is overridden. If the data item is a SimpleItem instance and the type is either Ellipse or Rectangle, the attached property for the ColumnSpan is set to 2:

```
if (itemdetail.Type.Equals(ItemType.Ellipse) ||
    itemdetail.Type.Equals(ItemType.Rectangle))
{
    element.SetValue(VariableSizedWrapGrid.ColumnSpanProperty, 2.0);
}
```

This defines how items are listed in a group, but there are also templates to define how groups are organized relative to each other. For this example, the groups are stacked horizontally in a VirtualizingStackPanel:

```
<GridView.ItemsPanel>
    <ItemsPanelTemplate>
        <VirtualizingStackPanel Orientation="Horizontal"/>
    </ItemsPanelTemplate>
</GridView.ItemsPanel>
```

Finally, the individual data items are defined using a **DataTemplate** that simply reuses the ItemDisplay user control:

```
<GridView.ItemTemplate>
    <DataTemplate>
        <local:ItemDisplay/>
    </DataTemplate>
</GridView.ItemTemplate>
```

The result is the layout you see in Figure 3.11. Note the elements are stacked in multiple rows and columns and that the ellipse group has wider space than the circles do. You can see the smaller group headings across the top and the default selection capabilities that are built into the GridView control.

ListView

The ListView control is similar to the GridView control. The main difference is that the default orientation is vertical instead of horizontal. It is designed for more narrow views, such as when the application is snapped.

> **▪ TIP**
>
> You'll learn about some more advanced layout features in Chapter 4, *Windows 8 Applications*. One example feature is the ability to switch between a full screen to a full window or a snap window. The snap window takes up a narrow strip on the display. It is a common practice to handle this special view by switching from a GridView implementation to a ListView implementation. You may also want to consider this type of transformation when the orientation of the display changes from portrait to landscape. The ability to adapt or tailor the application to the target device orientation and resolution is a fundamental trait of Windows 8 applications.

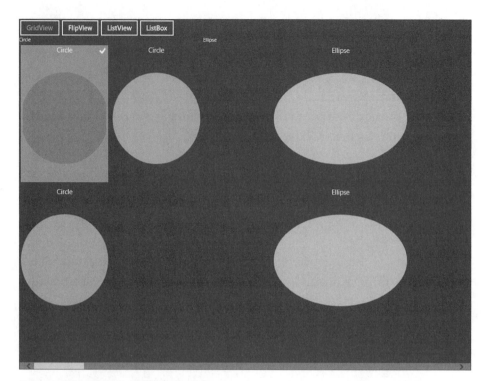

FIGURE 3.11: The **GridView** layout

Figure 3.12 shows the same shapes in the ListView configuration.

FlipView

The FlipView is a unique new control for iterating through elements in list. It will display one item at a time and allow you to swipe left or right to navigate the list. It comes with a built-in animation that will automatically slide the current item off the screen while sliding the new item into the current display. It is useful for close-up navigation of individual items or for flipping through items rapidly to see detail.

ListBox

The ListBox control is included to provide a comparison with the newer controls. It is capable of listing items but lacks the more advanced features of the ListView control. It does not provide the enhanced selection capabilities and does not support grouped data. When you migrate legacy programs to the Windows 8 platform, you'll likely want to replace any ListBox instances with the more feature-rich ListView control.

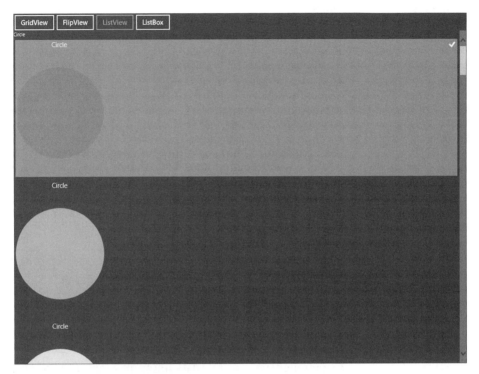

FIGURE 3.12: The list layout

Common Controls

When you understand the layout capabilities of XAML, you can begin to build your UI using a variety of built-in controls. All of the controls that are supplied for Windows 8 exist in the Windows.UI.Xaml.Controls namespace. Although you can easily insert the element tags for these controls in your XAML like any other object, it is important to note that the majority of controls are native WinRT objects with XAML projections. This ensures high performance while still providing the flexibility of the XAML engine.

Table 3.4 provides an alphabetical list of common controls with a brief description. Many of these controls will be explored in greater detail in other chapters of this book.

TABLE 3.4: Common Controls (*Indicates New Controls in the Windows Runtime)

Control	Description
AppBar*	Provides a toolbar for displaying application-specific commands. You'll learn more about it in Chapter 4.
Button	Provides a place for the user to click or tap and raises an event. It can also be bound to a command. You learn more about commands in Chapter 8, *Giving Your Application Charm*.
CheckBox	A simple control that can either be selected or cleared, usually used to manipulate Boolean values.
ComboBox	Provides a list of items the user can select from. In Windows 8, you are more likely to use a selectable list or grid to provide selection to have more control over the layout and touch experience.
HyperlinkButton	Provides text that is highlighted and marked up, usually to indicate it can be clicked to provide navigation.
Image	Host control for bitmap images.
MediaElement	Provides a surface to play back audio and video content.
MediaPlayer	Comprehensive control that allows playback and control of media content.
PasswordBox	Special text input control that masks the input so the user can securely enter a password or code.
PopupMenu*	Custom menu that presents commands you specify to the user.
ProgressBar	Displays a visual bar to the user to indicate progress.
ProgressRing*	Used to display indeterminate progress by showing an animated ring.
RadioButton	Allows mutually exclusive selection from a list of options.
RepeatButton	This is a special button that continuously raises events while it is pressed, unlike an ordinary button that raises a single Click event.

RichTextBlock	Provides a surface to display rich formatted text and graphics.
ScrollBar	Supplies a scroll bar with a sliding thumb.
SemanticZoom*	Allows the user to zoom between two views of a collection.
TextBlock	Used to display static text.
TextBox	Allows entry of one or multiple lines of text by the user.
Slider	Provides a bar with a thumb that allows the user to select from a range of values by moving the thumb.
ToggleButton	Button that can toggle between two states.
ToggleSwitch	Provides a switch that can toggle between two states.
ToolTip	A context window that pops up to display information for an element.
WebView*	Hosts web-based content.

These controls are all available to drop onto a XAML surface and define your UI. It is also possible to create custom controls or to group existing controls together and reuse them using user controls and templates. Although this section provided a brief overview of controls, you will learn about specific controls in far greater detail in later chapters of this book.

Summary

In this chapter, you learned about XAML, the unique markup language used to declare the UI for Windows 8 applications. You explored dependency properties and attached properties and discovered how they extend the core CLR properties to enhance XAML capabilities. You then examined how data-binding provides a way to separate the UI and presentation logic from the underlying data of your application.

Storyboards provide a way to animate elements on the screen. Styles and resources provide central repositories for look and feel information or "themes" for the application. Finally, layout controls provide different ways you can organize elements and lists and populate them with the common controls supplied by the Windows Runtime.

In the next chapter, you will learn about the unique characteristics of Windows 8 applications. You'll apply your knowledge of layouts and controls to build an application that responds to the orientation and screen resolution of the host device with help from a special class called the Visual State Manager. You'll explore how to handle user input in Windows 8 applications, wire in an application bar, provide context menus, and build a special "About page." Finally, you'll build reusable WinRT components that serve as building blocks for larger applications.

4

Windows 8 Applications

WINDOWS 8 APPLICATIONS SHARE COMMON TRAITS that make them ideal software for the variety of devices that Windows 8 runs on. They are fast and fluid and adapt easily to different display resolutions and modes. They respond to multiple forms of input and complex touch manipulations, and they provide a consistent user experience with a standard place for application-wide commands and guidelines for context menus.

In the last chapter, you learned about XAML, the unique declarative language that provides the capability to separate design from development and provides a powerful, extensible UI. In this chapter, you learn how to apply the combination of XAML and code to address the various traits that are unique to Windows 8 applications. Many of these traits are available and configurable through XAML.

Layouts and Views

Windows 8 applications adapt to various layouts and views. These include the orientation of the device (portrait or landscape) and the filled or snapped state when applications are running side-by-side. The Visual Studio 2012 built-in templates provide guidance to manage many of these transitions automatically. An easy way to test layout changes even if you don't have a tablet or accelerometer is by using the built-in simulator.

The Simulator

Access the Chapter 4 **Windows8Application** source from the book website at http://windows8applications.codeplex.com/.

Instead of debugging the application on your local machine, which is the default, use the debug target drop-down to select the simulator instead. You can see this selection in Figure 4.1.

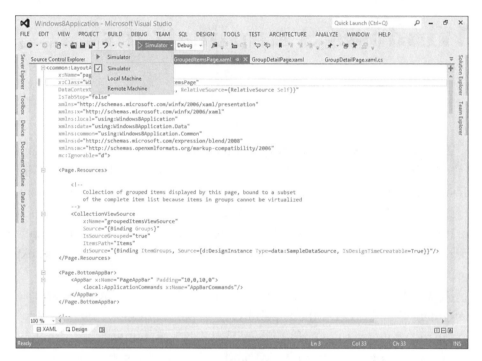

FIGURE 4.1: **Choosing the simulator for debug**

The simulator makes it easy to test different scenarios such as screen resolutions and orientation. It even provides touch emulation if you are developing on a machine that doesn't directly support touch. The simulator will provide a graphic that looks like a tablet complete with a Windows Key. A set of icons on the right side provide different functions. From top to bottom, these functions are

1. **Mouse Mode**—Use the pointer as a regular mouse.
2. **Touch Emulation**—Use the pointer as a touch surface. Click the mouse button to emulate a tap.

3. **Touch Emulation Pinch and Zoom**—This allows you to test pinch and zoom. Simply hold down the left mouse button and scroll the mouse wheel to zoom in or out (you can do the same thing in **Mouse Mode** by holding down **Ctrl** and then scrolling the mouse wheel).

4. **Touch Emulation Rotate**—Use this mode to emulate a touch rotation. Hold down the left mouse button and scroll the wheel to rotate in either direction.

5. **Rotate 90 Degrees Clockwise**—This emulates flipping the tablet between portrait and landscape mode.

6. **Rotate 90 Degrees Counterclockwise**—This emulates flipping the tablet between portrait and landscape mode.

7. **Change Resolution**—Emulate a different resolution. The resolution is simulated so you can emulate a higher resolution than you have available.

8. **Set Location**—Enter latitude, longitude, altitude, and margin of error to emulate a location for the simulator.

9. **Screenshot**—This handy feature takes a snapshot at the current simulator resolution.

10. **Configure Screenshot**—This allows you determine whether the screenshot copies to the clipboard and/or saves to a file and sets the save location.

11. **Help**—General help for the simulator.

The simulator offers a variety of options. For this example, set the resolution to **1366 × 768**. You should see the general application and some groups and group items, as shown in Figure 4.2. The simulator actually works by creating a remote desktop connection back to the device you are running the application on (as opposed to creating a virtual machine). This allows you to actually test the application on your own machine using the various touch inputs and form factors.

Now, with the application in focus (you can click or tap a blank area of the application to ensure it is focused), hold down the **Windows Key** and press the **period** (.). This will switch the application to the snapped view. If you have any other Windows 8 applications running, the next application will appear in the fill portion of the screen (the larger segment);

otherwise, it will remain empty while the current application shrinks to fit the snapped portion, as shown in Figure 4.3.

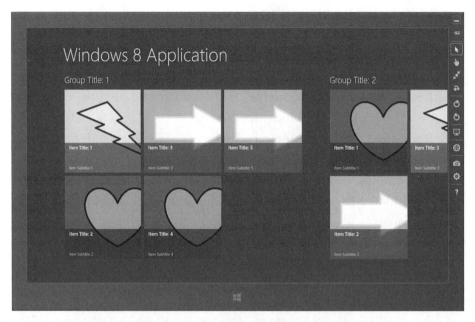

FIGURE 4.2: **Sample application running inside the simulator**

FIGURE 4.3: **The application in the snapped view**

The snapped view is a special compressed view used to provide at-a-glance information while another application has the primary focus. The vertically-oriented `ListView` control is the perfect control to use for this view instead of the horizontally-oriented `GridView`. The snapped view is only available when the width is at least 1366 pixels. Any smaller resolution such as 1024 ×768 will not allow the snapping feature. The snapped view is a fully functional view of your application but is always limited to 320 pixels in width. This is enough resolution to provide plenty of functionality and happens to be a common width for smartphones.

In addition to the snapped view, there is a 22 pixel-wide splitter that the user can use to unsnap the application by dragging it across the screen. This leaves exactly 1024 pixels for the remaining screen, so the filled view will have 1024×768 pixels available ($1366 - 320 - 22 = 1024$), which is the minimum resolution recommended for Windows 8 applications.

You'll notice in the sample application that the screen changed when you switched to a snapped view. Instead of a horizontal grid with items filling out rows and columns, it changed to a vertical list. This makes it easier to navigate and select items in the narrow snapped view. What is more interesting is how the application made the change. Built into the **Grid Application** template is XAML and code that takes advantage of a powerful class called the Visual State Manager.

The Visual State Manager

The Visual State Manager (VSM) is the key to success with separation of concerns between the design and UI/UX experience and program logic in Windows 8 applications. It works in conjunction with data-binding to help separate UI logic and concerns from the rest of your application.

The Visual State Manager handles the logic of states and transitions for controls. Controls are not limited to custom controls or control templates. The VSM works equally well for managing the state of pages and user controls as well. The target of the VSM is always an element that derives from the `Control` class, which includes controls like `Page` and `UserControl`, and the location of the VSM should always be the root of the template for the control. In the **Windows8Application** project, you'll find the element `VisualStateManager.VisualStateGroups` nested inside of the main grid of the **GroupedItemsPage.xaml** file.

The VSM defines groups, states, and optional transitions. A group is a set of mutually exclusive states. As the name implies, groups create an association between related states. In the application example, the page has several common states within the same group called `ApplicationViewStates`. These states include

- **FullScreenLandscape**—When the application is running in full screen mode and the tablet is in the landscape orientation
- **Filled**—When the application is taking the larger space beside another snapped application
- **FullScreenPortrait**—When the application is running in full screen mode and the tablet is in the portrait orientation
- **Snapped**—When the application is running in the 320 pixel-wide snapped mode

It is important that the states are mutually exclusive because the VSM only allows one state within a group at a given time. The groups represent a contract for the behavior of the page. You are given a set of states that the page will honor and must manage the page within the context of those states. The states are managed through a base class that the page inherits from. The VSM allows you to customize what happens to the visual appearance of the page in a given state.

To see how the states are managed, open the **Common** folder and examine the `LayoutAwarePage` class. The class is provided as part of the project template and hooks into the `ViewStateChanged` event that fires any time the orientation or snapped mode changes. The event handler simply interrogates the new view state and converts it to a string and then instructs the VSM to go to that state:

```
VisualStateManager.GoToState(layoutAwareControl, visualState, false);
```

Note that there is no UI logic in the state change. This is how the UI logic is kept separate from the application logic. The application logic simply manages the state. The UI changes for a state are declared in XAML using storyboards. If you use multiple groups for a control, you in effect have multiple storyboards executing against that control at the same time.

An important rule for groups is that they must be orthogonal to each other. Although a control can exist in multiple states (exactly one state for each group), the groups should not overlap which visual aspects they impact. This is a rule that cannot be enforced by the control contract because you are able to create whatever storyboards you like within a given state. Failure to follow this rule, however, can lead to unexpected results.

Groups are containers for related, mutually exclusive states. What is a *state*? A state has both a logical and physical definition. Logically it indicates a mutually exclusive status for the control. Physically it is the set of visual elements and attributes that represent the state. What is important about states is that they allow you to decouple the details of how the control appears in a given state from the state itself. In code, you can simply set the control to a given state and then let the VSM take care of how that state appears. This not only makes it easier to test and implement the control but also to extend and/or customize the control.

Take a look at the **GroupedItemsPage.xaml** file. A single group is defined without a name, and the first state is declared like this:

```
<VisualState x:Name="FullScreenLandscape"/>
```

The state is empty. This means the default XAML is sufficient to render the UI for that state. If you take a look at the XAML, you'll see a `SemanticZoom` control is defined in the first row of the grid (you'll learn more about semantic zoom later in this chapter). There is also a `ScrollViewer` declared for the same row but with its `Visibility` set to `Collapsed` so it won't render. This contains a `ListView` control that is used for the snapped view.

Now take a look at the declaration for the **Snapped** state. This is shown in Listing 4.1. There is a single `Storyboard` control with several animations. These animations aren't used for motion but instead take advantage of the fact that animations can change the value of dependency properties. The VSM uses animations to set the values of properties on controls (the reason why will be explained shortly).

LISTING 4.1: **The Definition for the Snapped State**

```xml
<VisualState x:Name="Snapped">
            <Storyboard>
                    <ObjectAnimationUsingKeyFrames
    Storyboard.TargetName="backButton"
    Storyboard.TargetProperty="Style">
                            <DiscreteObjectKeyFrame KeyTime="0"
    Value="{StaticResource SnappedBackButtonStyle}"/>
                    </ObjectAnimationUsingKeyFrames>
                    <ObjectAnimationUsingKeyFrames
    Storyboard.TargetName="pageTitle"
    Storyboard.TargetProperty="Style">
                            <DiscreteObjectKeyFrame KeyTime="0"
    Value="{StaticResource SnappedPageHeaderTextStyle}"/>
                    </ObjectAnimationUsingKeyFrames>

                    <ObjectAnimationUsingKeyFrames
    Storyboard.TargetName="itemListScrollViewer"
    Storyboard.TargetProperty="Visibility">
                            <DiscreteObjectKeyFrame KeyTime="0"
    Value="Visible"/>
                    </ObjectAnimationUsingKeyFrames>
                    <ObjectAnimationUsingKeyFrames
    Storyboard.TargetName="semanticViewer"
    Storyboard.TargetProperty="Visibility">
                            <DiscreteObjectKeyFrame KeyTime="0"
    Value="Collapsed"/>
                    </ObjectAnimationUsingKeyFrames>
            </Storyboard>
</VisualState>
```

In this example, the **Back** button and title styles are both changed. The SemanticZoom control is set to Collapsed so that the control and its children will disappear, and the ScrollViewer is set to Visible so it will appear with its content (when a control is Collapsed, it is no longer rendered within the visual tree; if it is Visible, it will be rendered even when the opacity is set to 0 or the color is Transparent). The animations will run for as long as the visual state is valid. When the state changes, the Storyboard will be stopped, and the properties will return to their default values (or the new values defined by the Storyboard controls for the new state).

The VSM uses Storyboard controls because they have the highest precedence for setting the value of a dependency property. Understanding how to manage states is as simple as understanding Storyboard controls. When your control goes to a specific state, the VSM will stop any Storyboard controls for other states within the same group (remember, states in a group are mutually exclusive) and then begin the Storyboard defined for the target state.

It is a best practice to set an initial state when the control is initialized to get the control on the "state graph" or in the collection of valid states. The LayoutAwarePage class does this in the StartLayoutUpdates method. Note the call to GoToState before exiting the method.

Transitions add flexibility to the Visual State Manager by allowing control over how a control moves (or transitions) between states. You can specify a transition to be applied any time the control moves to a specific state or restrict the transition only when moving to a state from another state. This is a very powerful feature.

The simplest transition uses the existing storyboard values and creates an interim animation to move between them. You simply specify a generated duration of time, and the Visual State Manager will take care of the rest. You can also create your own transition storyboards. The Visual State Manager will stop any transition storyboards as soon as the control has transitioned to the new state. It does not stop the state storyboards until the state changes.

Semantic Zoom

The main screen of the sample application arranges all of the items into groups. You might find that some lists end up holding a large number of items that may span dozens of groups. Although the built-in controls are designed to perform well with large amounts of data, it can be cumbersome for the user to navigate from one end of the list to another. To solve this problem, you can use a concept known as *semantic zoom*.

Semantic zoom is a technique that allows the user to zoom out from a list and navigate it at a higher level using an interface you provide. This is not a visual zoom because as the user zooms out, the actual interface changes. In the **Windows8Application** example, if you zoom out on the initial view either by touching two fingers to the tablet surface and drawing them apart or by holding down the **Ctrl** key and scrolling your mouse wheel or pressing the + or - keys, you will see the entire grid fade into a set of titles with group names.

The new view fades in when you zoom out, and disappears to be replaced by the detailed grid list when you zoom in. The zoomed-out view is shown in Figure 4.4. In this view, it is easy to see the full list of available groups. If you tap any of the groups, you will automatically zoom back in with the focus on the items for that group.

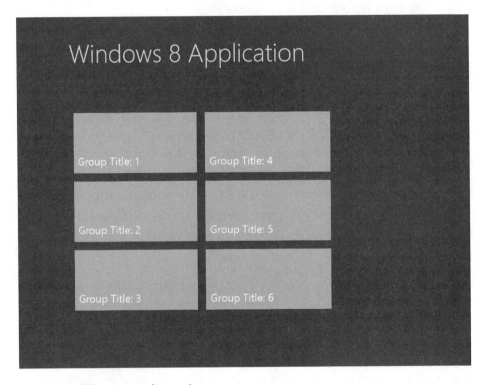

FIGURE 4.4: **The zoomed-out view**

This is a powerful feature and can be implemented in many different ways. A feed reader application might show the feed names and allow the user to zoom into the details. An application that manages contact lists could show the first letter of the last name, allowing you to quickly jump to the section of names that holds the contact you are looking for. Conceptually you are simply providing two different views based on the level of detail the user chooses to navigate at.

You implement semantic zoom using the SemanticZoom control. Open up the **GroupedItemsPage.xaml** file in the **Windows8Application** example. Find the SemanticZoom control. The SemanticZoom.ZoomedInView is the typical view that users will use to navigate your application. For this example, I simply took the default template, added the SemanticZoom control, and moved the GridView into the ZoomedInView section. When the user zooms out, the view switches to the SemanticZoom.ZoomedOutView. For this view, I created a set of tiles based on Microsoft's quickstart at http://msdn.microsoft.com/en-us/library/windows/apps/xaml/hh781234.aspx.

You may also wish to download the Windows 8 SDK Samples Semantic-Zoom example from http://code.msdn.microsoft.com/windowsapps/GroupedGridView-77c59e8e.

I simply updated the definition to include the title for the group. You can see the definition for the tile in the **MyStyles.xaml** dictionary file. I also used the OnNavigatedTo event to wire in the data source for the GridView. Take a look at the code-behind file named **GroupedItemsPage.xaml.cs**, and you will find the following method:

```
protected override void OnNavigatedTo(NavigationEventArgs e)
{
    this.DefaultViewModel["Groups"] = e.Parameter;
    this.groupGridView.ItemsSource =
        this.groupedItemsViewSource.View.CollectionGroups;
    base.OnNavigatedTo(e);
}
```

The code simply takes the set of groups from the CollectionViewSource defined in XAML and sets this as the source for the GridView in the ZoomedOutView. That's all there is to using the control. The control itself will handle responding to the user's "pinch and zoom" gestures (you can also hold down the **Ctrl** key and either scroll the mouse wheel or press the + or - keys) and swap between the various views. When the user taps on a particular item in the ZoomedOutView, the control will automatically switch to the ZoomedInView with the selected group in focus.

Microsoft provides the following guidelines for using SemanticZoom:

- Use the correct touch target size for elements that are interactive (you learn more about touch targets in the next section).

- Provide a suitable and intuitive region for the zoom.
- Use appropriate context for the view, for example:
  - Use group names for items in a grouped collection.
  - Use sort orders for ungrouped collections.
  - Use pages to represent collections of documents.
- Limit the number of pages or screens in the zoomed-out view to three so the user can quickly jump to content.
- Ensure that the pan direction is the same in both zoom levels.
- Don't use the zoom to change the scope of content (for example, showing one set of items in the zoomed-in view and another set in the zoomed-out view).
- Don't set a border on the child controls—if you need a border, only set it on the SemanticZoom control itself.

Read the full guidance online at http://msdn.microsoft.com/en-us/library/windows/apps/hh465319.aspx.

The SemanticZoom and GridView controls do a great job of handling default input and user interactions for you. There are often times when you are constructing your own controls and UIs that you must handle the input yourself. It's important to understand how Windows 8 applications handle different input events and what the expected behaviors for those events are. You learn more about handling user input in the next section.

Handling User Input

User input is an important component of WinRT applications. Windows 8 provides a touch-first experience and supports multiple methods of input. Touch-first means that your applications are designed to fully accommodate touch and don't contain elements that are only valid using the mouse, keyboard, or other methods. The touch approach is different from traditional input for several reasons.

Windows 8 provides multi-touch support, so you must be able to respond to more than one contact point on the screen. Your application must respond to manipulations and be designed for targets or areas of the application that will respond to touch because touch is not as precise as a mouse pointer. There is a much larger margin of error when you are dealing with the size of a fingertip compared to the traditional mouse-controller pointer.

Touch enables the user to interact with the device in several ways. Table 4.1 provides a list of common interactions and how they are invoked.

TABLE 4.1: Touch Interactions

Interaction	Description
Tap	One finger touches the screen briefly and then lifts.
Hold	One finger touches the screen and remains in place.
Drag	One or more fingers touch the screen and then move in the same direction while maintaining contact.
Pinch/Zoom	Two or more fingers touch the screen and move either closer together or farther apart while maintaining contact.
Rotate	Two or more fingers touch the screen and rotate around a common center point while maintaining contact.
Cross-slide	One finger touches an object and then drags it at a right angle to the panning direction (for example, in a grid list that can be panned side to side, a cross-slide involves dragging an item up or down).

You will find many of the Windows 8 controls have built-in support for the standard interactions. Although Windows 8 provides a touch-first experience, it is also important to support other methods of input including the stylus or pen, mouse, and keyboard. Table 4.2 shows some common actions and how they are invoked using different modes of input.

TABLE 4.2: Modes of Input

Action	Touch / Stylus / Pen	Mouse	Keyboard
Change Focus	No equivalent	No equivalent	Tab Key / Arrow Keys
Context Menu	Press and hold	Right-click	Menu Key
Drag and Drop	Cross-slide outside of the item row/column	Click and drag	Ctrl+C (cut) / Ctrl+V (paste)
Invoke	Tap	Click	Enter Key
Rotate	Touch Rotate	Must be manually handled—i.e., with a rotation button	Ctrl+. / Ctrl+,
Scroll	Drag	Click scrollbar or use mouse wheel	Arrow Keys
Scroll Rapidly	Drag with velocity	Click scrollbar track	Page Up / Page Down
Select	Cross-slide	Right-click	Space
Tooltip	Press and hold	Hover	Shift Focus and Wait
Zoom	Pinch	Ctrl + mouse wheel	Ctrl + / Ctrl -

One way the Windows 8 platform makes it easier to deal with events from multiple input devices is by surfacing a set of *pointer events* that are device-independent. Pointer events will fire in response to touch, stylus, mouse, or keyboard input. To see an example of this, open the **Touch** application. This application demonstrates various touch interactions.

Pointer Events

The sample application display is divided into two columns. The left column is a simple list that shows various touch events as they happen. The right column contains a graphic that uses shapes, images, and a symbol font. The grid that contains the graphic is set up to respond to various touch manipulations so you can pinch, zoom, rotate, and slide the graphic.

Compile, deploy, and run the application. You may want to use the simulator so you can experiment with different types of interactions including touch. You should see quickly that there are several events that fire regardless of the input used:

- **Tapped**—Fired based on a touch, stylus tap, or mouse click.
- **Double-Tapped**—Fired based on a double finger or stylus tap or a double mouse click.
- **Pointer Pressed**—Fired based on a touch, stylus tap, or mouse click.
- **Pointer Moved**—Fired based on a drag using either the finger, stylus, or mouse with the left button held down.
- **Pointer Released**—Fired when the finger or stylus is raised or when the left button on the mouse is released.

These events embody the vast majority of user interactions outside of scrolling and navigation. When you code using these core events, you ensure your application is responding consistently to user feedback from a variety of input devices. There are, however, a few pointer events that don't make sense for touch. The `PointerEntered` and `PointerExited` events fire when the pointer moves into the region listening to the event or exits the region. Both the mouse and stylus can fire these events because the cursor is continuously tracked even when it is not engaged (that is, the left mouse button is pressed or the stylus is in contact with the touch surface). There is no equivalent for touch because the events only recognize when contact is made.

This should enforce the concept of "touch-first." If you design a major feature of your application based on the events that only respond to mouse and stylus input, you will lose the ability for users to interact on touch devices. Any type of interaction that is specific to a particular form of input should provide a way to perform the same interaction using other inputs. You'll see an example of this when you learn about manipulations in the next section.

Manipulation Events

A manipulation is a touch event that involves one or more fingers. It begins when the first contact is made and ends when the last contact is released. A tap is a simple form of manipulation that involves a touch, a very brief hold, and a release. A pan is a more complex manipulation because it involves a touch, a drag or movement in the panning direction, and then a release. Pinch and zoom are even more complex manipulations that respond to the change in distance between multiple touch points.

Manipulations must take into account inertia. For touch to be intuitive, it should factor the velocity of the user interaction. For example, a slow pan is a precise way to slowly move through a list. If the user begins panning very rapidly, the implication is that they are trying to scroll through large amounts of data at once. The inertia of the pan should allow the list to keep scrolling even when the user lifts his finger, like spinning a wheel.

Manipulations can provide a large volume of data in a short period of time, so they are not enabled by default. To enable a control to begin tracking manipulations, you should set the `ManipulationMode` property. This is set to `All` for the `Grid` element named `TouchGrid` in the **MainPage.xaml** file. The possible values are defined by the `ManipulationModes` enumeration. The list of modes and their meaning is in Table 4.3.

TABLE 4.3: `ManipulationModes` Values

`ManipulationModes` Value	Description
None	Do not monitor manipulation events.
TranslateX	Permit manipulation events in the horizontal axis.
TranslateY	Permit manipulation events in the vertical axis.
TranslateRailsX	Permit horizontal manipulations using the rails mode.
TranslateRailsY	Permit vertical manipulations using the rails mode.
Rotate	Permit rotation manipulations.

Scale	Permit manipulations that change the scale of the target.
TranslateInertia	Apply inertia to translation manipulations.
RotateInertia	Apply inertia to rotation manipulations.
ScaleInertia	Apply inertia to scale manipulations.
All	Permit all manipulation modes and apply all inertias.
System	Reserved.

Rails mode refers to an optimization to improve the touch experience when the user can pan in multiple directions. Instead of following the user's touch direction exactly when they are panning horizontally or vertically, which could result in some "drift" in the perpendicular direction, the rails will lock the scroll direction when the finger is within a specific zone or rail. Any motion within that zone will lock to strict vertical or horizontal scrolling, while motion outside of that zone will handle the motion in all directions. To learn more about rails, read the guidelines for panning online at http://msdn.microsoft.com/en-us/library/windows/apps/hh465310.aspx.

You can set a specific manipulation mode through XAML simply by defining it on the element as in the example. If you wish to combine specific manipulations, you must programmatically set the value. This example combines the scale and rotation modes but does not apply inertia:

```
TouchGrid.ManipulationMode = ManipulationModes.Rotate |
    ManipulationModes.Scale;
```

You track manipulations by handling the ManipulationDelta event. This event fires throughout the manipulation and provides you with several data points. You are able to track changes in scale, rotation, and translation (drag) at both the cumulative (since the manipulation began) and delta (since the last manipulation event was fired) levels. In the example, the Grid element has a CompositeTransform applied to it. This is a transformation that allows scaling, rotation, and translation. The scale and translations are applied incrementally during the manipulation, and the rotation is applied based on the cumulative amount:

```
Transformation.ScaleX *= e.Delta.Scale;
Transformation.ScaleY *= e.Delta.Scale;
Transformation.TranslateX += e.Delta.Translation.X;
Transformation.TranslateY += e.Delta.Translation.Y;
Transformation.Rotation += e.Delta.Rotation;
```

This example is straightforward because it simply applies the manipulations directly to the grid. You will see it responds quite well to rotating, pinching, and zooming, as well as dragging. It also responds to inertia. If you flick the grid in a direction with a lot of velocity, the graphic will fly off the visible display. To reset the grid back to its original values, simply double-tap the display. The event handler will clear or reset any manipulations:

```
Transformation.ScaleX = 1.0;
Transformation.ScaleY = 1.0;
Transformation.TranslateX = 0;
Transformation.TranslateY = 0;
Transformation.Rotation = 0;
```

You can use the data from the manipulations to respond in whatever way makes sense for your application, whether it is by directly manipulating the onscreen element or performing some other function. It is important that you provide equivalent functionality for other forms of input. For example, the common way to handle pinch and zoom with the mouse is by using the scroll wheel; the keyboard method is to hold down the **Ctrl** key and use **+** and **-** to zoom in or out.

Mouse Support

The mouse support in this example is implemented by responding to the PointerWheelChanged event. This is another "abstracted" event, although it is most likely going to be fired by the wheel on a mouse. In fact, the actual property you inspect to see which direction the wheel was turned has "mouse" in the name. Take a look at the TouchGrid_PointerWheelChanged_1 event handler in the **MainPage.xaml.cs** file, and you'll see the code checks the MouseWheelDelta property to determine whether to increase or decrease the scale:

```
var factor = e.GetCurrentPoint((UIElement)sender)
    .Properties.MouseWheelDelta > 0
    ? 0.1 : -0.1;
Transformation.ScaleX += factor;
Transformation.ScaleY += factor;
```

If you use a mouse or run the simulator in mouse mode, you'll find that scrolling the mouse wheel will have the same effect as pinch and zoom. To be more consistent with the SemanticZoom control, you may want to implement the effect only when the user is holding down the **Ctrl** key while scrolling. Of course, it is also important to provide keyboard support. The next section explains how this is done for the same action (pinch and zoom).

Keyboard Support

Keyboard support is implemented using the KeyDown and KeyUp events. Multiple keys may be pressed at the same time, so the combination of events gives you the flexibility to track whatever key combinations are important to you. In the **Touch** example, you are able to scale the graphic by holding down the **Ctrl** key and then pressing **+** or **-**.

> **■ TIP**
>
> For the key events to work, the control they are attached to must have focus. This is usually done by either clicking an element or navigating to it with the pointer, tab, or arrow keys. Focus is not automatically set. Because the Grid element does not have a way to programmatically set focus, the key events for this example were placed on the ListBox control. To set the events directly on the Grid, you can create a custom Control or UserControl that contains a Grid as the main element. The Control class supports the Focus method and allows you set focus in code to successfully listen for key press events. You can use this technique for any of the base controls that don't directly support setting focus.

The first step is to wait until the ListBox control is loaded and set the focus so it can begin listening for key press events:

```
private void EventList_Loaded_1(object sender, RoutedEventArgs e)
{
    EventList.Focus(FocusState.Programmatic);
}
```

The next step is to track the state of the **Ctrl** key. When the key is pressed, a flag is set inside of the event handler for the KeyDown event:

```
if (e.Key.Equals(VirtualKey.Control) && !_isCtrlKeyPressed)
{
    _isCtrlKeyPressed = true;
    AddWithFocus("Ctrl Key pressed.");
}
```

When the key is released, the flag is reset:

```
private void EventList_KeyUp_1(object sender, KeyEventArgs e)
{
    if (e.Key.Equals(VirtualKey.Control))
    {
        _isCtrlKeyPressed = false;
        AddWithFocus("Ctrl key released.");
    }
}
```

Finally, if either the + or - key is pressed while the **Ctrl** key is held down, the scale is adjusted accordingly. Listing 4.2 shows the code for the full KeyDown event handler.

LISTING 4.2: An Event Handler for Keyboard Support

```
private void EventList_KeyDown_1(object sender, KeyEventArgs e)
{
    if (e.Key.Equals(VirtualKey.Control) && !_isCtrlKeyPressed)
    {
        _isCtrlKeyPressed = true;
        AddWithFocus("Ctrl Key pressed.");
    }
    else if (_isCtrlKeyPressed)
    {
        var factor = 0d;
        if (e.Key.Equals(VirtualKey.Add))
        {
            factor = 0.1;
        }
        else if (e.Key.Equals(VirtualKey.Subtract))
        {
            factor = -0.1;
```

```
        }
        Transformation.ScaleX += factor;
        Transformation.ScaleY += factor;
    }
}
```

The application now provides full support for all input methods, including touch, mouse, and keyboard.

Visual Feedback

Microsoft recommends that you provide visual feedback for all touch interactions in your application. Visual feedback gives users an indication of how the application is expected to work and helps identify content in the UI that will respond to interactions. All of the built-in controls for the Windows 8 platform provide touch feedback out of the box. If you build a custom control, you must provide the feedback on your own.

The guidelines for touch feedback include

- All controls must provide feedback.
- Even brief contact should provide feedback to help verify the touch interface is working, to show that a target was missed, and to indicate when an element does not respond to touch.
- Feedback should be immediate.
- Feedback should be restricted to the control or element that was touched.
- Feedback should not distract users from their intended actions.
- Panning or dragging should not trigger feedback.
- Targets should follow the touch contact throughout the duration of a manipulation.
- If the target is not moved, the touch should be tethered using a dashed line to the target to indicate the manipulation is associated with that target.

When the user touches and holds a UI element, contextual information should display based on the duration of the hold. A short hold that lasts less than 200 milliseconds should display a simple tooltip for clarification of actions. A long hold that lasts about 2 seconds should provide an information pop-up or a detailed list of available commands.

To see an example of an interaction, tap and hold any tile on your **Start** menu. Some items will show a brief tool tip that provides a more detailed description of the tile. You will also notice that the tile slides down briefly and exposes a check mark. This action is intended as guidance for how to select the tile. It is demonstrating the cross-slide action.

Now touch the tile, but instead of holding, slowly drag it down (this is the right angle to the pan direction for the **Start** menu). A gray checkmark will appear. Drag the tile further, and the checkmark will highlight. When you release the tile, it is selected. Repeat the action to unselect the tile. That is how to use cross-slide for selection, and the control itself provided a visual cue for the threshold. You can also start to drag the tile down and then drag it back to its original position to cancel the action.

Finally, touch the tile and drag it down—only this time keep dragging it even after the checkmark highlights. You will eventually cross the threshold. When that happens, the tile will snap to your finger, the **Start** menu will zoom out slightly, and the remaining tiles will move farther apart. This is the mode you can use to move the tile to a new position on the start menu. These interactions are summarized in Figure 4.5.

In the example, Tile 4 has already been selected. Tile 5 is being dragged. Because it has not crossed the threshold, it will only move vertically, and the checkmark is shown as a hint for the selection action. If the tile is dragged back, it will snap into place without being selected. Tile 6 was dragged beyond the threshold and can now be rearranged and moved in all directions.

Targeting

Targeting refers to building your UI elements to maximize touch interactions. There are several factors involved in creating successful targets. The first is to create targets that are large enough to contact. An extremely small target is difficult to select and will increase user error (not to mention frustration). Guidelines suggest your smallest target be 9 millimeters on the shortest side (48 pixels on a 135 pixel-per-inch display) and that all targets have a minimum padding of 2mm (about 10 pixels) between them.

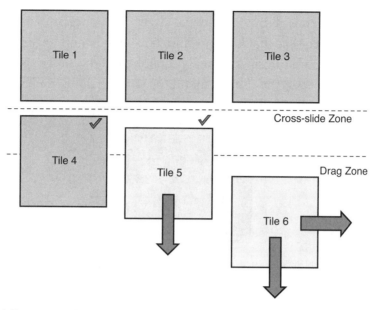

FIGURE 4.5: Cross-slide and drag

If a target is dragged less than 2.7 millimeters (about 14 pixels), the interaction should be handled as a tap. A greater distance should be handled as an actual drag. If you support the cross-slide action, the selection action begins when the user passes that threshold. The selection will change to a drag after the user moves the element 11 millimeters (about 60 pixels).

In addition to the *visual target*, which is the element you can see, there is an *actual target* that represents an area around the element that will still respond to touch. It is recommended that the visual target is about 60% the size of the actual target. The actual target can also provide a visual cue. To see this in action, go to the **Start** menu and look at your account information. An example is shown in Figure 4.6.

FIGURE 4.6: Account information

The picture and text provide a visual target. Now click anywhere within an imaginary rectangle that is large enough to contain both the text and the picture. The account information will highlight and reveal the actual target you can click to open the context menu for your account. You can see this in Figure 4.7.

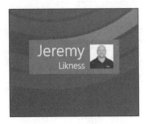

FIGURE 4.7: **Account information with actual target highlighted**

Another important aspect of targeting is to minimize the risk of critical errors. An element that has serious consequences should be grouped separately from other, more commonly used elements to avoid accidental activation. For example, if you have add, edit, and delete icons, you might consider grouping the add/edit icons together and placing the delete icon farther away to reduce the likelihood that the user accidentally taps it.

Context Menus

Context menus are short menus that provide clipboard commands (cut, copy, and paste) or custom commands, typically on objects that cannot be selected. They provide a short menu of commands. Context menus should never contain more than five commands. You can read the guidelines for context menus online at http://msdn.microsoft.com/en-us/library/windows/apps/hh465308.aspx.

The guidelines for context menus are to have short command names, use sentence capitalization (that is, "Clear list" instead of "Clear List"), and have a separator between related commands. The commands must be contextually relevant and should be ordered by importance with the most important commands at the bottom. If you are providing clipboard commands, they should always use the text and order:

- Cut
- Copy
- Paste

Context menus should be placed close the items they relate to and are often invoked by tapping or holding an item. In the **Touch** example, a context menu is attached to the ListBox control that lists the touch events. It is triggered by the DoubleTapped event.

The event handler defines a short block of code that creates a PopupMenu object, adds a command, and then waits for a response. It is also possible to create a context menu in XAML by using the Button.ContextMenu property. The contents include a ContextMenu with a list of MenuItem controls. The user can dismiss the menu by either selecting a command or moving the focus off the menu (for example, tapping or clicking another area of the application):

```
var contextMenu = new PopupMenu();
contextMenu.Commands.Add(new UICommand("Clear list",
    args => _events.Clear()));
var dismissed = await contextMenu.ShowAsync(
    e.GetPosition(EventList));
```

The UICommand takes a short name for the command and a delegate that is called when the command is selected. You can separate commands by adding an instance of the UICommandSeparator class to the list of the commands:

```
contextMenu.Commands.Add(new UICommandSeparator());
```

The commands will appear in the order they are added. You can query the return value of the ShowAsync method to determine what caused the menu to be dismissed. Some controls automatically provide context menus. For example, text selection provides a set of commands to cut, copy, and paste. Your application will likely provide a variety of commands that don't fit the narrow guidelines for the context menu. These commands most likely belong in the *Application Bar*.

The Application Bar

The **application bar** is a special control that is used to display commands to users on demand. It is not always visible by default, and the user must either swipe from the top or bottom edge of the screen or right-click to make it display. It is also possible to cause it to display programmatically. The application bar contains commands that are based on context—these can be global commands such as returning to the home page or commands specific to selected items.

In the **Windows8Application** example, a common `UserControl` provides application bar functionality. This provides a central location for the functionality and prevents duplicate code and XAML (you can place a separate application bar on every page if you like). You can host an application bar on the top, bottom, or both the top and bottom of the display. When the user swipes a second time or invokes an action, the application bar dismisses itself automatically. The application bar is implemented using the `AppBar` control.

Figure 4.8 shows the application bar for the main page before any item is selected. The **Add** and **Home** actions are disabled because there is no group selected and the user is already on the home screen. The application bar is defined using the `Page.BottomAppBar` element (you can use the `Page.TopAppBar` element for commands to appear on the top of the display).

Any application bar element must contain an `AppBar` control that will then host the XAML for the layout of your commands. Here is the definition from **GroupedItemsPage.xaml**:

```
<Page.BottomAppBar>
    <AppBar x:Name="AppBar" Margin="10,0,10,0">
        <local:ApplicationCommands x:Name="AppBarCommands"/>
    </AppBar>
</Page.BottomAppBar>
```

The XAML references a reusable `UserControl`. To see the definition of the layout for the application bar, open the **ApplicationCommands.xaml** file. You will see the commands displayed in the designer on a light gray background. The **Delete** command is a button on the left margin, and the **Add** and **Home** commands are on the extreme right margin. These are placed in `Grid` control for layout.

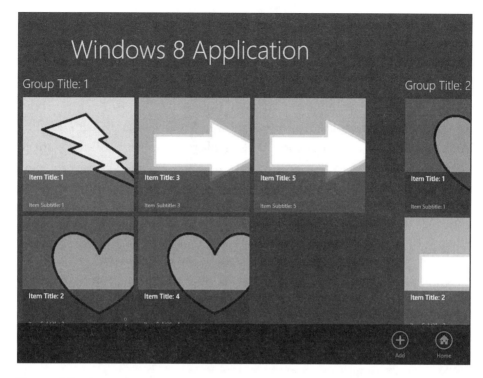

FIGURE 4.8: The application bar with commands disabled

You'll notice the commands are defined using a static resource:

```
<Button x:Name="Delete" HorizontalAlignment="Right"
    Style="{StaticResource DeleteAppBarButtonStyle}"
    Click="Delete_Click_1"/>
```

This resource is defined in the **Common/StandardStyles.xaml** file that is generated by the project template. These styles contain some of the most common commands. Each style provides a default icon and description. For example, the following XAML defines the help command (all of the styles target the Button control and are based on the AppBarButtonStyle resource):

```
<Style x:Key="HelpAppBarButtonStyle" ...>
    <Setter Property="AutomationProperties.Name" Value="Help"/>
    <Setter Property="Content" Value="&#xE11B;"/>
</Style>
```

If you don't see a style that matches the icon you need, you can simply create a new resource. It is not recommended that you manipulate the resources in the **StandardStyles.xaml** file without understanding what you are doing as this could potentially break the functionality of the application. To be safe, you can add your own dictionary to host the new styles and reference it from the **App.xaml** file (see **MyStyles.xaml**). Let's assume you are building an application that displays news articles and want to provide a command to change the font size. First, define a style for the new command:

```
<Style x:Key="FontAppBarButtonStyle" TargetType="Button"
    BasedOn="{StaticResource FontBarButtonStyle}">
</Style>
```

You can set an automation property (this is a unique identifier that helps with UI automation, used in various forms of testing and for accessibility) and name for the command:

```
<Setter Property="AutomationProperties.AutomationId"
    Value="FontAppBarButton"/>
<Setter Property="AutomationProperties.Name" Value="Font"/>
```

The last step is to locate the icon. If you have artistic skills or a designer on team, you may want to create the icon yourself. However, a more practical way is to take advantage of the built-in icons available for Windows 8 in the Segoe UI Symbol font. To browse the font, open the Windows 8 **Start** menu and type **charmap**. In the results pane, click **charmap.exe**. This will launch a tool that allows you to explore various fonts on your system. Select the Segoe UI Symbol font and scroll near the bottom. You will see quite a few icons. Figure 4.9 shows the icon that probably makes the most sense for a font command.

Note the code at the bottom. You can use this to set the symbol in your style by copying the portion after the plus (+) sign:

```
<Setter Property="Content" Value="&#xE185;"/>
```

Now you've got a style you can reference from anywhere.

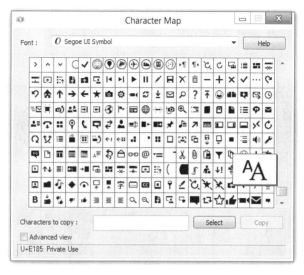

FIGURE 4.9: **How to select an icon using** `charmap.exe`

The code for the application bar control handles disabling or enabling icons based on selection. You can look at the **ApplicationCommands. xaml.cs** file to see the logic. For example, the delete command should only display if an item is currently selected:

```
var selected = App.CurrentItem;
Delete.Visibility = selected == null ?
    Visibility.Collapsed : Visibility.Visible;
```

You can see an example of the **Delete** command in the application bar in Figure 4.10. Notice that the **Add** command has been completely removed because it doesn't make sense in the context of a single item.

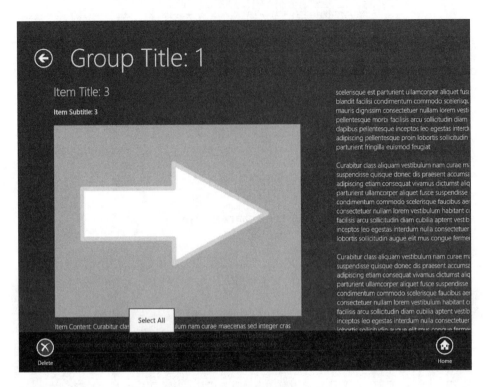

FIGURE **4.10**: The application bar with enabled commands

The implementation of the **Delete** command is a bit more complex. To prevent the user from accidentally deleting an item, it will show a confirmation to the user. If the user confirms the action and is on the detail page, the command will go back to the previous page as the current item will no longer exist after it is deleted. The dialog is set up like this:

```
var msg = new Windows.UI.Popups.MessageDialog("Confirm Delete",
    string.Format("Are you sure you wish to delete the item \"{0}\"",
            App.CurrentItem.Title));
```

The **OK** command is set up with a delegate that removes the current item from its group and then checks the current page to see if it needs to navigate back. You can take a look at the **App.xaml.cs** file to see the logic used to capture the page:

```
App.CurrentGroup.Items.Remove(App.CurrentItem);
if (App.NavigatedPage == typeof(ItemDetailPage))
{
    ((Frame)Window.Current.Content).GoBack();
}
```

The **Cancel** command will simply dismiss the application bar, so no delegate is passed to it:

```
msg.Commands.Add(new Windows.UI.Popups.UICommand("Cancel"));
```

The resulting dialog is shown in Figure 4.11.

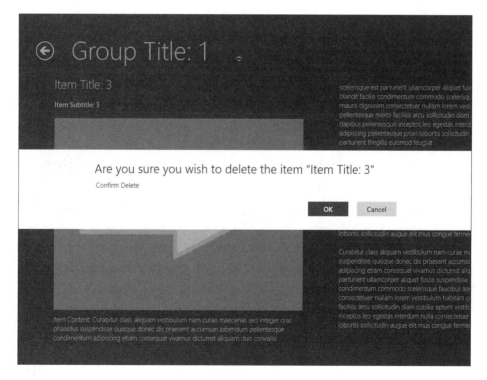

FIGURE 4.11: A confirmation dialog

The AppBar control can be programmatically opened or closed by setting the IsOpen property. The default behavior of the application bar is to disappear when the user interacts with the page anywhere outside of the application bar. If you set the IsSticky property to true, the application bar will remain until the user explicitly dismisses it using a right-click, **Ctrl+Z**, or the swipe gesture.

It is important to follow the guidelines for an application bar when you are organizing your command and controls. These guidelines are summarized in the following list:

- Global commands should be placed to the right.
- Commands should be separated on the left and right edges.
- Similar commands should be grouped together with separators.
- Context-specific commands should appear farthest to the left and appear or disappear as needed.
- Critical commands should be separated from other commands by extra space to avoid accidental activation.
- Do not use the application bar for settings—these are activated through the **Settings** charm.
- Do not use the application bar for search unless the search has a special context—instead, use the **Search** charm.
- Do not use the application bar for sharing content—use the **Share** charm instead.
- If the application bar becomes too crowded, you can move some commands to the top or bottom and extend commands with context menus.

Read the most current MSDN guidelines for application bars online at http://msdn.microsoft.com/en-us/library/windows/apps/hh465302.aspx.

Run the application again and practice adding and deleting items. One thing you should notice is what you get "for free" from the built-in grid controls. When you add or remove an item, it doesn't simply appear or disappear. As the existing items shift, they animate to their new locations in a fast and fluid motion. This all happens automatically as the result of you manipulating the underlying collections.

The application bar is not only limited to icons and commands. It might make sense to host other information in the application bar area. Examples include a status indicator (if you own a Windows Phone, you are familiar with the action of using an application bar to see the signal strength and remaining battery) or a thumbnail (take a look at Internet Explorer in Figure 4.12 and notice how it uses the application bar to facilitate switching between tabs or adding a new one).

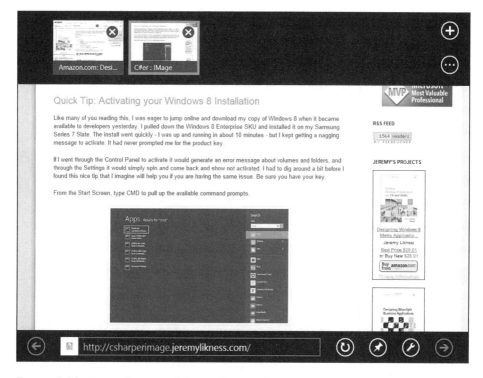

FIGURE 4.12: A creative use of the application bar in IE 10

Icons and Splash Screens

You may have noticed that the **Windows8Application** launches with a custom green splash screen. This serves two purposes: first, to affirm that I am at heart a developer and not a designer, and second, to demonstrate how you can customize the various icons and logos associated with your application.

To customize your tile and splash screen, double-click the **Package. appxmanifest** file to open package dialog. The settings for your icons and splash screen are on the Application UI tab, as shown in Figure 4.13. Here you can determine how and when the application name is displayed and what colors are used. You can provide logos for various tile configurations (the small logo is used in the zoomed-out view for the **Start** menu) as well as a splash screen logo and background color.

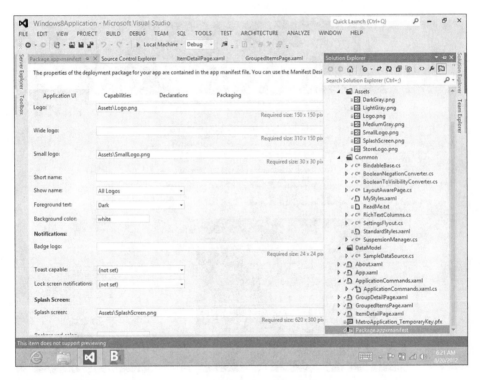

FIGURE 4.13: The Application UI tab for the package dialog

The dialog provides tips for the correct size. All of these items may be dynamic as well. You'll learn about how to provide a custom splash screen with your own elements in Chapter 5, *Application Lifecycle*. You'll learn about tiles and toast notifications in Chapter 7, *Tiles and Toasts*.

About Page

Information about your application, including settings, preferences, and the about page, should be accessed using the **Settings** charm. When you access settings, a **Permissions** option is always available that displays the application title, version, and publisher, as well as the list of permissions provided to the application. If you recall in Chapter 2, *Getting Started*, you had to provide permission for the application to use your web camera.

The first step to building pages that will display as part of the **Settings** charm is to create a class to facilitate panning the control in from the margin. This is known as a *flyout* and is not available "out of the box" for XAML applications. The class is quite simple to build and wraps the control in a Popup so it can overlay the edge of the application. Under the **Common** folder, you'll see the definition for the SettingsFlyout class that is in Listing 4.3 under the **Windows8Application**. There are two standard sizes for charm flyouts—narrow (346 pixels wide) and wide (646 pixels wide.)

LISTING 4.3: The SettingsFlyout Class

```
class SettingsFlyout
{
    private const int _width = 346;
    private Popup _popup;

    public void ShowFlyout(UserControl control)
    {
        _popup = new Popup();
        _popup.Closed += OnPopupClosed;
        Window.Current.Activated += OnWindowActivated;
        _popup.IsLightDismissEnabled = true;
        _popup.Width = _width;
        _popup.Height = Window.Current.Bounds.Height;

        control.Width = _width;
        control.Height = Window.Current.Bounds.Height;

        _popup.Child = control;
        _popup.SetValue(Canvas.LeftProperty,
            Window.Current.Bounds.Width - _width);
        _popup.SetValue(Canvas.TopProperty, 0);
        _popup.IsOpen = true;
    }
```

```
    private void OnWindowActivated(object sender,
        Windows.UI.Core.WindowActivatedEventArgs e)
    {
        if (e.WindowActivationState ==
            Windows.UI.Core.CoreWindowActivationState.Deactivated)
        {
            _popup.IsOpen = false;
        }
    }

    void OnPopupClosed(object sender, object e)
    {
        Window.Current.Activated -= OnWindowActivated;
    }
}
```

Take a look at **About.xaml** for the design. The **Settings** pages have a white background. The Grid is defined with transitions that provide the animated effect for the text to "fly-in" with the rest of the control. The special SettingsBackButtonStyle is a copy of the BackButtonStyle provided with the template and modified for display on the white background.

There are two commands wired into the page. The first command simply dismisses the parent (the SettingsFlyout class) and returns to the application settings. You must include a using statement for Windows.UI.ApplicationSettings for this to work:

```
    private void Button_Click_1(object sender, RoutedEventArgs e)
    {
        if (this.Parent.GetType() == typeof(Popup))
        {
            ((Popup)this.Parent).IsOpen = false;
        }
        SettingsPane.Show();
    }
```

The second command is triggered by a HyperlinkButton that is linked to my blog. It uses the Launcher class to open the Uri. This allows the Windows 8 platform to determine what application is registered to handle the Uri (most likely Internet Explorer 10) and then either pass the Uri to the application, or launch the application first.

```
private async void HyperlinkButton_Click_1(object sender,
    RoutedEventArgs e)
{
    await Windows.System.Launcher.LaunchUriAsync(
        new Uri("http://csharperimage.jeremylikness.com/"));
}
```

The final step is to actually register the new page with the **Settings** charm. When your application is launched you must hook into the CommandsRequested event on the SettingsPane object. This will fire when the **Settings** charm begins building the list of options after it is selected by the user. The registration is done in **App.xaml.cs**:

```
SettingsPane.GetForCurrentView().CommandsRequested +=
    App_CommandsRequested;
```

The event handler is passed a Request object that contains a list of commands. You can add your command to this list to make it display when the Settings charm is invoked:

```
var about = new SettingsCommand("about", "About", (handler) =>
{
    var settings = new SettingsFlyout();
    settings.ShowFlyout(new About());
});
args.Request.ApplicationCommands.Add(about);
```

Launch the application and try it for yourself. The About page is shown in Figure 4.14. To view it, simply swipe from the right side of the screen or hover your mouse pointer in the lower-right corner until the charm bar displays. Tap the **Settings** charm, and you'll see the new **About** command has been added in addition to the built-in **Permissions** command. Tap the **About** command, and you will see the new page animate into view.

You will use a similar technique to provide actual application settings and user preferences. You will learn more about storing and retrieving values in Chapter 5, and a detailed approach to handling application settings can be found in Chapter 6, *Data*.

FIGURE 4.14: **The About page**

Sensors

Touch input is not the only type of input that Windows 8 applications can process. Many Windows 8 devices contain special sensors that provide information like the physical orientation of the tablet or GPS coordinates. The Windows Runtime contains special APIs that allow you to tap into these sensors and build applications that respond to events like shaking the tablet, tilting the tablet, or providing contextual information based on the user's location. This section contains a brief overview of the available sensor APIs.

If you have a device with one of these sensors present, you can download and run sample applications that use the sensors from Microsoft's developer center. The following link will take you to a page to download a set of samples that includes a project for every sensor listed here (look for samples with Accelerometer, Gyrometer, Sensor, and Location in the title):

http://code.msdn.microsoft.com/windowsapps/Windows-8-Modern-Style-App-Samples

Accelerometer

The accelerometer provides information about the effect of gravity on the device across various axes. The API provides a current reading and generates an event when the reading changes. The event provides information about the acceleration in the X, Y, and Z planes. The code in Listing 4.4 demonstrates how to obtain a reading.

LISTING 4.4: Reading Values from the Accelerometer

```
async private void ReadingChanged(object sender,
    AccelerometerReadingChangedEventArgs e)
{
    await Dispatcher.RunAsync(CoreDispatcherPriority.Normal, () =>
    {
        AccelerometerReading reading = e.Reading;
        ScenarioOutput_X.Text = String.Format("{0,5:0.00}",
            reading.AccelerationX);
        ScenarioOutput_Y.Text = String.Format("{0,5:0.00}",
            reading.AccelerationY);
        ScenarioOutput_Z.Text = String.Format("{0,5:0.00}",
            reading.AccelerationZ);
    });
}
```

You can learn more about the accelerometer and run a sample application by reading the MSDN documentation found at http://msdn.microsoft.com/en-us/library/windows/apps/windows.devices.sensors.accelerometer.aspx.

Compass

The compass sensor, when present, provides a heading based on either True North or Magnetic North. *True North* is the direction to the geographic North Pole; *Magnetic North* is the direction to the magnetic north pole. The magnetic pole is not always in the same location because it shifts in response to changes in the Earth's magnetic core. Listing 4.5 shows how to read the compass headings.

LISTING 4.5: **Reading Compass Headings**

```
async private void ReadingChanged(object sender,
    CompassReadingChangedEventArgs e)
{
    await Dispatcher.RunAsync(CoreDispatcherPriority.Normal, () =>
    {
        CompassReading reading = e.Reading;
        ScenarioOutput_MagneticNorth.Text =
            String.Format("{0,5:0.00}",
            reading.HeadingMagneticNorth);
        if (reading.HeadingTrueNorth != null)
        {
            ScenarioOutput_TrueNorth.Text =
                String.Format("{0,5:0.00}",
                reading.HeadingTrueNorth);
        }
        else
        {
            ScenarioOutput_TrueNorth.Text = "No data";
        }
    });
}
```

You can learn more about the compass sensor online at http://msdn. microsoft.com/en-us/library/windows/apps/windows.devices.sensors. compass.aspx.

Geolocation

The geolocation API aggregates information from a variety of sources to provide an estimated location to your application. The information may come from the Windows Location Provider that uses a combination of Wi-Fi triangulation and IP address data to determine location, or it may come from sources like a built-in GPS device. The API draws on this information to provide the most accurate representation of location available.

Listing 4.6 demonstrates the use of the API to obtain information about the latitude and longitude of the device along with the estimated accuracy of the reading.

LISTING 4.6: **Obtaining Information About the Device Location**

```
Geoposition pos = await _geolocator.GetGeopositionAsync()
    .AsTask(token);
ScenarioOutput_Latitude.Text = pos.Coordinate.Latitude.ToString();
ScenarioOutput_Longitude.Text = pos.Coordinate.Longitude.ToString();
ScenarioOutput_Accuracy.Text = pos.Coordinate.Accuracy.ToString();
```

You can learn more about the geolocation API online at http://msdn.microsoft.com/en-us/library/windows/apps/windows.devices.geolocation.aspx.

Gyrometer

The gyrometer sensor provides information about angular velocity or how the device is being rotated. Like the other sensors, it provides an API to obtain the current reading as well as an event that fires when the reading changes. Listing 4.7 shows how to interpret the results from that event.

LISTING 4.7: **Reading the Gyrometer**

```
async private void ReadingChanged(object sender,
    GyrometerReadingChangedEventArgs e)
{
    await Dispatcher.RunAsync(CoreDispatcherPriority.Normal,
        () =>
    {
        GyrometerReading reading = e.Reading;
        ScenarioOutput_X.Text = String.Format("{0,5:0.00}",
            reading.AngularVelocityX);
        ScenarioOutput_Y.Text = String.Format("{0,5:0.00}",
            reading.AngularVelocityY);
        ScenarioOutput_Z.Text = String.Format("{0,5:0.00}",
            reading.AngularVelocityZ);
    });
}
```

You can learn more about the gyrometer online at http://msdn.microsoft.com/en-us/library/windows/apps/windows.devices.sensors.gyrometer.aspx.

Inclinometer

The inclinometer provides the pitch, roll, and yaw values of the device. This allows you to understand the orientation of the device relative to the ground (or more specifically, the direction that gravity is acting on the device). You use this sensor to determine if the device is twisted or tilted. For an explanation of pitch, roll, and yaw, refer to this article on the NASA website at http://www.grc.nasa.gov/WWW/K-12/airplane/rotations.html.

Listing 4.8 demonstrates code that reads the pitch, roll, and yaw values for the device.

LISTING 4.8: Reading the Inclinometer

```
async private void ReadingChanged(object sender,
    InclinometerReadingChangedEventArgs e)
{
    await Dispatcher.RunAsync(CoreDispatcherPriority.Normal,
        () =>
    {
        InclinometerReading reading = e.Reading;
        ScenarioOutput_X.Text = String.Format("{0,5:0.00}",
            reading.PitchDegrees);
        ScenarioOutput_Y.Text = String.Format("{0,5:0.00}",
            reading.RollDegrees);
        ScenarioOutput_Z.Text = String.Format("{0,5:0.00}",
            reading.YawDegrees);
    });
}
```

Learn more about the inclinometer online at http://msdn.microsoft.com/en-us/library/windows/apps/windows.devices.sensors.inclinometer.aspx.

Light Sensor

The ambient light sensor detects the quality and intensity of light in the device's environment. This enables your application to adjust the display, such as reducing the brightness when the user is in a dark environment. Reducing the brightness of the display can prolong the battery life for the device.

Listing 4.9 demonstrates reading values from the light sensor.

LISTING 4.9: Reading the Light Sensor

```
async private void ReadingChanged(object sender,
    LightSensorReadingChangedEventArgs e)
{
    await Dispatcher.RunAsync(CoreDispatcherPriority.Normal,
        () =>
    {
        LightSensorReading reading = e.Reading;
        ScenarioOutput_LUX.Text = String.Format("{0,5:0.00}",
            reading.IlluminanceInLux);
    });
}
```

You can learn more about the light sensor online at http://msdn.micro-soft.com/en-us/library/windows/apps/windows.devices.sensors.light-sensor.aspx.

Orientation Sensor

The orientation sensor provides a matrix that represents rotation and a Quaternion that can be used to adjust the user's perspective within an application. Unlike the simple orientation sensor that was used earlier in this chapter to change from portrait to landscape modes, the full orientation sensor is typically used in games to render the graphics differently based on the orientation of the tablet. A Quaternion is specific notation used to describe orientations and rotations.

Listing 4.10 illustrates how to obtain orientation readings.

LISTING 4.10: Reading the Orientation

```
async private void ReadingChanged(object sender,
    OrientationSensorReadingChangedEventArgs e)
{
    await Dispatcher.RunAsync(CoreDispatcherPriority.Normal,
        () =>
    {
        OrientationSensorReading reading = e.Reading;

        // Quaternion values
        SensorQuaternion quaternion = reading.Quaternion;
        ScenarioOutput_X.Text = String.Format("{0,8:0.00000}",
            quaternion.X);
        ScenarioOutput_Y.Text = String.Format("{0,8:0.00000}",
            quaternion.Y);
```

```
            ScenarioOutput_Z.Text = String.Format("{0,8:0.00000}",
                quaternion.Z);
            ScenarioOutput_W.Text = String.Format("{0,8:0.00000}",
                quaternion.W);

            // Rotation Matrix values
            SensorRotationMatrix rotationMatrix = reading.RotationMatrix;
            ScenarioOutput_M11.Text = String.Format("{0,8:0.00000}",
                rotationMatrix.M11);
            ScenarioOutput_M12.Text = String.Format("{0,8:0.00000}",
                rotationMatrix.M12);
            ScenarioOutput_M13.Text = String.Format("{0,8:0.00000}",
                rotationMatrix.M13);
            ScenarioOutput_M21.Text = String.Format("{0,8:0.00000}",
                rotationMatrix.M21);
            ScenarioOutput_M22.Text = String.Format("{0,8:0.00000}",
                rotationMatrix.M22);
            ScenarioOutput_M23.Text = String.Format("{0,8:0.00000}",
                rotationMatrix.M23);
            ScenarioOutput_M31.Text = String.Format("{0,8:0.00000}",
                rotationMatrix.M31);
            ScenarioOutput_M32.Text = String.Format("{0,8:0.00000}",
                rotationMatrix.M32);
            ScenarioOutput_M33.Text = String.Format("{0,8:0.00000}",
                rotationMatrix.M33);
        });
}
```

You can learn more about the orientation sensor online at http://msdn.
microsoft.com/en-us/library/windows/apps/windows.devices.sensors.
orientationsensor.aspx.

Summary

This chapter focused on the unique layouts and behaviors that define
Windows 8 applications. You learned about the Visual State Manager and
the role it plays in separating presentation logic from your application
code, explored the simulator to emulate features like location and touch,
and learned how to manage various orientations and view formats. The
SemanticZoom control was introduced as a way to enable the user to quickly
navigate through large data lists.

You learned the various nuances of touch input and how to manage
it from the Windows 8 environment. A sample application demonstrated

how to provide mouse, keyboard, and touch actions to invoke various commands, as well as how to enable and monitor manipulation events. You explored how the main example application provides a custom splash page and tiles, handles commands within the application using the AppBar control, and provides an About page through the **Settings** charm.

Windows 8 devices have the option of providing various sensors that obtain information about orientation, ambient light, acceleration, and location. There are a variety of APIs you can use to test for the presence of a sensor and obtain readings to enhance your application. These sensors allow you to respond to changes in the environment as well as provide contextual information to the user.

The development environment and project templates helped jumpstart a fairly comprehensive sample project that contains grouped items and provides functionality to navigate, add, and delete items. Under ordinary circumstances when you jump to other applications and leave the main application running, the current state will be preserved in memory, and swapping back to the application will return you to the same spot. There is no guarantee that it will remain in memory and the Windows Runtime can terminate your application.

Customers will expect to return to the same spot they left before the application was terminated. In the next chapter, you will learn about the Application Lifecycle and how to detect when your application is being suspended and when it is either returned to in memory or terminated and re-launched. You will also learn how the applications preserve the application state so that you can restore it and provide a seamless experience to the end user.

5

Application Lifecycle

IN THE TRADITIONAL WINDOWS ENVIRONMENT, THE USER MANAGES the lifetime of his applications. He launches the application, and it continues to run until he decides to close it. The problem with this model is that applications continue to drain system resources, including memory and CPU, even when they are not in the foreground. This impacts the performance of the application the user is using as well as drains the battery faster when the device is not plugged in.

It is easy to demonstrate this traditional behavior in the desktop mode of Windows 8. If you don't have a video file to use, browse to the following website that contains all of the video sessions from the Microsoft //BUILD event that launched Windows 8:

http://channel9.msdn.com/Events/BUILD/BUILD2011

(You may be reading this after the 2012 event; if so, then you should be able to reach the updated site and pull videos from there, too.)

Navigate to a video of your choice and use the download links to save a copy of either the mid-quality or high-quality video to your hard disk. This can take several minutes to hours depending on the size of the video. While you are waiting, launch the Task Manager. This is an application that provides a view of the applications running on your system. There are several ways to launch the Task Manager:

- From the Windows 8 **Start** menu, type **task manager** and select the program from the search results when it appears.
- On the desktop, right-click the taskbar and select the **Task Manager** option.
- From anywhere, hold down **Ctrl+Shift+Esc** at the same time

When you first launch the Task Manager, it will have a simple view, as shown in Figure 5.1.

FIGURE 5.1: **The simple Task Manager view**

The default view provides a simple list of running applications. To see a more advanced view, click the **More details** prompt in the lower left. This will provide the advanced view you see in Figure 5.2. It not only shows the running applications with specific information about their resource utilization, but also includes background processes that are running, such as drivers that your system uses to interface with various devices.

Make sure the Task Manager is running in the advanced view and is visible for you to watch. Now, launch the video you downloaded and start watching it by right-clicking the file in Windows Explorer and choosing **Play with Windows Media Player** to launch it. You should notice the CPU and memory for that application start to spike. The amount will vary depending on your system configuration. Now open an instance of

Notepad and stretch it so it completely covers the video. What you'll find is that the CPU usage will remain consistent even though you are no longer watching the video. The application actually goes through the task of processing the video when you've indicated you are no longer interested in that piece by bringing the Notepad application to the foreground.

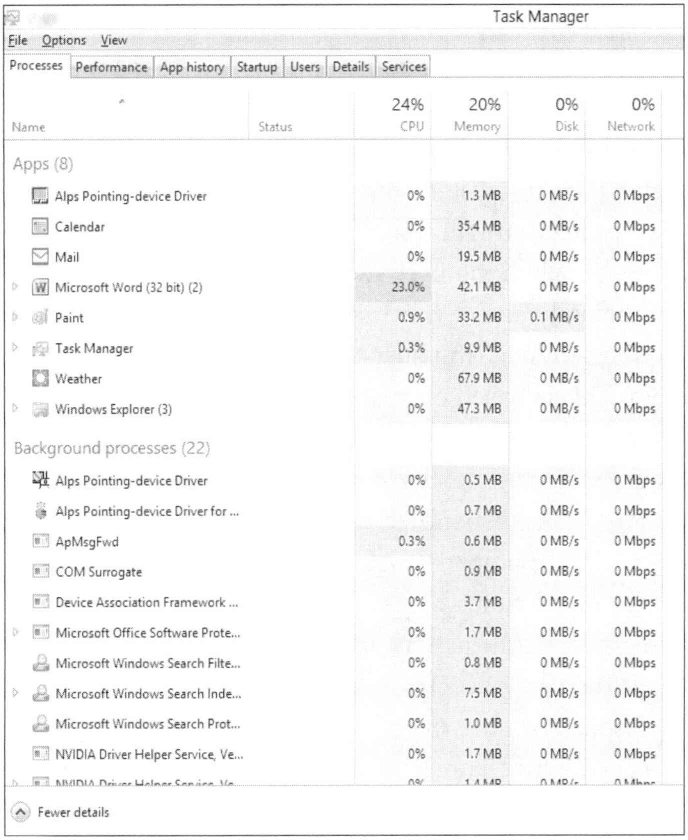

Task Manager

File   Options   View

Processes | Performance | App history | Startup | Users | Details | Services

Name	Status	24% CPU	20% Memory	0% Disk	0% Network
Apps (8)					
Alps Pointing-device Driver		0%	1.3 MB	0 MB/s	0 Mbps
Calendar		0%	35.4 MB	0 MB/s	0 Mbps
Mail		0%	19.5 MB	0 MB/s	0 Mbps
▷ W Microsoft Word (32 bit) (2)		23.0%	42.1 MB	0 MB/s	0 Mbps
▷ Paint		0.9%	33.2 MB	0.1 MB/s	0 Mbps
▷ Task Manager		0.3%	9.9 MB	0 MB/s	0 Mbps
Weather		0%	67.9 MB	0 MB/s	0 Mbps
▷ Windows Explorer (3)		0%	47.3 MB	0 MB/s	0 Mbps
Background processes (22)					
Alps Pointing-device Driver		0%	0.5 MB	0 MB/s	0 Mbps
Alps Pointing-device Driver for …		0%	0.7 MB	0 MB/s	0 Mbps
ApMsgFwd		0.3%	0.6 MB	0 MB/s	0 Mbps
COM Surrogate		0%	0.9 MB	0 MB/s	0 Mbps
Device Association Framework …		0%	3.7 MB	0 MB/s	0 Mbps
▷ Microsoft Office Software Prote…		0%	1.7 MB	0 MB/s	0 Mbps
Microsoft Windows Search Filte…		0%	0.8 MB	0 MB/s	0 Mbps
▷ Microsoft Windows Search Inde…		0%	7.5 MB	0 MB/s	0 Mbps
Microsoft Windows Search Prot…		0%	1.0 MB	0 MB/s	0 Mbps
NVIDIA Driver Helper Service, Ve…		0%	1.7 MB	0 MB/s	0 Mbps
▷ NVIDIA Driver Helper Service, Ve…		0%	1.4 MB	0 MB/s	0 Mbps

⌃ Fewer details

FIGURE 5.2: The advanced Task Manager view

This scenario changes in Windows 8 applications. The user decides which applications will run in the foreground, and only one application can run in the foreground at a time (with the exception of the snapped view, which allows two applications with one taking up a small strip of space). The system will then determine what happens to the other background applications. If you don't build your application correctly, you will create negative side effects that cause a bad user experience. The management of applications in the Windows Runtime is called Process Lifetime Management (PLM).

Process Lifetime Management

Windows 8 applications only run when they are in the foreground. This allows the user to focus on the primary application she wishes to interact with. Applications in the background go into a suspended state in which the threads for the application are literally frozen in place. The application will no longer take up system resources or impact battery life. Most of the time, the application will remain in memory. This allows fast application switching, so when the user swipes back to a different application, it resumes immediately as if it were already running.

There is a case where the suspended application may be terminated by the system. This is based on system resources. For example, if the foreground application requires a large chunk of memory that will potentially result in a low memory state, the system may terminate one or more applications that are in the suspended state. It will target background applications based on their memory consumption and terminate the ones taking up the most resources first.

To see this process in action, launch the Windows 8 Start menu by pressing the **Windows** Key. Open the Task Manager and overlay it on the Windows 8 display. Be sure to go under **Options** and ensure that **Always on Top** is checked. Now launch an application and then return to the **Start** menu and launch another application. Repeat this process several times. You should notice after a few seconds that the applications will show a Suspended status. If the status is not showing, go into **View→Status values** and select **Show suspended status**. Figure 5.3 shows the result of launching several applications with the Weather application in the foreground. Notice that the other Windows 8 applications are in a Suspended status.

If the system experiences low resources, many of the applications in Suspended status might be terminated and will be removed from the Task Manager list. You can also emulate a suspension from Visual Studio 2012 in debug mode. You learn how later in this chapter, but first, it's important to understand the full PLM lifecycle. The life of an application begins with *activation*.

FIGURE 5.3: **Windows 8 applications in the Suspended status**

Activation

Activation is the first step in an application lifecycle. In previous versions of Windows, activation typically happened as the result of the user launching the application, either through the **Start** menu or by typing the name of the program at a command prompt. In Windows 8, an application is always activated through a contract. You learned about the mechanics of activation in Chapter 2, *Getting Started*.

The most common contract is the **Launch** contract. This is the contract that is invoked when you tap a tile from the **Start** menu. The **Launch** contract activates the application and calls the OnLaunched method. Another contract that may activate your application is the **Share** contract if your application is a share target like **ImageHelper** from Chapter 2. There are several other contracts that can activate the application. The **Windows8Application2** is based on the application from Chapter 4, *Windows 8 Applications,* and has been updated to support the **Search** contract. You can download it from this book's website at http://windows8applications.codeplex.com/.

Adding this contract to a Windows 8 application is straightforward. This has already been done in the sample application, but if you were starting with a new application, you would right-click the project node in the **Solution Explorer** and choose **Add→New Item** or hold down **Ctrl+Shift+A**. Choose the **Search Contract** option and name the search results page, as shown in Figure 5.4.

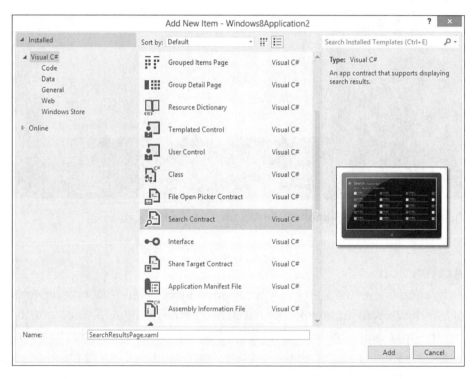

FIGURE 5.4: **Adding the Search contract to a project**

When you add the new item, several things happen behind the scenes. In addition to a new Page, a method called OnSearchActivated is added to the **App.xaml.cs** file to handle incoming search requests. It provides a code snippet to move into the OnLaunched event to handle queries from within the running application. The Declarations section of the package for the application is also updated to include the **Search** declaration.

When the plumbing is in place, the templates can be used to provide search capabilities. In the example, the search results show on the page with a set of filters by group. This will enable the user to specify a search across all items or restrict the search to items within a particular group. The search is also set up to handle incoming requests regardless of whether or not the application is currently running.

When the application is activated by any contract, it will display a splash screen. The initial splash screen is composed of the background color and a static image (you learned how to specify these in Chapter 4 and will learn how to specify a custom one later in this chapter). The application is notified of activation when the appropriate method in **App.xaml.cs** is called based on the contract (OnLaunching for the **Launch** contract, OnSearchActivated for the **Search** contract, and so on).

The application is given about 15 seconds to show the first page. Failure to show the first page within this timeframe will result in the application being terminated, and it will appear as a crash to the end user. This is important to know because applications that require large amounts of data to be downloaded or initialized prior to showing the first page must handle the delay appropriately. It is possible to do this by providing an extended splash screen. You learn about extended splash screens later in this chapter.

When the application is activated, it becomes the foreground application and will run until the user switches to a different application, including the desktop. When the user switches, the application will be notified via the Suspending event. This notifies the application that it is about to be suspended and allows the developer to insert any code that is necessary to preserve state prior to termination.

Suspension

In the normal course of operation, your application will become suspended as soon as it is no longer in the foreground. It is not easy to force a suspension of the application during testing, so Visual Studio 2012 provides a way to manually suspend your program for debugging purposes. To understand suspension, load the **Windows8Application2** project.

Open the **App.xaml.cs** file and place a breakpoint next to the highlighted line of code in the OnSuspending method:

```
private static async void OnSuspending(object sender,
    SuspendingEventArgs e)
{
    var deferral = e.SuspendingOperation.GetDeferral();
    Debug.WriteLine(string.Format("{0} remaining",
        e.SuspendingOperation.Deadline - DateTime.Now));
    await SuspensionManager.SaveAsync();
    deferral.Complete();
}
```

Launch the application in debug mode. In the toolbar, you should see an icon that looks like a pause button with an application behind it (don't confuse this with the Pause button for debug that forces a "Break All"). The tooltip is shown in Figure 5.5. Use that icon to emulate a suspension of your application. When you click it, you'll notice the line of code is highlighted as the OnSuspending method in the application object is called. Note the value that is written to the Output window (if you can't see it, hold down **Ctrl+Alt+O** for "Output") and then press **Continue**.

The Deadline is an offset that provides the time remaining for the suspension to complete. If your application does not complete any necessary tasks within that timeframe, it will be terminated. When performing asynchronous tasks, you must ask for a deferral. With the arguments passed to the event, you can request a deferral and then perform a list of asynchronous operations such as saving your application state to disk. The sample application saves state as events happen, so it has no extra work to perform when the application is being suspended. When the application is ready for suspension, it will call the Complete method to finish suspension.

■ TIP

So far you've learned how to use the debugger in Visual Studio 2012 to debug applications run locally or within the simulator. There is another option to debug to a remote machine. This is particularly useful when you have a slate device to test touch operations on but prefer to develop from a laptop or desktop. To debug remotely, you must first launch a special application on the remote device that configures the debug environment. You can then specify the remote machine from the Remote Machine option. You may have to authenticate before the debugging session begins. Full instructions to set up this feature are available online at http://msdn.microsoft.com/en-us/library/bt727f1t(v=vs.110).aspx.

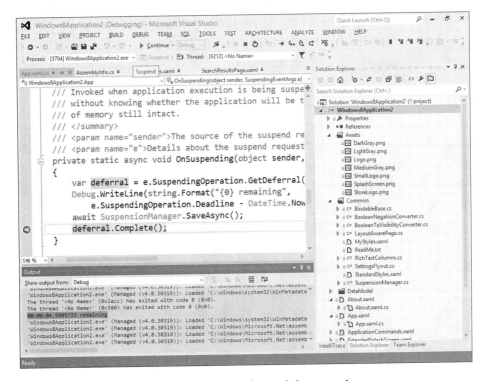

FIGURE 5.5: Suspending an application from debug mode

At this stage the application is still in memory, but it is not consuming any resources. If you launch the Task Manager, you'll see the CPU utilization at 0%. The application is no longer impacting battery life and is simply waiting. If you then resume operation (either by bringing the application back to the foreground or by pressing the **Resume** option located in the same drop-down as **Suspend** in Visual Studio 2012), the application will be "fast-switched" and resumed with no perceptible delay.

The kernel provides one additional service for suspended applications. There are times when the application may be in a critical section of code, such as releasing locks on files. The kernel will not suspend the application while it is in a critical code section (usually when control has passed to a WinRT component) and instead will wait until the application exits that section to avoid system-wide deadlocks.

You may have noticed another option next to **Suspend** and **Resume** that has the text **Suspend and shutdown**. This icon is used to terminate your application. This will simulate what happens when the application is in a suspended state and system resources force the runtime to shut down your application to free up memory.

Termination

When the system needs memory, the active user is switched, the system is shut down, or your application crashes, the Windows Runtime will terminate the application. There is no event to notify you when it is terminating. This is why it is important to save state either while the application is running or when the OnSuspending event handler is called.

Typical application behavior is to start at the first screen whenever it is launched for the first time or after the user has closed it. You should only launch the application into saved state when you are resuming from a termination event. Fortunately, the previous state of the application is always passed to the OnLaunched event. This allows you to check the previous state and take action based on whether the user is swapping back to a terminated application or re-launching it after closing it.

Resume

The application can register for the Resuming event. This event is only fired if the application was still in memory when the user returned it to the foreground. There is no need to restore any state because all of the application threads, stack, and storage were maintained. So why is this event even available?

The main reason is for applications that provide timely data to refresh their information. Imagine a weather application that is suspended when you swap to a game that you play for several hours. The application remains in memory with all of its threads frozen in place. You then return to the application. What do you expect to see? Without the Resuming event, you would simply see the stale information the application displayed earlier in the day. This event will allow the weather application to fetch the latest forecast and show you the current weather status, including any alerts that may have been issued.

If an application is terminated, then it is relaunched when the user comes back to it. The Resuming event is not fired. Instead, the application can check the previous state to determine what logic to apply when it is launched. Take a look at the ExtendedSplashScreen_Loaded method in **ExtendedSplashScreen.xaml.cs**, and you will see the following check:

```
if (_activationArgs.PreviousExecutionState ==
    ApplicationExecutionState.Terminated)
```

If the application was terminated, the previous state is queried and the user is returned to the place he left off. You learn how the state is saved and restored later in this chapter. Otherwise, the application initializes and places the user in the **Start** screen. The other valid states you can check for include ClosedByUser, NotRunning, Running, and Suspended.

Figure 5.6 provides a general overview of the application lifecycle.

The following list of guidelines will help you build your application to provide the best user experience possible while managing PLM:

- **Incrementally save user data**—This keeps you from having to save everything at once when the application is suspended and risk timing out.
- **Save and restore application state**—This is important to ensure the user has a consistent experience when she returns to the application.
- **Only save/restore session metadata (where the user is/navigation)**—Any other data should be handled elsewhere by your application.

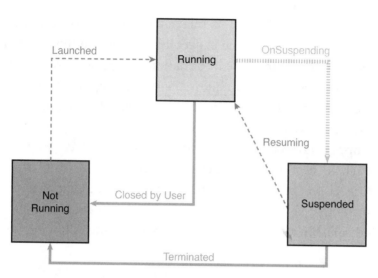

FIGURE 5.6: Overview of the application lifecycle

Now that you are familiar with the lifecycle, you can use the code in the templates to manage the application state. It will help to understand how navigation in Windows 8 applications works. When a previously suspended application is launched from the **Start** screen, it will resume the application rather than treating the launch as a "fresh start."

Navigation

There are two primary types of navigation in Windows 8 applications: hierarchical and flat. In hierarchical applications, you start with a high level view and drill down to a specific area. In the example applications, you've dealt with groups of collections and drilled into collections and then specific items. A flat navigation is like the traditional wizard and guides you through various steps of the process.

When you launch a mail application for the first time, you likely start with a flat navigation scenario. A wizard will guide you through the process of entering the information about your mail server and your credentials, testing the connection, and adding it to the accounts list. When you begin using the mail application, your view is hierarchical. You start with a view of accounts and messages and then drill down into individual messages.

For Windows 8 applications built using XAML and C#, the default container for your application is the Frame. Take a look at the **Windows8Application2** example in the **ExtendedSplashScreen.xaml.cs** file. The code for the ExtendedSplashScreen_Loaded method creates the Frame, hooks into an event, and then navigates to a page. The splash screen performs some work before wiring up the main application navigation (you will learn more about the custom splash screen later in this chapter):

```
var rootFrame = new Frame();
rootFrame.Navigating += rootFrame_Navigating;
// additional code here
rootFrame.Navigate(target, parameter);
```

The Frame object is a visual container that supports navigation. The unit of navigation within the Frame is a Page. The Page is a special control that is designed to work with navigation. Think of it as a container for the visual elements you wish to present for a specific area of the application. The Frame object allows you to navigate by passing in the type of Page you wish to display, as well as an optional parameter. In the example for the sample application, the target defaults to the type of the main page that shows the various groups and passes in the name for the collection of groups from the data source:

```
if (!rootFrame.Navigate(typeof(GroupedItemsPage), "ItemGroups"))
```

Calling the Navigate method on the Frame will create an instance of the target page. When the target Page is loaded, the OnNavigatedTo method is called. This allows you to set up your UI. The sample application uses this method to wire the data to the underlying view model (you'll learn more about view models in Chapter 9, *MVVM and Testing*) as well as set the source for items on the control.

The Frame keeps a journal of Page objects that you navigate to. This allows it to function similar to a web browser because you can choose to go back to previous Page instances or move forward when you've navigated backwards. These actions are supported by the GoBack and GoForward methods, and you can check to see if the actions are possible by interrogating the CanGoBack and CanGoForward properties on the Frame object.

Open **GroupDetailPage.xaml**. The XAML for the back button looks like this:

```
<Button x:Name="backButton" Click="GoBack"
    IsEnabled="{Binding Frame.CanGoBack,
    ElementName=pageRoot}"
    Style="{StaticResource BackButtonStyle}"/>
```

The button is enabled only when a previous page exists in the journal. If it is enabled and the user clicks the button, it invokes the GoBack method. This method is defined in the base LayoutAwarePage class that in turn derives from Page:

```
protected virtual void GoBack(object sender, RoutedEventArgs e)
{
    if (this.Frame != null && this.Frame.CanGoBack)
        this.Frame.GoBack();
}
```

Figure 5.7 shows the typical flow when a navigation event occurs. The Frame is instructed to Navigate to a new Page called **Page 2**. The Navigating event is fired for the Frame. The **Page 1** object is informed of the navigation through the OnNavigatingFrom event. If there is a reason to prevent the navigation from taking place (for example, the user has entered data on a form and not yet saved it), **Page 1** can cancel the navigation by setting the Cancel flag on the event.

When **Page 1** declines to cancel the navigation, the Frame unloads **Page 1** and fires the Navigated event. It informs **Page 1** that it has been unloaded through the OnNavigatedFrom method. It then places an instance of **Page 2** onto the visible frame and notifies **Page 2** via the OnNavigatedTo event. The Frame may create a new instance of **Page 2** or reuse an existing instance. **Page 1** is now part of the journal, so CanGoBack is enabled, and a call to GoBack on the Frame will result in **Page 1** being shown again.

You can control how the Frame manages instances of pages through the CacheSize property. This represents a number of pages that will be stored in the cache. Any pages in cache are simply reused instead of having new instances created. For a Page to participate in the cache, you must set the NavigationCacheMode on the Page object to either Enabled or Required. When it is set to Required, it will be cached regardless of the CacheSize setting on the Frame object and will not count against the CacheSize total.

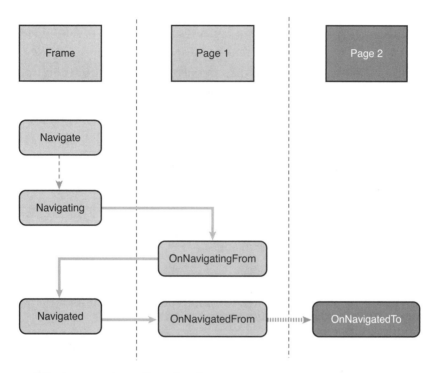

FIGURE 5.7: An overview of navigation events

Understanding how navigation works makes it easy to manage the location of the user. The built-in templates in Visual Studio 2012 provide a special helper class called the SuspensionManager that assists with saving and restoring state. When the application is loaded, the root Frame object is registered with the SuspensionManager in **App.xaml.cs**:

```
SuspensionManager.RegisterFrame(rootFrame, "AppFrame");
```

This sets up the SessionManager to observe the frame as the user navigates. It then saves the navigation stack as well as parameters that are passed to pages so that it can restore both the user location and the navigation history when the application is resumed. The state is saved to a local cache using the Application Data API.

Application Data API

The Application Data API provides a way to manage data specific to a particular application. You can use it to store state, preferences, local cache, and other settings. The Windows Runtime manages application-specific storage and isolates it per user and per application from other users and applications on the system. The data persists through application updates and is removed when the application is uninstalled.

There are three types of local data that are available to your application. Table 5.1 lists these types and describes what they are used for.

TABLE 5.1: Application Data Storage Types

Store	Description
Local	Exists for the application and user on the current device. Persists between application launches and system reboots.
Roaming	Exists for the application and user on all devices. This storage is limited to about 100 kilobytes of data. It requires a Windows Account.
Temporary	This store may be removed by the system at any given time and is typically used for local "work files" or other temporary data that does not need to persist between application launches.

Each store provides two types of access. The first type, *application settings*, allows for any WinRT data type to be stored. You can store data as single values, composite values, or in containers to segregate sets of data from each other. This storage is intended for small sets of data. According to the documentation, the settings are actually stored in the registry. Read the documentation for application data online here at http://msdn.micro-soft.com/en-us/library/windows/apps/hh464917.aspx.

The second type is *application files*. These are files in the traditional sense that you can read and write to. Each store has a space allocated for storage per application and user. You are able to create directories up to 32 levels deep and read or write as many files as you like. The files written to the temporary store can be removed at any time. The files written to the roaming store when the user is logged in with a Windows account (such as Live) are synchronized across devices but must fit within the quota that you can query using `ApplicationData.RoamingStorageQuota`.

The application is in control of local data, so it typically will not change except as a result of application code. Roaming data is different because the user may change data on one device while running an instance of the application on another device. When application data is synchronized, these changes will raise the `DataChanged` event. Your application can use this event to react to changes and refresh the data on the local device. You can also explicitly signal a data change by calling `SignalDataChanged`.

The **Windows8Application2** example uses the local settings to store the navigation location for the application and this is the default for the `SuspensionManager`. The reason it uses the local settings instead of the roaming settings is because when the user adds a new item, it is only stored locally. The items list can potentially become quite large, so it doesn't make sense to store it in the roaming settings. You will learn more about data in Chapter 6, *Data*, and how to manage large collections across devices.

The application storage settings are extremely easy to use. If you were not concerned about the navigation history and parameters passed to various pages, you could easily save the current page by updating the `NavigatedPage` property in **App.xaml.cs** like this:

```
set
{
    _navigatedPage = value;
    ApplicationData.Current.LocalSettings.Values["NavigatedPage"]
        = value.ToString();
}
```

That's really how simple it is—you simply choose a key for the property and set the value. It is also possible to store groups of values together. If you need an atomic operation that ensures either all of a group of values is stored or none are, use the `ApplicationDataCompositeValue`. This simply prepares an atomic group of values for storage with a single setting. In the **App.xaml.cs** file the current group, and item could be stored like this:

```
private void PersistCurrentSettings()
{
    var value = new ApplicationDataCompositeValue();
    value.Add("Group", _currentGroup == null ? string.Empty :
```

```
        _currentGroup.UniqueId);
    value.Add("Item", _item == null ? string.Empty : _item.UniqueId);
    ApplicationData.Current.LocalSettings.Values["Current"] = value;
}
```

Reading back values is straightforward as well. To restore the current page, the application would simply read in the value of the type as a string and then convert it to an actual type for navigation:

```
target = Type.GetType(ApplicationData.Current.LocalSettings
    .Values["NavigatedPage"].ToString(), true);
```

The navigation would be combined with the value of the current item or group. Composite values are retrieved like this:

```
var value = ApplicationData.Current.LocalSettings.Values["Current"]
    as ApplicationDataCompositeValue;
```

The value could then be restored and queried against the internal collections to retrieve the full object:

```
var currentItemId = value["Item"];
CurrentItem = (from g in DataSource.ItemGroups
                from i in g.Items
                where i.UniqueId.Equals(currentItemId)
                select i).FirstOrDefault();
```

The query uses Language-Integrated Query syntax, or LINQ. You can learn more about LINQ online at http://msdn.microsoft.com/en-us/library/bb397926(v=vs.110).aspx.

It is also possible to separate settings in different containers. You can use the `ApplicationDataContainer` class for this. The store provides a `CreateContainer` method as well as a list of current `Containers`. When you reference a specific container, you can access the `Values` dictionary to set and retrieve settings specific to that container.

Storage is not limited to simple key-value pairs. You can also create folders and files. Instead of saving individual pages and parameters as suggested here, it is possible to use the generic `SuspensionManager` helper to handle most of your navigation scenarios. The `SuspensionManager` declares a simple file name to store all of the state for the application:

```
private const string sessionStateFilename = "_sessionState.xml";
```

It then uses the DataContractSerializer to create an image of the stored navigation state. This class can inspect all of the properties and values in a class instance and turn them into an XML representation. Here is the code that does this by transforming the instance into an in-memory XML document:

```
MemoryStream sessionData = new MemoryStream();
DataContractSerializer serializer =
    new DataContractSerializer(typeof(Dictionary<string, object>),
        _knownTypes);
serializer.WriteObject(sessionData, _sessionState);
```

Next, the code is written to storage. The Application Data API is used to create an instance of the file, and then the stream that was serialized is written to disk:

```
StorageFile file = await ApplicationData.Current.LocalFolder
    .CreateFileAsync(sessionStateFilename,
        CreationCollisionOption.ReplaceExisting);
using (Stream fileStream = await file.OpenStreamForWriteAsync())
{
    sessionData.Seek(0, SeekOrigin.Begin);
    await sessionData.CopyToAsync(fileStream);
    await fileStream.FlushAsync();
}
```

To restore state when the user returns to the application, the reverse operation is performed:

```
StorageFile file = await ApplicationData.Current.LocalFolder
    .GetFileAsync(sessionStateFilename);
using (IInputStream inStream = await file.OpenSequentialReadAsync())
{
    DataContractSerializer serializer = new DataContractSerializer(
    typeof(Dictionary<string, object>), _knownTypes);
    _sessionState = (Dictionary<string, object>)serializer
        .ReadObject(inStream.AsStreamForRead());
}
```

Compile and run the application and then navigate into a group and an item. Terminate the application by either dragging it off the bottom edge of the display or by pressing **Alt+F4**. Now open the **File Explorer** and navigate to the following:

```
C:\users\{username}\AppData\Local\Packages\{packagename}
```

Replace {username} with your user name and {packagename} with the name of the package from the **Package name** value on the **Packaging** tab of the application manifest. On my machine, the path resolves to this:

```
C:\Users\Jeremy\AppData\Local\Packages\
➥34F9460F-0BA2-4952-8627-439D8DC45427_req6rhny9ggkj
```

Open the **LocalState** folder and you should see the **_sessionState.xml** file. There you can see the stored contents for the state of the application. An example XML element that holds the navigation history looks like this:

```
<KeyValueOfstringanyType>
<Key>Navigation</Key>
<Value i:type="a:string" xmlns:a="http://www.w3.org/2001/XMLSchema">
➥1,3,2,33,Windows8Application2.GroupedItemsPage,12,10,ItemGroups,32,
➥Windows8Application2.GroupDetailPage,12,7,Group-2,31,
➥Windows8Application2.ItemDetailPage,12,14,Group-2-Item-2
</Value>
</KeyValueOfstringanyType>
```

You will learn more about storing and retrieving data in Chapter 6, *Data*.

Connected and Alive

Just because applications are suspended and potentially terminated when they are in the background doesn't mean they can't remain connected or provide the appearance of running. One effective way to keep applications current and provide real-time feedback to the user is through the use of tiles and notifications. You will learn more about these in Chapter 7, *Tiles and Toasts*.

There are also other ways that applications may remain running. The following list shows just a few that are available:

- **Audio**—Certain applications such as podcasts and music players can register to play audio in the background with a basic set of audio controls even when the application is not running.
- **Download**—The Background Transfer API can be used to download large amounts of data in a power-friendly manner.

- **Lock Screen**—Special lock screen applications can provide basic information to a user even when her tablet is locked (for example, the mail application can show the number of unread mail messages).
- **Sockets**—The ControlChannelTrigger class can be used to register for network events that will notify the application even when it is suspended.

It is a misconception that Windows 8 applications stop when they are swapped to the background. The combination of services provided through the platform enable them to remain connected and current regardless of whether they are running in the foreground. The use of these APIs enables your application to preserve system resources and battery lifetime by responding to events in a smart way.

Custom Splash Screen

Earlier in this chapter, you learned that the application must display the first page on launch within a given timeframe, or the application will be terminated. When you require more time to set up the application, you can show a custom splash screen while you are initializing the application. In this section, you learn how to configure a custom splash screen.

The **Windows8Application2** simulates a long startup operation by waiting for a loop to complete. This loop runs slowly in debug mode because it writes each value to the debugger:

```
await Task.Run(() =>
                {
                    for (var x = 0; x < 2000; x++)
                    {
                        Debug.WriteLine(x);
                    }
                });
```

This loop is intended to simulate common operations an application may perform at startup. These include connecting to web services to download content and reading items that are serialized from cache. If the application takes too long to perform these tasks, the application will be terminated by Windows 8 after 15 seconds.

To fix these issues, a custom splash screen is used to load the data first before rendering the initial grid. In **App.xaml.cs**, the OnLaunched method sets an instance of ExtendedSplashScreen as the main visual when the application is launched and passes in the current splash screen:

```
var splashScreen = args.SplashScreen;
var eSplash = new ExtendedSplashScreen(splashScreen, false, args);
splashScreen.Dismissed += eSplash.DismissedEventHandler;
Window.Current.Content = eSplash;
Window.Current.Activate();
```

The ExtendedSplashScreen control keeps a reference to the original splash screen. It contains a copy of the same image that is displayed and uses the position from the system-provided splash screen to align the image. The image will appear in the exact same place to create a seamless transition from the splash screen image to the extended splash screen that displays.

When the control is loaded, it simply calls the Initialize method on the data source and waits asynchronously for the items to load. When all items are loaded, the control replaces the visual with a Frame object for navigation and navigates to the first page. All of this logic would normally exist in the **App.xaml.cs** code-behind file but was moved to the ExtendedSplashScreen control so it can be deferred until the data is completely loaded.

A ProgressRing control is positioned just below the splash screen image to indicate to the user that work is being performed. To see the progress indicator, run the application in debug mode. You will see the splash screen image with a spinning progress ring. It will continue to animate even though the program is paused because the operation is handled asynchronously so it does not block the UI thread. This example showed a very simple feedback mechanism, but applications with more complex initialization can show a progress bar and display textual feedback to the user as components are loaded. You will see more detailed examples of this in later chapters; here, the splash screen simply executes the delay and then launches into the main page.

Summary

In this chapter, you learned about the application lifecycle and the role that Process Lifetime Management (PLM) plays. Applications can be suspended and terminated but have mechanisms to save and restore state that can synchronize between multiple devices. You learned about the frame-based navigation that Windows 8 applications use and how to take advantage of local storage to preserve the user's location in the application. Local storage allowed you to save and restore data specific to the user and application.

You also learned how to create a custom splash screen to allow applications to initialize without being terminated if it takes longer than about five seconds to display the first page. This chapter touched briefly on application data by demonstrating the local file system. There are many ways Windows 8 applications can create and consume data, from web-based services to local files. The next chapter, *Data*, will cover these approaches to data.

6

Data

D ATA IS CENTRAL TO MOST APPLICATIONS, AND understanding how
to manage data and transform it into information the user can interact with is critical. Windows 8 applications can interact with data in a variety of ways. You can save local data, retrieve syndicated content from the
Web, and parse local resources that are stored in JSON format. You can
query XML documents, use WinRT controls to direct the user to select files
from the file system, and manipulate collections of data using a structured
query language.

In this chapter, you learn about the different types of data that are available to your Windows 8 application and techniques for manipulating,
loading, storing, encrypting, signing, and querying data. You'll find that
the WinRT provides several ready-to-use APIs that make working with
data a breeze. This chapter explores these APIs and how to best integrate
them into your application.

Application Settings

You were exposed to application settings in Chapter 5, *Application Lifecycle*.
Common cases for using application settings include

- Simple settings that are accessed through the **Settings** charm and can
  be synchronized between machines (Roaming)

- Local data storage persisted between application sessions (Local)
- Local persistent cache to enable occasionally disconnected scenarios (Local)
- Temporary cached data used as a workspace or to improve performance of the application (Temporary)

The settings use a simple dictionary to store values and require the values you store to be basic WinRT types. It is possible to store more complex types. In Chapter 5, you learned how to manually serialize and de-serialize an item by writing to a file in local storage. You serialize complex types using a serialization helper. An example of this exists in the SuspensionManager class that is included in the project templates. You can search for the file **SuspensionManager.cs** on your system to browse the source code.

The SuspensionManager class uses the DataContractSerializer to serialize complex types in a dictionary:

```
DataContractSerializer serializer =
    new DataContractSerializer(typeof(Dictionary<string, object>),
        knownTypes_);
serializer.WriteObject(sessionData, sessionState_);
```

The serializer (in this case, the DataContractSerializer class) automatically inspects the properties on the target class and composes XML to represent the class. The XML is written to a file in the folder allocated for the current application. Similar to the various containers for application settings (local, roaming, and temporary), there is a local folder specific to the user and application that you can use to create directories and read and write files. Accessing the folder is as simple as

```
StorageFile file =
    await ApplicationData.Current.LocalFolder.
CreateFileAsync(filename,
    CreationCollisionOption.ReplaceExisting);
```

You can access a roaming or temporary folder as well. The Create CompletionOption is a feature that allows you generate filenames that don't conflict with existing data. The options (passed in as an enum to the file method) include:

- FailIfExists—The operation will throw an exception if a file with that name already exists.

- GenerateUniqueName—The operation will append a sequence to the end of the filename to ensure it is a unique, new file.

- OpenIfExists—If the file already exists, instead of creating a new file, the operation will simply open the existing file for writing.

- ReplaceExisting—Any existing file will be overwritten. The example will always overwrite the file with the XML for the dictionary.

After the dictionary has been written, the serialization helper is used to de-serialize the data when the application resumes after a termination:

```
DataContractSerializer serializer =
    new DataContractSerializer(typeof(Dictionary<string, object>),
        knownTypes_);
sessionState_ = (Dictionary<string, object>)serializer
    .ReadObject(inStream.AsStreamForRead());
```

The local storage can be used for more than just saving state. As demonstrated in Chapter 5, you may also use it to store data. It can also be used to store assets like text files and images. A common design is to use local storage to save cloud-based data that is unlikely to change as a local cache. This will allow your application to operate even when the user is not connected to the Internet and in some cases may improve the performance of the application when the network is experiencing high latency. In the next section, you learn more about how to access and save data using the Windows Runtime.

Accessing and Saving Data

Take a moment to download the **Wintellog** project for Chapter 6, *Data,* from the book website at http://windows8applications.codeplex.com/.

You may need to remove TFS bindings before you run the project. This is a sample project that demonstrates several techniques for accessing and saving data. The application takes blog feeds from various Wintellect employees and caches them locally on your Windows 8 device. Each time you launch the application, it scans for new items and pulls those down.

These blogs cover cutting-edge content ranging from the latest information about Windows 8 to topics like Azure, SQL Server, and more. You may
recognize some of the blog authors including Jeff Prosise, Jeffrey Richter,
and John Robbins.

You learned in Chapter 5 about the various storage locations and how
you can use either settings or the file system itself. The application currently uses settings to track the first time it runs. That process takes several
minutes as it reads a feed with blog entries and parses the web pages for
display. An extended splash screen is used due to the longer startup time.
You can see the check to see if the application has been initialized in the
ExtendedSplashScreen_Loaded method in **SplashPage.xaml.cs**:

```
ProgressText.Text = ApplicationData.Current.LocalSettings.Values
    .ContainsKey("Initialized") && (bool)ApplicationData.Current.
LocalSettings.Values["Initialized"]
    ? "Loading blogs..." :
"Initializing for first use: this may take several minutes...";
```

After the process is completed, the flag is set to true. This allows the
application to display a warning about the startup time the first time it
runs. Subsequent launches will load the majority of data from a local cache
to improve the speed of the application:

```
ApplicationData.Current.LocalSettings.Values["Initialized"]
    = true;
```

There are several classes involved with loading and saving the data.
Take a look at the StorageUtility class. This class is used to simplify the
process of saving items to local storage and restoring them when the application is launched. In SaveItem, you can see the process to create a folder
and a file and handling potential collisions as described in Chapter 5 (extra
code has been removed for clarity):

```
var folder = await ApplicationData.Current.LocalFolder
                 .CreateFolderAsync(folderName,
    CreationCollisionOption.OpenIfExists);
var file = await folder.CreateFileAsync(item.Id.GetHashCode().
➥ToString(),
    CreationCollisionOption.ReplaceExisting);
```

Notice that the method itself is marked with an `async` keyword, and the file system operations are preceded by `await`. You learn about these keywords in the next section. Unlike the example in Chapter 5 that manually wrote the properties to storage, the `StorageUtility` class takes a generic type to make it easier to save any type that can be serialized. The code uses the same engine that handles complex types transmitted via web services (you will learn more about web services later in this chapter). This code uses the `DataContractJsonSerializer` to take the snapshot of the instance that is saved:

```
var stream = await file.OpenAsync(FileAccessMode.ReadWrite);
using (var outStream = stream.GetOutputStreamAt(0))
{
    var serializer = new DataContractJsonSerializer(typeof(T));
    serializer.WriteObject(outStream.AsStreamForWrite(), item);
    await outStream.FlushAsync();
}
```

The file is created through the previous call and used to retrieve a stream. The instance of the `DataContractJsonSerializer` is passed the type of the class to be serialized. The serialized object is written to the stream attached to the file and then flushed to store this to disk. The entire operation is wrapped in a `try … catch` block to handle any potential file system errors that may occur. This is common for cache code because if the local operation fails, the data can always be retrieved again from the cloud.

▪ GENERICS 101

Generics are a very important feature of the C# language. They provide the ability to create a template for type-safe code without committing to a specific type. The `SaveItem<T>` method is a template for saving an instance of an unknown type. When it is called from the `BlogDataSource` class, the compiler inspects the type that is passed and generates code specific for that type. The definition is an open generic and the call closes the generic with a specific type. You may be familiar with generics in collections, like List<T>, but they can be used in far more powerful and flexible solutions. Learn more about generics online at: http://bit.ly/csharpgenerics.

To see how the serialization works and where the files are stored, run the application and allow it to initialize and pass you to the initial grouped item list. Hold down the **Windows Key** and press **R** to get the run dialog. In the dialog, type the following:

```
%userprofile%\AppData\Local\Packages
```

Press the **Enter** key, and it will open the folder.

This is where the application-specific data for your login will be stored. You can either try to match the folder name to the package identifier or type **Groups** into the search box to locate the folder used by the Wintellog application. When you open the folder, you'll see several folders with numbers for the name and a single folder called **Groups**, similar to what is shown in Figure 6.1.

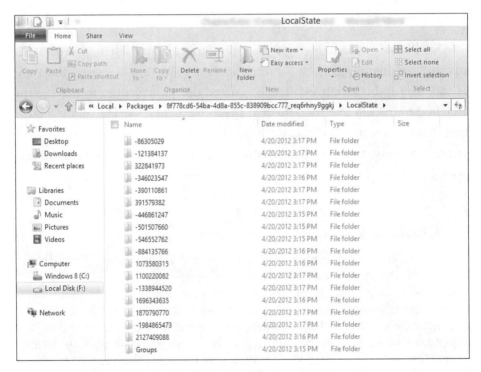

FIGURE 6.1: The local cache for the Wintellog application

To simplify the generation of filenames, the application currently just uses the hash code for the unique identifier of the group or item to establish a filename. A hash code is simply a value that makes it easier to compare complex objects. You can read more about hash codes online at http://msdn.microsoft.com/en-us/library/system.object.gethashcode.aspx.

Hash codes are not guaranteed to be unique, but in the case of strings, it is highly unlikely that the combination of a group and a post would cause a collision. The **Groups** folder contains a list of files for each group. Navigate to that folder and open one of the items in **Notepad**. You'll see the JSON serialized value for a `BlogGroup` instance.

▪ JAVASCRIPT OBJECT NOTATION (JSON)

JSON is an open standard for storing text-based information. The default serialization engine for web services uses Extensible Markup Language (XML) to store values in a structured document. JSON uses a different approach that has become popular because it takes less space and is easier to read and understand than XML. It uses valid JavaScript syntax to describe objects, so the code can be executed by a JavaScript interpreter to easily create an object. You can search for the keywords "JSON Visualizer" to find several websites that will allow you to paste JSON and see a visual interpretation of the object it represents. The standard is defined online at http://json.org/.

The JSON is stored in a compact format on disk. The following example shows the JSON value for my blog, formatted to make it easier to read:

```
{
    "Id" : "http://www.wintellect.com/CS/blogs/jlikness/default.aspx",
    "PageUri" :
    "http://www.wintellect.com/CS/blogs/jlikness/default.aspx",
    "Title" : "Jeremy Likness' Blog",
    "RssUri" : "http://www.wintellect.com/CS/blogs/jlikness/rss.aspx"
}
```

The syntax is straightforward. The braces enclose the object being defined and contain a list of keys (the name of the property) and values (what the property is set to). If you inspect any of the serialized posts (those are contained in a folder with the same name as the group hash code), you will notice the `ImageUriList` property uses a bracket to specify an array:

```
"ImageUriList" : [
    "http://www.wintellect.com/.../Screen_thumb_42317207.png",
    "http://www.wintellect.com/.../someotherimage.png" ]
```

You may have already looked at the BlogGroup class and noticed that not all of the properties are being stored. For example, the item counts are always computed when the items are loaded for the group, so they do not need to be serialized. This particular approach requires that you mark the class as a DataContract and then explicitly tag the properties you wish to serialize. The BlogGroup class is tagged like this:

```
[DataContract]
public class BlogGroup : BaseItem
```

Any properties to be serialized are tagged using the DataMember attribute:

```
[DataMember]
public Uri RssUri { get; set; }
```

If you have written web services using Windows Communication Foundation (WCF) in the past, you will be familiar with this format for tagging classes. You may not have realized it could be used for direct serialization without going through the web service stack. The default DataContractSerializer outputs XML, so remember to specify the DataContractJsonSerializer if you want to use JSON.

▪ TIP

It is common to put code that initializes a class in the constructor for that class. When you use the serialization engines provided by the system, the constructor is not called. This actually makes sense because the implication is that the class was already created and is serialized in a state that reflects the initialization. If you do need code to run when the class is deserialized, you can specify a member for the engine to call by tagging it with the OnDeserialized attribute. In the Wintellog example, you can see an instance of this in the BlogItem class. This ensures an event is registered regardless of whether the class was created using the new keyword or was deserialized.

The process to restore is similar. You still reference the file but this time open it for read access. The same serialization engine is used to create an instance of the type from the serialized data:

```
var folder = await ApplicationData.Current.LocalFolder
    .GetFolderAsync(folderName);
var file = await folder.GetFileAsync(hashCode);
var inStream = await file.OpenSequentialReadAsync();
var serializer = new DataContractJsonSerializer(typeof(T));
var retVal = (T)serializer.ReadObject(inStream.AsStreamForRead());
```

You can see when you start the application that the process of loading web sites, saving the data, and restoring items from the cache takes time. In the Windows Runtime, any process that takes more than a few milliseconds is defined as asynchronous. This is different from a synchronous call. To understand the difference, it is important to be familiar with the concept of *threading*.

The Need for Speed and Threading

In a nutshell, threading provides a way to execute different processes at the same time (concurrently). One job of the processor in your device is to schedule these threads. If you only have one processor, multiple threads take turns to run. If you have multiple processors, threads can run on different processors at the same time.

When the user launches an application, the system creates a main application thread that is responsible for performing most of the work, including responding to user input and drawing graphics on the screen. The fact that it manages the user interface has led to a convention of calling this thread the "UI thread." By default, your code will execute on the UI thread unless you do something to spin off a separate thread.

The problem with making synchronous calls from the UI thread is that all processing must wait for your code to complete. If your code takes several seconds, this means the routines that check for touch events or update graphics will not run during that period. In other words, your application will freeze and become unresponsive.

The Windows Runtime team purposefully designed the framework to avoid this scenario by introducing asynchronous calls for any methods that might potentially take longer than 50 milliseconds to execute. Instead of running synchronously, these methods will spin off a separate thread to perform work and leave the UI thread free. At some point when their work is complete, they return their results. When the new await keyword is used, the results are marshaled automatically to the calling thread, which in many cases is the UI thread. A common mistake is to try to update the display without returning to the UI thread; this will generate an exception called a cross-thread access violation because only the UI thread is allowed to manage those resources.

Managing asynchronous calls in traditional C# was not only difficult, but resulted in code that was hard to read and maintain. Listing 6.1 provides an example using a traditional event-based model. Breakfast, lunch, and dinner happen asynchronously, but one meal must be completed before the next can begin. In the event-based model, an event handler is registered with the meal so the meal can flag when it is done. A method is called to kick off the process, which by convention ends with the text Async.

LISTING 6.1: Asynchronous Meals Using the Event Model

```
public void EatMeals()
{
    var breakfast = new Breakfast();
    breakfast.MealCompleted += breakfast_MealCompleted;
    breakfast.BeginBreakfastAsync();
}
void breakfast_MealCompleted(object sender, EventArgs e)
{
    var lunch = new Lunch();
    lunch.MealCompleted += lunch_MealCompleted;
    lunch.BeginLunchAsync();
}
void lunch_MealCompleted(object sender, EventArgs e)
{
    var dinner = new Dinner();
    dinner.MealCompleted += dinner_MealCompleted;
    dinner.BeginDinnerAsync();
}
void dinner_MealCompleted(object sender, EventArgs e)
{
    // done;
}
```

This example is already complex. Every step requires a proper registration (subscription) to the completion event and then passes control to an entirely separate method when the task is done. The fact that the process continues in a separate method means that access to any local method variables is lost and any information must be passed through the subsequent calls. This is how many applications become overly complex and difficult to maintain.

The Task Parallel Library (TPL) was introduced in .NET 4.0 to simplify the process of managing parallel, concurrent, and asynchronous code. Using the TPL, you can create meals as individual tasks and execute them like this:

```
var breakfast = new Breakfast();
var lunch = new Lunch();
var dinner = new Dinner();
var t1 = Task.Run(() => breakfast.BeginBreakfast())
    .ContinueWith(breakfastResult => lunch.
BeginLunch(breakfastResult))
    .ContinueWith(lunchResult => dinner.BeginDinner(lunchResult));
```

This helped simplify the process quite a bit, but the code is still not easy to read and understand or maintain. The Windows Runtime has a considerable amount of APIs that use the asynchronous model. To make developing applications that use asynchronous method calls even easier, Visual Studio 2012 provides support for two new keywords called async and await.

Understanding async and await

The async and await keywords provide a simplified approach to asynchronous programming. A method that is going to perform work asynchronously and should not block the calling thread is marked with the async keyword. Within that method, you can call other asynchronous methods to launch long running tasks. Methods marked with the async keyword can have one of three return values.

All async operations in the Windows Runtime return one of four interfaces. The interface that is implemented depends on whether or not the operation returns a result to the caller and whether or not it supports tracking progress. Table 6.1 lists the available interfaces.

TABLE 6.1: Interfaces Available for async **Operations**

	Reports Progress	Does Not Report Progress
Returns Results	IAsyncOperationWithProgress	IAsyncOperation
Does Not Return Results	IAsyncActionWithProgress	IAsyncAction

In C#, there are several ways you can both wrap calls to asynchronous methods as well as define them. Methods that call asynchronous operations are tagged with the async keyword. Methods with the async keyword that return void are most often event handlers. Event handlers require a void return type. For example, when you want to run an asynchronous task from a button tap, the signature of the event handler looks like this:

```
private void button1_Click(object sender, RoutedEventArgs e)
{
    // do stuff
}
```

To wait for asynchronous calls to finish without blocking the UI thread, you must add the async keyword so the signature looks like this:

```
private async void button1_Click(object sender, RoutedEventArgs e)
{
    // do stuff
    await DoSomethingAsynchronously();
}
```

Failure to add the async modifier to a method that uses await will result in a compiler error. Aside from the special case of event handlers, you might want to create a long-running task that must complete before other code can run but does not return any values. For those methods, you return a Task. This type exists in the System.Threading.Tasks namespace. For example:

```
public async Task LongRunningNoReturnValue()
{
    await TakesALongTime();
    return;
}
```

Notice that the compiler does the work for you. In your method, you simply return without sending a value. The compiler will recognize the method as a long-running Task and create the Task "behind the scenes" for you. The final return type is a Task that is closed with a specific return type. Listing 6.2 demonstrates how to take a simple method that computes a factorial and wrap it in an asynchronous call. The DoFactorialExample method asynchronously computes the factorial for the number 5 and then puts the result into the Text property as a string.

LISTING 6.2: Creating an Asynchronous Method That Returns a Result

```
public long Factorial(int factor)
{
    long factorial = 1;

    for (int i = 1; i <= factor; i++)
    {
        factorial *= i;
    }

    return factorial;
}

public async Task<long> FactorialAsync(int factor)
{
    return await Task.Run(() => Factorial(factor));
}

public async void DoFactorialExample()
{
    var result = await FactorialAsync(5);
    Result = result.ToString();
}
```

Note how easy it was to take an existing synchronous method (Factorial) and provide it as an asynchronous method (FactorialAsync) and then call it to get the result with the await keyword (DoFactorialExample). The Task.Run call is what creates the new thread. The flow between threads is illustrated in Figure 6.2. Note the UI thread is left free to continue processing while the factorial computes, and the result is updated and can be displayed to the user.

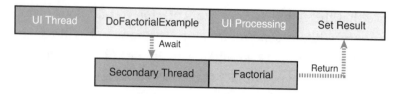

FIGURE 6.2: **Asynchronous flow between threads**

The examples here use the Task Parallel Library (TPL) because it existed in previous versions of the .NET Framework. It is also possible to create asynchronous processes using Windows Runtime methods like ThreadPool. RunAsync. You can learn more about asynchronous programming in the Windows Runtime in the development center at http://msdn.microsoft. com/en-us/library/windows/apps/hh464924.aspx. For a quickstart on using the await operator, visit http://msdn.microsoft.com/en-us/library/ windows/apps/hh452713.aspx.

Lambda Expressions

The parameter that was passed to the Task.Run method is called a *lambda expression*. A lambda expression is simply an anonymous function. It starts with the signature of the function (if the Run method took parameters, those would be specified inside the parenthesis) and ends with the body of the function. I like to refer to the special arrow => as the *gosinta* for "goes into." Take the expression from the earlier code snippet that is passed into Task. Run:

```
()=>Factorial(factor)
```

This can be read as "nothing goes into a call to Factorial with parameter factor." You can use lambda expressions to provide methods "on the fly." In the previous examples showing lunch, breakfast, and dinner, special methods were defined to handle the completion events. A lambda expression could also be used like this:

```
breakfast.MealCompleted += (sender, eventArgs)
        =>
    {
        // do something
    };
```

In this case, the lambda reads as "the `sender` and `eventArgs` goes into a set of statements that do something." The parameters triggered by the event are available in the body of the lambda expression, as are local variables defined in the surrounding methods. Lambda expressions are used as a short-hand convention for passing in delegates.

There are a few caveats to be aware of when using lambda expressions. Unless you assign a lambda expression to a variable, it is no longer available to reference from code, so you cannot unregister an event handler that is defined with a lambda expression. Lambda expressions that refer to variables within the method capture those variables so they can live longer than the method scope (this is because the lambda expression may be referenced after the method is complete), so you must be aware of the side effects for this. You can learn more about lambda expressions online at http://msdn.microsoft.com/en-us/library/bb397687(v=vs.110).aspx.

IO Helpers

The `PathIO` and `FileIO` classes provide special helper methods for reading and writing storage files. The `PathIO` class allows you to perform file operations by passing the absolute path to the file. Creating a text file and writing data can be accomplished in a single line of code:

```
await PathIO.WriteTextAsync("ms-appdata:///local/tmp.txt", "Text.");
```

The `ms-appdata` prefix is a special URI that will point to local storage for the application. You can also access local resources that are embedded in your application using the `ms-appx` prefix. In the sample application, an initial list of blogs to load is stored in JSON format under **Assets/Blogs.js**. The code to access the list is in the `BlogDataSource` class (under the **DataModel** folder)—the file is accessed and loaded with a single line of code:

```
var content = await PathIO
    .ReadTextAsync("ms-appx:///Assets/Blogs.js");
```

The `FileIO` class performs similar operations. Instead of taking a path and automatically opening the file, it accepts a parameter of type `IStorageFile`. Use the `FileIO` helpers when you already have a reference to the file or need to perform some type of processing that can't be done by simply referencing the path.

Table 6.2 provides the list of available methods you can use. All of the methods take an absolute file path for the `PathIO` class and an `IStorageFile` object (obtained using the storage API) for the `FileIO` class:

TABLE 6.2: File Helper Methods from the `PathIO` and `FileIO` Classes

Method Name	Description
AppendLinesAsync	Appends lines of text to the specified file
AppendTextAsync	Appends the text to the specified file
ReadBufferAsync	Reads the contents of the specified file into a buffer
ReadLinesAsync	Reads the contents of the specified file into lines of text
ReadTextAsync	Reads the contents of the specified file into a single string as text
WriteBufferAsync	Writes data from a buffer to the specified file
WriteBytesAsync	Writes the byte array to the specified file
WriteLinesAsync	Writes the text lines to the specified file
WriteTextAsync	Writes the text to the specified file

Take advantage of these helpers where it makes sense. They will help simplify your code tremendously.

Embedded Resources

There are several ways you can embed data within your application and read it back. A common reason to embed data is to provide seed values for a local database or cache, configuration items, and special files such as license agreements. You can embed any type of resource, including images and text files. The applications you have worked with already include image resources.

To specify how a resource is embedded, right-click the resource name in the **Solution Explorer** and select **Properties** or select the item and press **Alt + Enter**. Figure 6.3 shows the result of highlighting the file **Blogs.js** in the **Assets** folder and selecting the **Properties** dialog. Note the **Build Action** and **Copy to Output Directory** properties.

FIGURE 6.3: Properties for a resource

When you set the action to Content, the resource is copied into a folder that is relative to the package for your application. In addition to the storage containers you learned about in Chapter 5, every package has an install location that contains the local assets you have specified the Content build action for. This will include resources such as images.

You can find the location where the package is installed using the Package class:

```
var package = Windows.ApplicationModel.Package.Current;
var installedLocation = package.InstalledLocation;
var loc = String.Format("Installed Location: {0}",
    installedLocation.Path);
```

An easier way to access these files is to use the ms-appx prefix. Open the **BlogDataSource.cs** file. The **Blogs.js** file is loaded in the LoadLiveGroups method. It is loaded by using the special package prefix, like this:

```
var content = await PathIO.ReadTextAsync(
    "ms-appx:///Assets/Blogs.js");
```

It is also possible to embed resources directly into the executable for your application. These resources are not visible in the file system but can still be accessed through code. To embed a resource, set the **Build Action** to **Embedded Resource**. Accessing the resource is a little more complex.

To read the contents of an embedded resource, you must access the current assembly. An assembly is a building block for applications. One way to get the assembly is to inspect the information about a class you have defined:

```
var assembly = typeof(BlogDataSource).GetTypeInfo().Assembly;
```

The assembly is what the resource is embedded within. Once you have a reference to the assembly, you can grab a stream to the resource using the GetManifestResourceStream method. There is a trick to how you reference the resource, however. The resource will be named as part of the namespace for your assembly. Therefore, a resource at the root of a project with the default namespace Wintellog will be given the path:

```
Wintellog.ResourceName
```

The reference to the **ReadMe.txt** file in the **Common** folder is therefore Wintellog.Common.ReadMe.txt. This file is not ordinarily embedded in the project; the properties have been updated to illustrate this example. After you have retrieved the stream for the resource, you can use a stream reader to read it back. When the assembly reference is obtained, you can return the contents like this:

```
var stream = assembly.GetManifestResourceStream(txtFile);
var reader = new StreamReader(stream);
var result = await reader.ReadToEndAsync();
return result;
```

You will typically use embedded resources only when you wish to obfuscate the data by hiding it in the assembly. Note this will not completely hide the data because anyone with the right tools will be able to inspect the assembly to examine its contents, including embedded resources. Embedding assets using the Content build action not only makes it easier to inspect the assets from your application, but also has the added advantage of allowing you to enumerate the file system using the installed location of the current package when there are multiple assets to manage.

Collections

Collections are the primary structures you will use to manipulate data within your application. These classes implement common interfaces that provide consistent methods for querying and managing the data in the collection. Collections are often bound to UI controls. In the **Wintellog** example, a collection of blogs provides the grouped few and is bound to the GridView control. A collection of posts within the blogs feed the detail view within a group.

The Windows Runtime has a set of commonly used collection types. These types are mapped automatically to .NET Framework types by the CLR. In code, you won't reference the Windows Runtime types directly. Instead, you manipulate the .NET equivalent, and the CLR handles conversion automatically. Table 6.3 lists the Windows Runtime type and the .NET equivalent along with a brief description and example classes that implement the interface.

TABLE 6.3: Collection Types in the Windows Runtime and .NET

WinRT	.NET Framework	Example	Description
IIterable<T>	IEnumerable<T>	Most collection types	Provides an interface to support iteration for a collection
IIterator<T>	IEnumerator<T>	Exposed via collection type	The interface for performing iteration over a collection
IVector<T>	IList<T>	List<T>	A collection that can be individually accessed via an index
IVectorView<T>	IReadOnlyList<T>	ReadOnly Collection<T>	Version of an indexed collection that cannot be modified
IMap<K,V>	IDictionary<K,V>	Dictionary<K,V>	A collection of values that are referenced by keys

IMapView<K,V>	IReadOnly Dictionary<K,V>	ReadOnly Dictionary<K,V>	Version of a collection with key/value pairs that cannot be modified
IBindableIter-able	IEnumerable	Exposed via non-generic collections	Supports iteration over a non-generic collection
IBindableVector	IList	Custom classes that implement IList	Supports a non-generic collection that can be refer-enced by index

One important list that is not mapped to the Windows Runtime is the ObservableCollection<T>. This is a special list because it works with the data-binding system you learned about in Chapter 3, *Extensible Application Markup Language (XAML)*. The ObservableCollection<T> implements the INotifyCollectionChanged interface, which is designed to notify listeners when the list changes—for example, when items are added or removed or the entire list is refreshed.

For performance, the data-binding system does not constantly examine the lists you bind to UI controls. Instead, the initially bound list is used to generate the controls on the display. When you manipulate the list, the data-binding system receives a notification through the CollectionChanged event and can use the list of added and removed items to refresh the controls being displayed. Without the interface, the only way to have a list refresh the UI is to raise a PropertyChanged event for the property that exposes the list. This is inefficient because it results in the entire list being refreshed rather than only the items that changed.

Language Integrated Query (LINQ)

One major advantage of using collections is the ability to write queries against them using Language Integrated Query (LINQ). This feature extends the language syntax of C# to provide patterns for querying and updating data. LINQ itself works with providers for different types of data storage, such as a database backend (SQL) or an XML document. The

LINQ to Objects provider supports classes that implement the IEnumerable interface and therefore can be used with most collections.

LINQ to Objects is implemented as a set of extension methods to the existing IEnumerable interface. These extension methods are declared in the System.Linq namespace. Extension methods enable you to add methods to existing types without having to create a new type. They are a special type of static method that use a special this modifier for the first parameter. You can learn more about extension methods online at http://msdn.microsoft.com/en-us/library/bb383977(v=vs.110).aspx.

There are three fundamental steps involved with a LINQ query. The first step is to provide the data source or collection you will query against. The second step is to provide the query, and the final step is to execute the query. It's important to understand that creating a query does not actually invoke any action against the data source. The query only executes when you need it and then only processes results as you obtain them. This is referred to as *deferred execution*.

LINQ supports a variety of query operations. It also supports multiple syntaxes for querying data. The BlogDataSource class in the **Wintellog** project has a method called LinqExamples. This method is never called, but you can use it to see the various types of LINQ queries and syntaxes. The first syntax is referred to as *LINQ query syntax* and resembles the T-SQL syntax you may be used to working with in databases. The second syntax is method-oriented and is referred to as *method syntax*. The method syntax is constructed using lambda expressions.

The following series of examples shows both syntaxes, starting with the query syntax.

Queries

You can use simple queries to parse collections and return the properties of interest. The following examples produce a list of strings that represent the titles from the blog groups:

```
var query = from g in GroupList select g.Title;
var query2 = GroupList.Select(g => g.Title);
```

Filters

Filters allow you to restrict the data returned by a query. You can filter using common functions that compare and manipulate properties. In the following examples, the list is filtered to only those groups with a title that starts with the letter "A."

```
var filter = from g in GroupList
                where g.Title.StartsWith("A")
                select g;
var filter2 = GroupList.Where(g => g.Title.StartsWith("A"));
```

Sorting

You can sort in both ascending and descending order and across multiple properties if needed. The following queries will sort the blogs by title:

```
var order = from g in GroupList
            orderby g.Title
            select g;
var order2 = GroupList.OrderBy(g => g.Title);
```

Grouping

A powerful feature of LINQ is the ability to group similar results. This is especially useful in Windows 8 applications for providing the list for controls that support groups. The following queries will create groups based on the first letter of the blog title:

```
var group = from g in GroupList
            group g by g.Title.Substring(0, 1);
var group2 = GroupList.GroupBy(g =>
            g.Title.Substring(0, 1));
```

Joins and Projections

You can join multiple sources together and project to new types that contain only the properties that are important to you. The following query syntax will join the items from one blog to another based on the date posted and then project the results to a new class with source and target properties for the title:

```
var items = from i in GroupList[0].Items
            join i2 in GroupList[1].Items
            on i.PostDate equals i2.PostDate
            select new
            {   SourceTitle = i.Title, TargetTitle = i2.Title };
```

Here is the same query using lambda expressions:

```
var items2 = GroupList[0].Items.Join(
    GroupList[1].Items,
    g1 => g1.PostDate,
    g2 => g2.PostDate,
    (g1, g2) => new { SourceTitle = g1.Title,
        TargetTitle = g2.Title });
```

This section only touched the surface of what is possible with LINQ expressions. You can learn more about LINQ by reading the articles and tutorials available online at http://msdn.microsoft.com/en-us/library/bb383799(v=vs.110).aspx.

Web Content

The Windows Runtime makes it easy to download and process web content. To access web pages, you will use the HttpClient. The class is similar to the WebClient class that Silverlight developers may be familiar with. This class is used to send and receive basic requests over the HTTP protocol. It can be used to send any type of standard HTTP request including GET, PUT, POST, and DELETE. The client returns an instance of HttpResponseMessage with the status code and headers of the response. The Content property contains the actual contents of the web page that was retrieved if the operation was successful.

⬛ NETWORK ACCESS

Using the `HttpClient` requires that you provide the appropriate capabilities to your application. There are different capabilities to use based on the location of the target web server. If the web server is located on your home or private network, you will set the **Private Networks (Client & Server)** capability. In most cases, you will be accessing a server that is located on the public Internet. This will require you to set the **Internet (Client)** capability, which is set by default when you create a new project.

The `BlogDataSource` class contains a helper method that provides an instance of `HttpClient`. The method sets a buffer size to allow for large pages to be loaded and provides a user agent for the request to use. User agents are most often used to identify the browser making the web request. In the case of programmatic access, you can pass an agent that provides information about the application and expected compatibility. Passing an agent that is compatible with mobile devices may result in the web server returning a page that is optimized for mobile browsing.

The Windows Runtime makes it easy to fetch a page asynchronously and process the results. The following two lines of code fetch the client and retrieve the page:

```
var client = GetClient();
var page = await client.GetStringAsync(item.PageUri);
```

Images are not always embedded within the RSS feed, so the code retrieves the target page for the entry and then parses it for images. This is done using regular expressions. The syntax for a regular expression provides a concise way to match patterns in strings of text. This makes it ideal for parsing tokens like HTML tags out of the source document.

■ REGULAR EXPRESSIONS

Regular expressions provide a powerful syntax for finding and replacing patterns in text. The first regular expression parsers were provided as part of early Unix-based distributions and were integrated into text editors and command-line utilities to parse large amounts of data. The .NET Framework provides the System.Text.RegularExpressions. Regex object to process text with regular expressions. Most operations involve two strings: a target string containing the text or process and a pattern string that contains the regular expression itself. To learn more about the regular expression syntax and how to use it in .NET, visit http://msdn.microsoft.com/en-us/library/hs600312.aspx.

The first expression parses all image tags from the source for the web page:

```
public const string IMAGE_TAG = @"<(img)\b[^>]*>";
private static readonly Regex Tags = new Regex(IMAGE_TAG,
    RegexOptions.IgnoreCase | RegexOptions.Multiline);
var matches = Tags.Matches(content);
```

Each tag is then parsed to pull the location of the image from the src attribute. This is used to construct an instance of an Uri that is added to the ImageUriList property of the blog post. This property is implemented as an ObservableCollection to provide notification when new images are added. A random image is displayed for each post. The image is hosted on the Internet, but Windows 8 will use a cached copy of the image when the user is offline if it has been downloaded previously.

Syndicated Content

Syndicated content is information that is available to other sites through special feeds. These feeds are most often presented in an XML format using either RSS (stands for RDF Site Summary, although it is commonly referred to as Real Simple Syndication—RDF is an abbreviation of Resource Description Framework) and Atom. Both formats have evolved as standard XML-based ways for blogs, websites, and other content providers to expose data in a consistent way so that other programs can download and consume the data.

The RSS specification is available online at http://www.rssboard.org/rss-specification.

The Atom publishing protocol is available online at http://atompub.org/.

Both formats provide a way to specify a *feed*, which is a set of related entries (topics, articles, or posts). Each entry may have a post date, information about the author, a set of links that reference the original source, and rich content such as images and videos. To parse the data in the past, you would either have to read the specifications and write your own special XML parser or find a third-party parser that would do it for you.

The Windows Runtime provides the SyndicationClient class to make it easy for you to interact with feeds. This class exists in the Windows.Web.Syndication namespace. The class can be used to asynchronously retrieve feed information and can be provided credentials to connect with sources that require authentication. When passed a URL, it is capable of parsing feeds in Atom (0.3 and 1.0) and RSS (0.91, 0.92, 1.0, and 2.0) format and presenting them using a common object model.

The sample program retrieves the feed just using four lines of code. Two lines are not required and are used to take advantage of the browser cache and provide a custom user agent to the host website when requesting the data. A helper method named GetSyndicationClient returns the client with some default properties set in the BlogDataSource class:

```
private static SyndicationClient GetSyndicationClient()
{
    var client = new SyndicationClient
                        { BypassCacheOnRetrieve = false };
    client.SetRequestHeader("user-agent", USER_AGENT);
    return client;
}
```

Using the client is as simple as calling a method to retrieve the feed by passing the location of the feed:

```
var client = GetSyndicationClient();
var feed = await client.RetrieveFeedAsync(group.RssUri);
```

The result of the operation, if successful, is a `SyndicationFeed` object. The instance contains information about the location of the feed, categories or tags hosted by the feed, contributors to the feed, links associated with the feed, and of course the items that are posted to the feed. Each `SyndicationItem` in the feed hosts the location of the item, categories or tags specific to that item, the title and content of the item, and an optional summary.

You can follow the code in the example to see how easy it is to parse the feed and retrieve the necessary data. There is no need for you to specify the format of the feed because the class will figure this out automatically from the feed itself. Syndication is a powerful way to expose content and consume it in Windows 8 applications.

Streams, Buffers, and Byte Arrays

The traditional method for reading data from a file, website, or other source in .NET is to use a stream. A stream enables you to transfer data into a data structure that you can read and manipulate. Streams may also provide the ability to transfer the contents of a data structure back to the stream to write it. Some streams support seeking, finding a position within a stream the same way you might skip ahead to a different scene on a DVD movie.

Streams are commonly written to byte arrays. The byte array is the preferred way to reference binary data in .NET. It can be used to manipulate data like the contents of a file or the pixels that make up the bitmap for an image. Many of the stream classes in .NET support converting a byte array to a stream or reading streams into a byte array. You can also convert other types into a byte array using the `BitConverter` class. The following example converts a 64-bit integer to an array of 8 bytes (8 bytes x 8 bits = 64 bits) and then back again:

```
var bigNumber = 4523452345234523455L;
var bytes = BitConverter.GetBytes(bigNumber);
var copyOfBigNumber = BitConverter.ToInt64(bytes, 0);
Debug.Assert(bigNumber == copyOfBigNumber);
```

The Windows Runtime introduces the concept of an **IBuffer** that behaves like a cross between a byte array and a stream. The interface itself only provides two members: a *Capacity* property (the maximum number of bytes that the buffer can hold) and a *Length* property (the number of bytes currently being used by the buffer). Many operations in the Windows Runtime either consume or produce an instance of IBuffer.

It is easy to convert between streams, byte arrays, and buffers. The methods to copy a stream into a byte array or send a byte array into a stream already exist as part of the .NET Framework. The WindowsRuntimeBufferExtensions class provides additional facilities for converting between buffers and byte arrays. It exists in the System.Runtime. InteropServices.WindowsRuntime namespace. It provides another set of extension methods including AsBuffer (cast a Byte[] instance to an IBuffer), AsStream (cast an IBuffer instance to a Stream), and ToArray (cast an IBuffer instance to a Byte[] instance).

Compressing Data

Storing large amounts of data can take up a large amount of disk space. Data compression encodes information in a way that reduces its overall size. There are two general types of compression. *Lossless compression* preserves the full fidelity of the original data set. *Lossy compression* can provide better performance and a higher compression ratio, but it may not preserve all of the original information. It is often used in image, video, and audio compression where an exact data match is not required.

The Windows 8 Runtime exposes the Compressor and Decompressor classes for compression. The **Compression** project provides an active example of compressing and decompressing a data stream. The project contains a text file that is almost 100 kilobytes in size and loads that text and displays it with a dialog showing the total bytes. You can then click a button to compress the text and click another button to decompress it back.

The compression task performs several steps. A local file is opened for output to store the result of the compressed text. There are various ways to encode text, so it first uses the Encoding class to convert the text to a UTF8 encoded byte array:

```
var storage = await ApplicationData.Current.LocalFolder
    .CreateFileAsync("compressed.zip",
    CreationCollisionOption.ReplaceExisting);
var bytes = Encoding.UTF8.GetBytes(_text);
```

You learned earlier in this chapter how to locate the folder for a specific user and application. You can examine the folder for the sample application to view the compressed file after you click the button to compress the text. The file is saved with a zip extension to illustrate that it was compressed, but it doesn't contain a true archive, so you will be unable to decompress the file from Windows Explorer.

▪ ENCODING

Text and characters in various cultures and languages is stored internally as a series of bits and bytes. The way these bits are encoded can vary between different encoding schemes. One of the earliest schemes is known as ASCII and uses a sequence of 7-bit characters to encode text. More modern schemes include UTF-8 (uses sequences of 8-bit bytes, sometimes up to 3 bytes when needed) and UTF-16 (uses sequences of 16-bit integers). The .NET Framework provides the Encoding class to make it easier to work with various formats. You can read more about the class online at http://msdn.microsoft.com/en-us/library/86hf4sb8(v=vs.110).aspx.

The next lines of code open the file for writing, create an instance of the Compressor, and write the bytes. The code then completes the compression operation and flushes all associated streams:

```
using (var stream = await storage.OpenStreamForWriteAsync())
{
    var compressor = new Compressor(stream.AsOutputStream());
    await compressor.WriteAsync(bytes.AsBuffer());
    await compressor.FinishAsync();
}
```

When the compression operation is complete, the bytes are read back from disk to show the compressed size. You'll find the default algorithm cuts the text file down to almost half of its original size. The decompression operation uses the Decompressor class to perform the reverse operation and retrieve the decompressed bytes in a buffer (it then saves these to disk so you can examine the result).

```
var decompressor = new Decompressor(stream.AsInputStream());
var bytes = new Byte[100000];
var buffer = bytes.AsBuffer();
var buf = await decompressor.ReadAsync(buffer, 999999,
   InputStreamOptions.None);
```

When you create the classes for compression, you can pass a parameter to determine the compression algorithm that is used. Table 6.4 lists the possible values.

TABLE 6.4: Compression Algorithms

CompressAlgorithm Member	Description
InvalidAlgorithm	Invalid algorithm. Used to generate exceptions for testing.
NullAlgorithm	No compression is applied, and the buffer is simply passed through. Used primarily for testing.
Mszip	Uses the MSZIP algorithm.
Xpress	Uses the XPRESS algorithm.
XpressHuff	Uses the XPRESS algorithm with Huffman encoding.
Lzms	Uses the LZMS algorithm.

The Windows Runtime makes compression simple and straightforward. Use compression when you have large amounts of data to store and are concerned about the amount of disk space your application requires. Remember that compression will slow down the save operation, so be sure to experiment to find the algorithm that provides the best compression ratio and performance for the type of data you are storing. Remember that you must pass the same algorithm to the decompression routine that you used to compress the data.

Encrypting and Signing Data

Many applications store sensitive data that should be encrypted to keep it safe from prying eyes. This may be information about the user or internal data for the application itself. Other information may need to be signed. Signing generates a specialized hash of data that provides a unique signature. If the original data is tampered with, the signature of the data will change. You can verify the signature against the original to determine if the data was modified in any way.

Encryption and signing is handled in the Windows Runtime by the `CryptographicEngine` class. This class provides services to encrypt, decrypt, sign, and verify the signature of digital content. The **EncryptionSigning** project contains some simple examples of performing these operations. The main code is located in the **MainPage.xaml.cs** file.

Encryption and decryption operations require a special *key*. Think of a key as a password for the encryption and decryption operations. There are two types of keys you can use. The most straightforward is called a *symmetric key*, which uses the same password or "secret" to both encrypt and decrypt the information.

To produce a key, you use the `SymmetricKeyAlgorithmProvider` class. You initialize the class by calling `OpenAlgorithm` with the name of the algorithm you wish to use. You then call `CreateSymmetricKey` to generate the key for the encryption operation. This same key must be used to decrypt the data later on. You can read the list of valid algorithms in the MSDN documentation at http://msdn.microsoft.com/en-us/library/windows/apps/windows.security.cryptography.core.symmetrickeyalgorithmprovider.openalgorithm.aspx.

In the example application, the **RC4** stream cipher is used to encrypt and decrypt the data. The user is prompted for one of two passwords, and then the passwords are repeated 100 times to fill a buffer. You can use any source data that can be converted to an array of bytes for the key. A helper utility is included in the code to help convert a string to an instance of `IBuffer`:

```
var buffer = CryptographicBuffer
    .ConvertStringToBinary(str.Trim(),
    BinaryStringEncoding.Utf8);
return buffer;
```

The `CryptographicBuffer` class provides a set of helper utilities for encryption, decryption, and signing operations. It supports comparing two instances of a buffer, converting between strings and binary arrays using various encodings, decoding and encoding using **Base64**, and generating a buffer of random data. In this example, it is used to encode the string using UTF8 to a buffer that is returned.

> ## ▪ BASE64
>
> Base64 is an encoding scheme that supports converting binary data to ASCII. This enables you to transmit binary data in a medium that supports only strings and text. If you want to store the bitmap for an image in a JSON object, you can encode it using Base64 and then decode it when you deserialize the JSON string. The size of the encoded text will always be greater than the source image because the conversion to ASCII requires that it does not use all of the bits available in a character byte. The most common scheme is to encode 3 bytes (24 bits) to 4 bytes (32 bits). For this reason, Base64 is sometimes referred to as 3-to-4 encoding.

Using the helper method, the code produces the key like this:

```
var result = await GetPassword();
var provider = SymmetricKeyAlgorithmProvider.OpenAlgorithm("RC4");
var key = provider.CreateSymmetricKey(AsBuffer(result));
```

When the key is generated, it is a simple step to encrypt the source text with the key. The result is encoded using Base64 so that it can be updated to the `TextBlock` in the right column for display:

```
var encrypted = CryptographicEngine.Encrypt(key,
    AsBuffer(BigTextBox.Text), null);
_encrypted = encrypted.ToArray();
BigTextBlock.Text = CryptographicBuffer
    .EncodeToBase64String(encrypted);
```

When you encrypt the text, the decrypt button is enabled. The user is given the option to select a password again for the decryption. If the user chooses a password that is different from the one used in the encryption operation, the decrypt process will fail or produce illegible output. The decryption process produces a key the same way the encryption process does and then simply calls the Decrypt method on the CryptographicEngine class:

```
var decrypted = CryptographicEngine.Decrypt(key,
    _encrypted.AsBuffer(), null);
BigTextBox.Text = AsText(decrypted).Trim();
```

It is also possible to encrypt and decrypt using an *asymmetric key*. The AsymmetricKeyAlgorithmProvider is used to generate asymmetric keys. Asymmetric encryption uses two different keys, a "public" key and a "private" key to perform encryption and decryption. This allows you to encrypt the data with your private secret but provide a public key for decryption. It allows third parties to decrypt the data while keeping your secrets safe.

You can learn more about asymmetric keys and see sample code online at http://msdn.microsoft.com/en-us/library/windows/apps/windows.security.cryptography.core.asymmetrickeyalgorithmprovider.openalgorithm.aspx.

The key used to sign data can be generated using the MacAlgorithmProvider class. This class represents a Message Authentication Code (MAC). You can create the key using any one of the popular algorithms including Message-Digest Algorithm (MD5), Secure Hash Algorithm (SHA), and Cipher-based MAC (CMAC). The key is generated much the same way as the encryption key. In the example project, a default password is used to generate the key for the signature:

```
var provider = MacAlgorithmProvider.OpenAlgorithm("HMAC_SHA256");
var key = provider.CreateKey(
    AsBuffer(MakeBigPassword(PASSWORD1)));
```

The signing process generates a buffer the same way the encryption process does. The difference is that you can use the buffer output by encryption to decrypt the message and produce the original. The signature is one-way—you cannot recreate the message from the signature. It's only function is to compare against an existing message to determine whether or not it has been tampered with.

The signature is generated with a call to the `Sign` method on the `CryptographicEngine` class:

```
_signature = CryptographicEngine.Sign(key,
    AsBuffer(BigTextBox.Text)).ToArray();
```

The signature is verified with a call to `VerifySignature` that will return true if the text has not been altered since the signature was generated:

```
var result = CryptographicEngine.VerifySignature(key,
    AsBuffer(BigTextBox.Text),
    _signature.AsBuffer());
```

To see how this works, launch the sample application and tap the **Sign** button. Now tap the **Verify** button to see that the text has not been altered. Now add a space or other character to the text in the left column and tap **Verify** again. This time you should receive a message that the text has been tampered with.

Windows 8 provides a set of powerful algorithms for encrypting, decrypting, and signing data. The process is made extremely simple through the use of the `CryptographicEngine`, `CryptographicBuffer`, and key provider classes. Use encryption to secure data both internal to your application and for transport over the Internet and use signatures to verify that data has not been tampered with in-transit.

Web Services

A web service is a method for communication between devices over the Internet. The most common protocol for communication is the Simple Object Access Protocol (SOAP) that was designed in 1998. If you've worked with SOAP, you know there is nothing simple about it, and a new protocol known as Representational State Transfer (REST) is quickly gaining popularity.

Web services are important for communications in applications. Many enterprise systems expose web services for consumption by client software like this Windows 8 application. One advantage of using SOAP is that it provides a discovery mechanism through the Web Services Description Language (WSDL) that allows the client application to determine the signature and structure of the API. You can learn more about the WSDL specification online at http://www.w3.org/TR/wsdl.

Open the **WeatherService** project to see an example of using web services. The example uses a free web service to obtain weather information. Connecting to the service was as simple as right-clicking the **References** node of the **Solution Explorer**, choosing **Add Service Reference**, and entering the URL for the service. The result is shown in Figure 6.4.

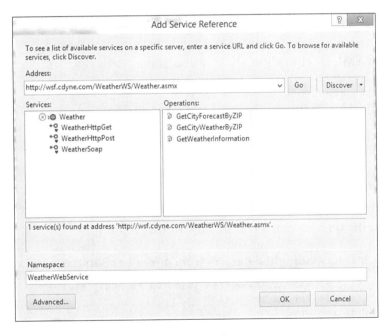

FIGURE 6.4: Adding a SOAP-based web service

When the service is added, a client proxy is generated automatically. The proxy handles all of the work necessary to make a request to the API and return the data and presents these as asynchronous implementations of the server interfaces. In the example application, the user is prompted to enter a zip code. When the button is clicked, the zip code is validated and, if there are no errors, passed to the web service. The following line of code is all that is needed to create a proxy for connecting to the web service and to call it with the zip code (note the convention of using Async at the end of the method name):

```
var client = new WeatherWebService.WeatherSoapClient();
var result = await client.GetCityForecastByZIPAsync(
    zip.ToString());
```

If the result does not indicate a successful call, a dialog is shown that indicates there was a problem. Otherwise, the results are bound to the grid and shown through data-binding. This is all it takes to data-bind the results from the web service call:

```
ResultsGrid.DataContext = result;
```

The XAML is set to show the city and state:

```
<StackPanel Orientation="Horizontal">
    <TextBlock Text="{Binding City}"/>
    <TextBlock Text=","/>
    <TextBlock Text="{Binding State}"/>
</StackPanel>
```

Listing 6.3 shows the full XAML for the individual forecast items. The "description" field is purposefully misspelled because this is how it came across in the web service as of the time of this writing.

LISTING 6.3: Data-Binding the Results from a Weather Service

```
<ListView Grid.Row="1" ItemsSource="{Binding ForecastResult}">
    <ListView.ItemTemplate>
        <DataTemplate>
            <StackPanel Orientation="Horizontal">
                <TextBlock Text="{Binding Date,
➥Converter={StaticResource ConvertDate}}"
                            Width="200"/>
                <TextBlock Text="{Binding Description}"
➥Width="150" Margin="5 0 0 0"/>
                <Image Source="{Binding Description,
➥Converter={StaticResource ConvertImage}}"/>
                <TextBlock Text="{Binding Temperatures.MorningLow}"
➥Margin="5 0 0 0" Width="50"/>
                <TextBlock Text="{Binding Temperatures.DaytimeHigh}"
➥Margin="5 0 0 0" Width="50"/>
            </StackPanel>
```

```
        </DataTemplate>
      </ListView.ItemTemplate>
  </ListView>
```

The weather service documentation provided a set of icons that correspond to the description. The `ImageConverter` class takes the description and translates it to a file name so it can return the image:

```
var filename =
    string.Format("ms-appx:///Assets/{0}.gif",
        ((string) value).Replace(" ", string.Empty).ToLower());
return new BitmapImage(new Uri(filename, UriKind.Absolute));
```

Figure 6.5 displays the result of my request for the weather forecast of my hometown (Woodstock, Georgia) via its zip code.

FIGURE 6.5: The weather forecast for Woodstock, Georgia

OData Support

The Open Data Procotol (OData) is a web protocol used for querying and updating data. It is a REST-based API built on top of Atom that uses JSON or XML for transporting information. You can read more about OData online at http://www.odata.org/.

Windows 8 applications have native support for OData clients once you download and install the client from:

http://go.microsoft.com/fwlink/?LinkId=253653

To access OData services, you simply add a service reference the same way you would for a SOAP-based web service. A popular OData service to use for demonstrations is the Netflix movie catalog. You can browse the service directly by typing http://odata.netflix.com/catalog/ into your browser.

In most browsers, you should see an XML document that contains various tags for collections you may browse. For example, the collection referred to as **Titles** indicates you can browse all titles using the URL, http://odata.netflix.com/catalog/Titles.

The **Netflix** project shows a simple demonstration of using this OData feed. The main URL was added as a service reference the same way the weather service was added in the previous example. The first step in using the service is to create a proxy to access it. This is done by taking the generated class from adding the service and passing in the service URL:

```
var netflix =
    new NetflixCatalog(
        new Uri(
            "http://odata.netflix.com/Catalog/",
            UriKind.Absolute));
```

Next, set up a collection for holding the results of an OData query. This is done using the special DataServiceCollection class:

```
private DataServiceCollection<Title> _collection;
...
_collection = new DataServiceCollection<Title>(netflix);
TitleGrid.ItemsSource = _collection;
```

Finally, specify a query to filter the data. This query is passed to the proxy and will load the results into the collection. In this example, the query will grab the first 100 titles that start with the letter "Y" in order of highest rated first:

```
var query = (from t in netflix.Titles
                where t.Name.StartsWith("Y")
                orderby t.Rating descending
                select t).Take(100);
_collection.LoadAsync(query);
```

Finally, as data comes in, you have the option to page in additional sets of data. This is done by checking the collection for a *continuation*. If one exists, you can request that the service load the next set. This allows you to page in data rather than pull down an extremely large set all at once:

```
if (_collection.Continuation != null)
{
    _collection.LoadNextPartialSetAsync();
}
```

Run the included sample application. You should see the titles and images start to appear asynchronously in a grid that you can scroll through. As in the previous example, the results of the web service are bound directly to the grid:

```
<Image Stretch="Uniform" Width="150" Height="150">
    <Image.Source>
        <BitmapImage UriSource="{Binding BoxArt.LargeUrl}"/>
    </Image.Source>
</Image>
<TextBlock Text="{Binding Name}" Grid.Row="1"/>
```

The Windows 8 development environment makes it easy and straight-forward to connect to web services and pull data in from external sources. Many existing applications expose web services in the form of SOAP, REST, and OData feeds. The built-in support to access and process these feeds makes it possible to build Windows 8 applications that support your existing functionality when it is exposed via web services.

Summary

This chapter explored a variety of ways you can deal with data in your Windows 8 applications. You learned how to save and retrieve data from file storage, access it over the Web, and syndicate it through RSS and Atom feeds. You learned about the built-in tools that make it easy to encrypt and sign data. Finally, you saw how easy it is to connect to existing SOAP and OData web services by generating proxies and retrieving data asynchronously from external APIs.

In the next chapter, you will learn how to keep your application alive even when it is not running through the use of tiles and notifications. Tiles provide information to the user at a glance on their Start screens and can be refreshed even when the application is not running. Notifications can be generated from within the application or by an external source to inform the user when important events happen and provide a contextual link back into the application.

7

Tiles and Toasts

WINDOWS 8 APPLICATIONS CAN REMAIN ALIVE AND connected even when they are not running in the foreground. This is obvious when you look at your Windows 8 **Start** screen. Unlike the boring collection of static icons you are probably used to, the Windows 8 **Start** screen is alive and animated. The weather tile provides the current temperature and an image that indicates weather conditions at a glance. Social networking tiles show the latest tweets directed your way. Email tiles display the number of unread emails and scroll the subjects. If you own a Windows Phone, you are likely already familiar with the concept of active tiles and use them on a daily basis.

All of these features are delivered through tiles. Tiles are baked into the Windows Runtime. The APIs exist to easily deliver information in a variety of formats and templates. More importantly, you can update tiles and send notifications even when your application is not in the foreground or actively running. This enables you to keep the application alive and relevant at all times.

Basic Tiles

You are already familiar with basic tiles. The package manifest for your application on the Application UI tab allows you to specify a 150 x 150 pixel square logo and a 310 x 150 large logo. This is the static or default tile.

The wide logo is optional and when provided enables choosing between a smaller or wider icon. The wider icon is useful because it gives you more surface area for providing information when you update the tiles. You can see an example of defining these tiles in Figure 7.1.

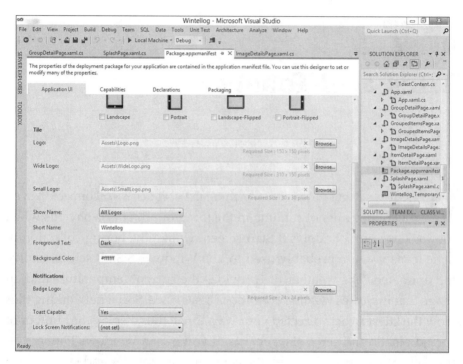

FIGURE 7.1: **Defining the logos for tiles**

Both types of tiles support live updates. Live tiles are updated either from your application or from the cloud and overwrite the basic template. They can overlay the basic template with simple information like badges and badge counts or completely replace the basic template. There are a variety of templates to choose from with image, text, and combination formats.

Live Tiles

Live tiles provide you with the ability to create a dynamic experience for your application, even when it is not running. The Windows Runtime makes it easy for you to define a tile format and publish information to that tile. It's as easy as providing some simple XML and calling a helper class. The most difficult part of the process is choosing which tile format to use.

You can download a sample application that provides a list of the available tile formats online at http://code.msdn.microsoft.com/ windowsapps/App-tiles-and-badges-sample-5fc49148.

Download the source, compile the application, and run it. You will be presented with several different scenarios. Select the fifth scenario, and you can cycle through the available templates and specify images and text to update the tile. Figure 7.2 shows a snapshot of the images provided with the sample to give you an idea of the variety of formats that are available. The sample also comes with a set of tile extensions that you can reuse to make it easier to set up tiles and badges.

FIGURE 7.2: **Various tile templates**

The predefined templates include images, text, and combinations of images and text. The "peek" templates provide animations and swap between one format and the other. With each template, you specify the text and the path to the image (if the template supports images) in an XML document and pass that document to the Windows Runtime.

A detailed listing of each tile template, a sample image, and the associated XML is available online at http://msdn.microsoft.com/en-us/library/windows/apps/hh761491.aspx.

Download the updated **Wintellog2** application from the book website at http://windows8applications.codeplex.com/.

For this chapter, the application has been updated to provide a few new key features, including the following:

- Introduction of the ImageUriManager class for better resolution of images for each blog post
- Inclusion of application bars to browse images, jump back to home, and open posts in a browser
- Addition of Semantic Zoom to the main page to quickly access various blogs

The application is still missing some key features such as integration with **Search** and **Share** charms. These will be implemented for Chapter 8, *Giving Your Application Charm*. In this chapter, the application has also been enhanced to provide badges and tiles. It provides a new feature to pin either a blog or a specific post to the **Start** menu. The tiles are updated from the SplashPage class.

After loading the list of posts from cache and the Internet, the application queries the five most recent posts and sorts them in ascending order by post date:

```
var query = from i in
        (from g in list
            from i in g.Items
            orderby i.PostDate descending
            select i).Take(5)
    orderby i.PostDate
    select i;
```

There are two ways you can update tiles. The default mode will always replace the current tile with the most recent tile you specify. Another approach is to provide tiles to a notification queue. When the queue is enabled, up to five of the most recent updates will be cycled for the tile. This allows you to provide multiple pieces of content, such as the titles of unread emails or in the case of the sample application, the titles of the five most recent posts.

The `TileUpdateManager` class is provided by the Windows Runtime and used to configure tiles. The following code enables the notification queue:

```
TileUpdateManager.CreateTileUpdaterForApplication()
    .EnableNotificationQueue(true);
```

The query is iterated for each post, and two tiles are created using the extension methods provided by the Windows 8 Code Samples. A square tile allows the image to "peek" in and wraps the title text:

```
var squareTile = new TileSquarePeekImageAndText04();
squareTile.TextBodyWrap.Text = item.Title;
squareTile.Image.Alt = item.Title;
squareTile.Image.Src = item.DefaultImageUri.ToString();
```

Wide tiles should always specify a square tile as a fallback in case the user opts to use the smaller tile size (to change the size of a tile, simply select it on the start screen and the option will appear to make it wider or smaller depending on the current size and the sizes the applications supports). The application bar for this action is shown in Figure 7.3.

Here is the code for the wide tile that references the square tile in **SplashScreen.xaml.cs**:

```
var wideTile = new TileWideSmallImageAndText03();
wideTile.SquareContent = squareTile;
wideTile.Image.Alt = item.Title;
wideTile.Image.Src = item.DefaultImageUri.ToString();
wideTile.TextBodyWrap.Text = item.Title;
```

FIGURE 7.3: **Specifying tile options on the Start screen**

To see how the extension classes help generate the XML for the tiles, place a breakpoint after the wide tile is created on the line that generates the notification:

```
var notification = wideTile.CreateNotification();
```

Run the application and allow it to hit the breakpoint. Open the Immediate Window by navigating to **Debug→Windows→Immediate Window** or holding down **Ctrl+Alt+I**. This is a window that allows you to enter statements and variables to evaluate as the application is running. In the Immediate Window type **wideTile** (case sensitive) and press **Enter**. You will see the contents of the class dumped, as shown in Figure 7.4. You can use wideTile.GetContent() to show only the XML.

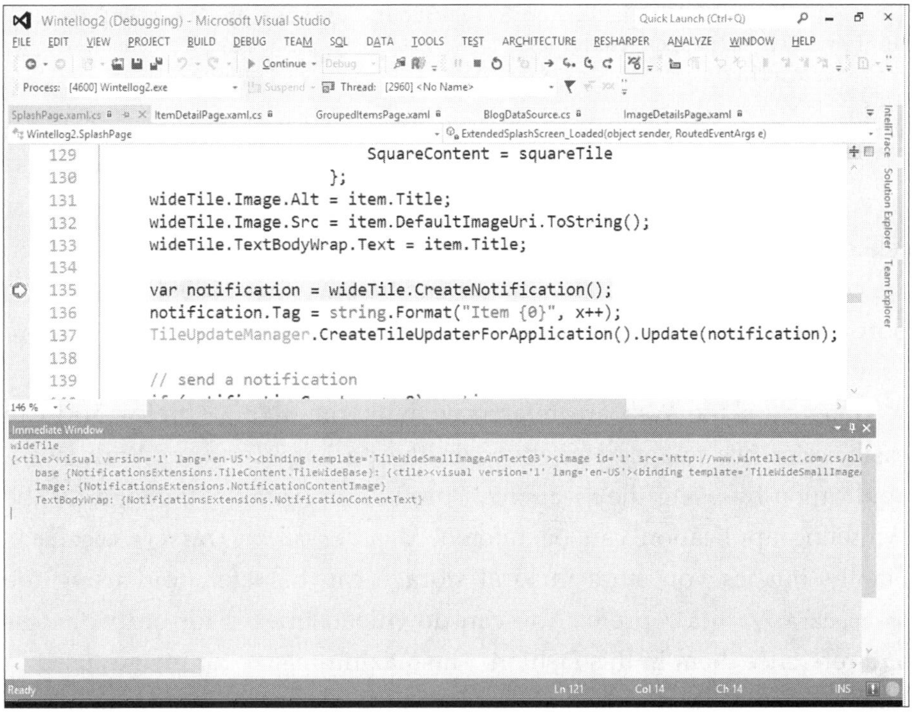

FIGURE 7.4: **Using the Immediate Window in debug mode**

The contents of the tile include the XML snippet shown in Listing 7.1.

LISTING 7.1: **The XML for a Wide Tile with a Square Tile**

```
<tile>
   <visual version='1' lang='en-US'>
      <binding template='TileWideSmallImageAndText03'>
         <image id='1' src='http://lh6.ggpht.com/
➡-V8-lch3ip3U/T33GescOOHI/AAAAAAAAAps/vuQXHOJYqz0/
➡slbookcover%25255B3%25255D.png?imgmax=800'
   alt='Designing Silverlight Business Applications
➡Officially Released'/>
         <text id='1'>Designing Silverlight Business Applications
➡Officially Released</text>
      </binding>
      <binding template='TileSquarePeekImageAndText04'>
         <image id='1' src='http://lh6.ggpht.com/-V8-
➡lch3ip3U/T33GescOOHI/AAAAAAAAAps/vuQXHOJYqz0/
➡slbookcover%25255B3%25255D.png?imgmax=800'
   alt='Designing Silverlight Business Applications
➡Officially Released'/>
```

```
        <text id='1'>Designing Silverlight Business Applications
➥Officially Released</text>
      </binding>
    </visual>
</tile>
```

As you can see, the XML is straightforward. It contains bindings that relate to the various tile sizes. The binding specifies the template and then the contents for the template. Images and text tags have identifiers to support tiles that allow for multiple entries. There are three possible ways to provide images.

Images on the Web are referenced with the `http://` prefix. You can easily reference images embedded in the package for your Windows 8 application by using the `ms-appx:///` prefix (for example, the logo for the Wintellog application can be referenced as `ms-appx:///Assets/Logo.png`). Finally, images you store in local storage can be referenced using the `ms-appdata:///local/` prefix. You can download images for offline access and reference them in this fashion. The maximum size for images used in tiles is 150 kilobytes.

Choosing the correct tile size is based on a few parameters. The square tile is intended for short summary messages and infrequently updated notifications. The wide tile size is recommended when your application has interesting notifications that are updated frequently. This wider size is intended to convey the "connected and alive" Windows 8 theme.

Other guidelines for using tiles from Microsoft include

- Don't use multiple tiles to link to subareas in your application—it is more appropriate to use a secondary tile (these are discussed later).
- Don't use tiles to provide extras or accessories for your application.
- Don't create a special tile for troubleshooting or configuring settings—use the **Settings** charm for this (you'll learn more about this in Chapter 8).
- Don't design your tile with a call to action to launch the application—this is implied by the tile's availability on the **Start** screen.
- Don't advertise using tiles.

- Don't embed information that is relative to the current time in a tile update, like "10 minutes ago," because the content will become stale; instead use absolute dates and times.

To read Microsoft's complete set of Windows 8 design guidelines for tiles, visit http://msdn.microsoft.com/en-us/library/windows/apps/hh465403.aspx.

When you turn on notification queuing, there is an extra property to set on the tile. This is the tag property. Tags are used to uniquely identify "slots" in the notification queue. Using tags, you can update the tile that appears in a given slot by submitting a new tile with the same tag. The sample application defines five unique slots that are always updated with the five most recent posts.

Badges

In addition to live tiles, the Windows Runtime supports the concept of badge notifications. Badges are small icons that appear on the surface of the tile. They are typically used to convey summary or status information. There are two types of badge notifications: a number (for example, showing the count of new items) and a glyph (for example, showing a status like active or new or warning). Badges can overlay both square and wide tiles and will appear in the lower–right corner of the tile except when right-to-left languages are used.

■ TIP

The reference application provides badges to indicate new posts. The first time you run the application, you should see the badge count for all of the posts that were downloaded. After that, you may want to test the badge functionality even when new posts aren't available. To do this, simply find the local storage for the application (you learned how to do this in previous chapters) and navigate into the folder for any of the groups. Delete a few of the items in the folder to force the application to reload the posts. When you launch the application the next time, it will pull down those items again and update the badge to indicate the new items.

The numeric badge can display any number from 1 through 99. In the reference application, the badge is used to display a count of new posts that were downloaded since the last time the application was launched. First, a count of new items is calculated. The range is capped at 99:

```
var totalNew = list.Sum(g => g.NewItemCount);
if (totalNew > 99)
{
    totalNew = 99;
}
```

The badge is then updated using the extension methods from the Windows 8 Code Samples under the **NotificationExtensions** folder. If new items exist, the numeric-style badge is sent:

```
if (totalNew > 0)
{
    var badgeContent = new BadgeNumericNotificationContent(
        (uint)totalNew);
    BadgeUpdateManager.CreateBadgeUpdaterForApplication()
        .Update(badgeContent.CreateNotification());
}
```

The XML for this is simple and straightforward. This is the XML for a badge showing a 3 count:

```
<badge version="1" value="3"/>
```

If no new items exist, the badge is simply cleared:

```
BadgeUpdateManager.CreateBadgeUpdaterForApplication().Clear();
```

You can also provide badges that are glyphs. You can use the `BadgeGlyphNotificationContent` class for this. You can only pick one of the pre-existing status glyphs provided by the Windows Runtime:

- None
- Activity
- Alert
- Available

- Away
- Busy
- New Message
- Paused

- Playing
- Unavailable
- Error

You can see sample images for each glyph online at http://msdn. microsoft.com/en-us/library/windows/apps/hh761458.aspx.

Microsoft also provides the following guidelines for badges:

- Numeric badges should only be used when the item count is meaningful; if you are likely to have a high number count, consider using a glyph instead.
- The numbers on badges should be relative to the last time the user launched the application rather than when the application was first installed.
- If your application supports different types of notifications, it makes sense to use the glyph for new messages rather than providing an ambiguous count.
- Only use glyphs when the status the glyph represents is likely to change.

Badges work in conjunction with live tile updates. The reference application will scroll through the most recent posts while also showing a badge that indicates the number of new posts. The combination of new content and a badge to indicate it exists is a common scenario. One change you could make is to show only the new posts instead of the five most recent to align the tile content with the badge count.

Secondary Tiles

Launch the reference application and navigate to a group or item. Open the application bar, and you will see an option to **Pin to Start,** as shown in Figure 7.5.

When you select that option, a new tile will appear on the **Start** menu. It shows the application logo with the title of the blog. When you click the tile, the application will load and then navigate directly to that blog. The same behavior will occur when you pin an item: Launching the tile will take you directly to that item.

FIGURE 7.5: **The option to pin a blog to the Start menu**

The additional tiles are referred to as *secondary tiles* because they provide new ways to launch the application outside of the main tile. They are used to promote interesting content or deep links into a location within the application. You are not able to create secondary tiles programmatically. Only the user can create tiles, so the command to pin the item will initiate a dialog that allows the user to create the tile. Users are also able to easily remove the tile from the start screen by selecting the tile and choosing the **Unpin from Start** command in the application bar.

Secondary tiles must use the standard square logo but can optionally choose the wide logo format. They are capable of showing notifications and badges (these should be filtered specifically to the content; for example only new items for that specific blog). Secondary tiles are automatically removed when the application is uninstalled.

When you click the command to pin a group, the following code is executed:

```
var group = DefaultViewModel["Group"] as BlogGroup;
var title = string.Format("Blog: {0}", group.Title);
App.Instance.PinToStart(sender,
    string.Format("Wintellog.{0}", group.Id.GetHashCode()),
```

```
title,
title,
string.Format("Group={0}", group.Id));
```

The first line finds the current group, and the second line creates a title. The `PinToStart` method is a helper method that makes it easy to prompt the user to create the secondary tile. It takes in the UI element (the button on the application bar) that the tile was requested from, a unique identifier for the tile (in this case, we use the hash code for the group's identifier), a short name, a display name, and a set of arguments. The arguments are stored with the tile and passed to the application when it is launched. This allows the application to determine where to navigate or deep link when it is launched.

The helper method creates a few links to embedded assets for the various logo sizes:

```
var logo = new Uri("ms-appx:///Assets/Logo.png");
var smallLogo = new Uri("ms-appx:///Assets/SmallLogo.png");
var wideLogo = new Uri("ms-appx:///Assets/WideLogo.png");
```

Next, the secondary tile object is created, and some properties are set. The Windows Runtime provides a class in the `Windows.UI.StartScreen` namespace for this:

```
var tile = new SecondaryTile(id, shortName, displayName, args,
    TileOptions.ShowNameOnLogo | TileOptions.ShowNameOnWideLogo,
    logo);
tile.ForegroundText = ForegroundText.Dark;
tile.SmallLogo = smallLogo;
tile.WideLogo = wideLogo;
```

The last bit of code takes the parent element that the tile was requested from and computes the area on the screen. This is passed to the special dialog, referred to as a *flyout*, as information to help arrange where it will appear. A flyout is simply a lightweight dialog that appears in context and dismisses easily, similar to using the **Charm Bar**. A method on the tile is called to request the user to confirm placing it on the **Start** screen.

```
var element = sender as FrameworkElement;
var buttonTransform = element.TransformToVisual(null);
var point = buttonTransform.TransformPoint(new Point());
var rect = new Rect(point,
    new Size(element.ActualWidth, element.ActualHeight));
await tile.RequestCreateForSelectionAsync(rect,
    Windows.UI.Popups.Placement.Left);
```

You can see the result of tapping the **Pin to Start** button in Figure 7.6. Note the flyout appears on the left side above where the user tapped. The user is also able to edit the text that will appear on the tile before pinning it. Flyouts are an important element of the Windows 8 UI. Although there are no built-in controls for flyouts, Tim Heuer has released a toolkit named Callisto that includes an implementation of the control that you can reuse in your own projects, which can be found at https://github.com/timheuer/callisto.

FIGURE 7.6: **The flyout dialog for pinning a secondary tile**

In this case, the arguments passed to the tile include the group and the identifier for the group, like this:

```
Group=http://feeds2.feedburner.com/CSharperImage
```

When the extended splash page is done loading all of the content, it checks the arguments passed into the application. If the arguments start with the text Group, the code parses out the identifier for the group and then calls the group detail page with the ID:

```
if (_activationArgs.Arguments.StartsWith("Group"))
{
    var group = _activationArgs.Arguments.Split('=');
    rootFrame.Navigate(typeof (GroupDetailPage), group[1]);
}
```

The application responds to secondary tiles by parsing the launch arguments. If you try to set a breakpoint and modify those arguments, you will find they are read-only. So how can you debug a secondary tile? It is easy to debug an application that you launch, whether from the primary tile or a secondary tile. First, right-click the Windows 8 application in the solution explorer and choose **Properties** or press **Alt+Enter**. This will open the properties dialog for the project. Navigate to the **Debug** tab and check the box next to **Do not launch, but debug my code when it starts**. This is shown in Figure 7.7.

Now you can press **F5** to start debugging; the debugger will start, but the application will not launch. Press the **Windows Key** to open the **Start** screen and navigate to the secondary tile. Tap the tile, and the application will launch. The debugger will attach to the process automatically and stop at any breakpoints you have set. You will now be able to view the arguments passed in from the secondary tile and troubleshoot the application as needed in that context.

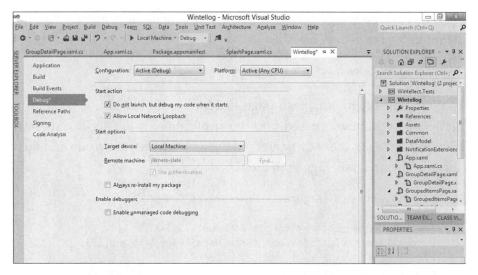

FIGURE 7.7: **Setting the application to debug without automatically launching**

Toast Notifications

Toast notifications enable you to send transient messages outside of the application. Although they can be initiated from within the application, a far more common use is from an external source. In the next section, you learn more about push notifications and how to update your application even when it is not running.

The user has complete control over toast notifications. When the user activates the **Settings** charm, he is always presented with a **Permissions** command. Selecting this command results in options similar to the ones you see in Figure 7.8.

Notifications can be sent immediately or scheduled for later use. For example, a calendar application might set a reminder for an event. The notification can be scheduled from within the application but will still appear even if the application is no longer running. The reference application takes advantage of this to schedule toast notifications for new items. This is not how the application would typically be designed but is included as a way to illustrate how toast notifications work.

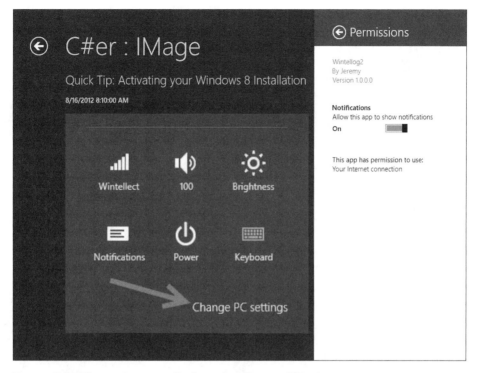

FIGURE 7.8: The user-controlled setting for notifications

The first step to creating a toast notification is to enable toast capabilities in the application. To do this, open the **Package.appmanifest** and navigate to the Application UI tab. Make sure the setting for **Toast Capable** is set to **Yes**. This setting is shown in Figure 7.9.

When you have enabled notifications, you can build your toasts. The reference application uses the extensions provided by the Windows 8 Code Samples mentioned earlier in this chapter. There are eight templates provided for notifications. Table 7.1 lists the templates and describes how they appear.

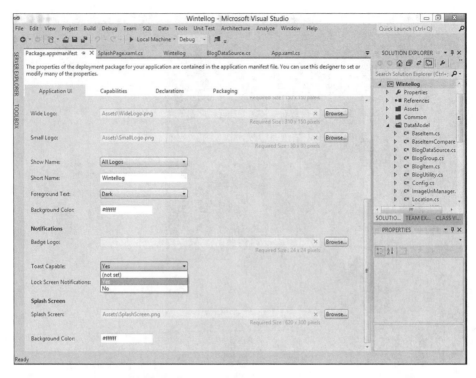

FIGURE 7.9: **Enabling notification for an application**

TABLE 7.1: **Toast Templates**

Template	Description
ToastText01	A single string that can wrap over three lines.
ToastText02	A single line of bold text following by a string that can wrap over two lines.
ToastText03	A line of bold text that can wrap over two lines followed by a single string of regular text.
ToastText04	A single line of bold text followed by two lines of regular text.
ToastImageAndText01	A large image with a single string that wraps over three lines.
ToastImageAndText02	A large image, a single line of bold text, and a string of regular text that wraps over two lines.

ToastImageAndText03	A large image, one string of bold text that wraps over two lines, and one line of regular text.
ToastImageAndText04	A large image, one string of bold text on a single line, and two lines of regular text.

In the `SplashPage` code-behind, you can see the code to create a toast notification. Although this code would most likely live on a server used to push notifications to the client, it is contained here within the application for illustration purposes. The code creates a template and sets the values used by the template:

```
var notificationTemplate =
    ToastContentFactory.CreateToastImageAndText02();
notificationTemplate.TextHeading.Text = item.Group.Title;
notificationTemplate.TextBodyWrap.Text = item.Title;
notificationTemplate.Image.Src = item.DefaultImageUri.ToString();
notificationTemplate.Image.Alt = item.Title;
```

Notifications are similar to secondary tiles because they can also pass arguments to the application for context. The `Launch` property is used to set the arguments. The reference application uses the same format for notifications as it did for secondary tiles:

```
notificationTemplate.Launch = string.Format("Item={0}", item.Id);
```

This takes advantage of the fact that the code to process the parameters already exists. If you want to distinguish between a notification and a secondary tile launch, you can add additional information to the arguments to parse when they are received. The `ToastNotificationManager` provides the functionality you need to schedule toasts. It will create an instance of the notification object that you can query to see if toasts are enabled:

```
var notifier = ToastNotificationManager.CreateToastNotifier();
if (notifier.Setting == NotificationSetting.Enabled) { ... }
```

If you want to know why notifications are not enabled, you can query the `Setting` enumeration that provides the following values:

- **Enabled**—Toasts are enabled, and notifications will be sent/received.
- **DisabledByGroupPolicy**—An administrator has disabled all notifications through a group policy.
- **DisabledByManifest**—The application did not declare toasts by setting **Toast Capable** to **Yes**.
- **DisabledForApplication**—The user has explicitly disabled notifications for this application.
- **DisabledForUser**—The user or administrator has disabled all notifications for the user on the device.

When you have established that toasts are allowed and created the template, you can simply generate the notification from the template and show the toast:

```
var toast = notificationTemplate.CreateNotification();
notifier.Show(toast);
```

If you want to schedule the notification instead (as the reference application does), you simply specify a time for the toast to display and create a ScheduledToastNotification. Instead of calling Show, you pass the instance to the AddToSchedule method:

```
var toast = notificationTemplate.CreateNotification();
var date = DateTimeOffset.Now.AddSeconds(30);
var scheduledToast = new ScheduledToastNotification(toast.Content,
    date);
notifier.AddToSchedule(scheduledToast);
```

To test the toast notification, you can navigate to the local storage for the application and delete one or two posts. Run the application. When the application is done initializing and displays the first page, close it (drag it from top to bottom or press **Alt+F4**). Wait about 30 seconds, and you should see the toast display. You can either dismiss the toast or click it. Because the toast was configured with parameters for the item it shows, clicking the toast will launch the application and take you to the specific item shown by the notification. Figure 7.10 shows several notifications appearing over the weather application.

FIGURE 7.10: Toast notifications overlaying the weather application

To dismiss the toast, you can swipe the toast from the screen, hover the mouse pointer over the top right to see a close button, or wait and it will eventually go away. Tapping or clicking on the toast will bring you into the application.

▪ TIP

When the application is not running, the toast notification will launch the application and pass the specified arguments. If the application is running when the notification appears, it is possible to respond to user interactions. You can perform logic when the user taps the notification by hooking into the `Activated` event on the notification instance you receive when you call `CreateNotification`. When the toast is dismissed, whether by the user or due to timing out, you can respond by hooking into the `Dismissed` event. The event arguments provide a reason for the toast being dismissed.

You can also change the duration and content of the audio that is played by the toast. This is done by setting the Audio.Content property on the template. Sources include the tone for instant messages, alarms, calls, mail, reminders, SMS, and silent. Setting the Duration property to ToastDuration. Long will cause the toast to display for 25 seconds rather than the default period of 7 seconds.

All of the examples for tiles and toasts so far have been demonstrated from within the application itself. This is not always practical because there are many times you will want to update the application when it is not running. Weather applications may update the tiles as the weather changes and send toasts when there are weather alerts. How can you keep the application connected and alive when it is not running? The answer is with push notifications.

Windows Notification Service

The Windows Notification Service (WNS) enables the delivery of tile and toast notifications over the Internet. This is how you can keep your application current and fresh, even when it is not running. The service handles all of the communication with your application and even takes care of tricky situations such as when the device is behind a firewall. It is designed to scale to millions of users and, best of all, is a free service for your application.

There are five steps involved in using the WNS service. These steps are the same whether you wish to send tiles, toasts, or simple badge updates. The steps are illustrated in Figure 7.11.

The steps can be broken down as follows:

1. The application requests a channel. This is a unique URI used to communicate with the specific application on a specific Windows 8 device.

2. The WNS assigns a channel and sends this information back to the application.

3. The application must now communicate this channel to the host that will manage updates—most often this is a web server you or your company creates to track channels and send updates. Often you will send the channel URI with a unique identifier for the device so you can tie updates back to the original device.

4. When your host service wishes to send an update, it posts the content for the update to WNS using the channel URI that was provided.

5. The Windows 8 device maintains an ongoing communication link with WNS that will work even from behind a firewall. When an update is present, it will acquire the update and use it to update the badge or tile or to generate a notification.

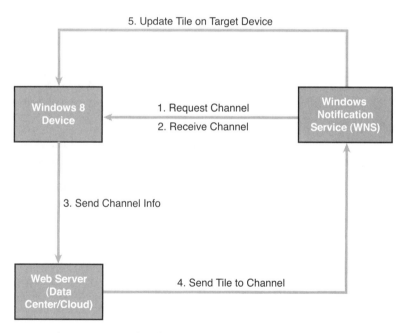

FIGURE 7.11: The steps involved with using the Windows Notification Service

The ongoing link is maintained by the application, but it can expire after a time. It is a good practice to consistently establish and store the link each time the application is launched or resumed. This will ensure the service has the most up-to-date value.

In addition to providing the scale necessary to communicate with a large number of devices, WNS also addresses security. Although any Windows 8 application can request and establish a channel with WNS, sending a message requires an authorization that includes a special code. This code is unique and based on the combination of a unique security identifier for the application and a shared secret you generate.

There are two ways to obtain the credentials you need to interact with WNS. The preferred method is through the Windows Store, using a developer account. You can learn more about the developer center online at http://msdn.microsoft.com/en-us/windows/apps/.

To access your developer account or create a new one, select the Dashboard tab and follow the prompts. As of this writing, the store is closed to general registration, and the steps involved may change when Windows 8 is finally released. After you create your account, you can follow the steps outlined at http://msdn.microsoft.com/en-us/library/windows/apps/hh465407.aspx to obtain your security credentials.

If you do not have a developer account or simply want temporary access for testing, you can navigate to the Windows Live Application Management site at http://go.microsoft.com/fwlink/?linkid=227235.

This site requires a Windows Live Account. After you sign in, you will be prompted to obtain information from the application manifest. Specifically, you will be prompted to enter the **Package Display Name** and **Publisher** from the **Packaging** tab in the manifest. Figure 7.12 shows this information for the Wintellog application.

The **Package Display Name** is **Wintellog**, and the **Publisher** (*not* the **Publisher Display Name**) is **CN=Jeremy**. Enter these values in the fields to proceed. When you accept the terms and submit the form, you will see a page similar to what's shown in Figure 7.13.

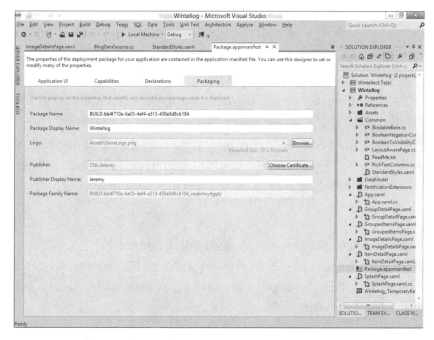

FIGURE 7.12: Package information

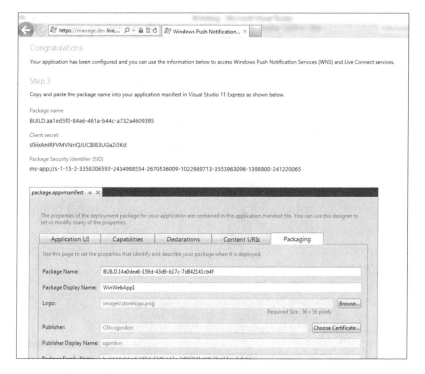

FIGURE 7.13: The credentials provided for WNS

Three key pieces of information are provided:

- The **Package Name** must be updated in your manifest. If you already have a value there, overwrite it with the one that is supplied.
- The **Client Secret** is a special code you will use to authorize your push notifications and should be stored on the host server.
- The **Package Security Identifier** is unique to the particular package and also used for authentication. The secret and identifier will be used to match the package itself when a request to push information is made.

When you have the necessary information, you can begin sending push notifications. The first step is to request a channel. The reference application does this when the application starts and saves it for later use (this code is in the **App.xaml.cs** file):

```
Channel = await PushNotificationChannelManager
    .CreatePushNotificationChannelForApplicationAsync();
```

That call is fairly simple and straightforward. If an exception is thrown, the application will store the exception. When the channel is generated, it is typically sent to the host server to store and reference for later communication with the client. I'm not going to ask you to stand up a web service and provide a host, so this example will simply save the channel so you can copy and paste into a helper application. You learn about a trivial way to stand up a site to manage notification registration later in this chapter.

From the main Wintellog page (the GroupedItemsPage), you can open the application bar and you will see a command labeled **Show Channel**. When you tap this command, it will copy the channel to the clipboard. This is done using a DataPackage. This is the same class used to communicate information through the **Share Contract**, only here it is used to populate the clipboard instead:

```
var dataPackage = new DataPackage();
dataPackage.SetText(App.Instance.Channel.Uri);
Clipboard.SetContent(dataPackage);
```

You will see a dialog appear that indicates it was successfully copied or that displays an error if the channel was not acquired. Now that you have the channel, you can compile and run the **PushNotificationTest** application. This is a special application that simulates what a host web service would do when sending push notifications to the Wintellog2 application. The main page is shown in Figure 7.14.

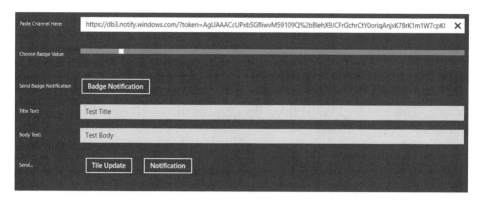

FIGURE 7.14: The push notification test application

Your first step is to position the cursor inside the **Paste Channel Here** input and paste the channel you copied to the clipboard from the Wintellog2 application. Now you should be able to send updates. For example, move the slider to any value and tap the **Badge Notification** button. If you receive a success dialog, go back to the **Start** screen and look at the tile for the Wintellog2 application. It should reflect the number you selected. You can also enter your own text and use it to either update the tile or generate a notification.

The source for the **PushNotificationTest** application demonstrates what your host service would do in order to send notifications. The diagram in Figure 7.11 was somewhat simplified because there is an authentication step required before the push notification can be send. The authentication uses the OAuth protocol to obtain a special code that is used for the notification. OAuth is a popular open protocol for secure authorization that you can learn more about online at http://oauth.net/.

The application defines a contract that is used to communicate with the service:

```
[DataContract]
public class OAuthToken
{
    [DataMember(Name = "access_token")]
    public string AccessToken { get; set; }
    [DataMember(Name = "token_type")]
    public string TokenType { get; set; }
}
```

This is where the secret and security identifier you obtained earlier come into play (the ones that I used are hard-coded in the reference application). The first step is to create the content the service needs to provide the access code:

```
var body =
    String.Format("grant_type=client_credentials&client_id={0}
➥&client_secret={1}
➥&scope=notify.windows.com", urlEncodedSid, urlEncodedSecret);
```

The request is always the same with the exception of the client identifier and secret. These are taken from their raw format and encoded for transport over the web. For example, the secret is encoded like this:

```
const string SECRET = "4n3ZeAodQpNmAQiBIpl2Pb6gcyKetITN";
var urlEncodedSecret = WebUtility.UrlEncode(SECRET);
```

Your host application would likely contain this somewhere in a secured configuration file or database record and then access it as needed. The message is formatted using a special class that helps encapsulate messages that are sent over HTTP. In this case, the content is string-based, so the StringContent helper class is used:

```
var httpBody = new StringContent(body,
Encoding.UTF8, "application/x-www-form-urlencoded");
```

An instance of the HttpClient is then used to post the request. The result should be a token that contains the access code necessary for sending push notifications:

```
var client = new HttpClient();
var response = await client.PostAsync(
    new Uri("https://login.live.com/accesstoken.srf", UriKind.
Absolute),
    httpBody);
var oAuthToken = GetOAuthTokenFromJson(
    await response.Content.ReadAsStringAsync());
return oAuthToken.AccessToken;
```

The token is always requested from https://login.live.com/accesstoken.srf by sending the secret and the client identifier. When the token is received, you can extract the access code and use it for push notification calls. The nice thing about notification calls is that they use the exact same XML you generated locally to update your tiles, badges, and to send notifications. The only difference is that the XML is pushed to a special channel obtained by the application.

For example, the code to send the badge notification uses the same extensions provided by the SDK to post the badge to the cloud:

```
var badge = new BadgeNumericNotificationContent(
    (uint)BadgeValue.Value);
await PostToCloud(badge.CreateNotification().Content, "wns/badge");
```

The only difference between this and a call to generate a notification is the content and the type:

```
var tile = TileContentFactory.CreateTileSquareText02();
tile.TextHeading.Text = title;
tile.TextBodyWrap.Text = text;
await PostToCloud(bigTile.CreateNotification().Content);
```

The call to PostToCloud extracts the XML from the notification and prepares a message to post to WNS:

```
var content = xml.GetXml();
var requestMsg = new HttpRequestMessage(HttpMethod.Post, uri);
requestMsg.Content =
    new ByteArrayContent(Encoding.UTF8.GetBytes(content));
```

Next, the headers are set. The overall package is XML, but the specific package type will map to wns/badge, wns/tile, or wns/notification depending on what you intend to push. The access code that was retrieved is placed in the authentication header:

```
requestMsg.Content.Headers.ContentType =
    new MediaTypeHeaderValue("text/xml");
requestMsg.Headers.Add("X-WNS-Type", type);
requestMsg.Headers.Authorization =
    new AuthenticationHeaderValue("Bearer", _accessCode);
```

Finally, there is nothing left to do but send the message. The response is queried to display the status in case the call was not successful:

```
var responseMsg = await new HttpClient().SendAsync(requestMsg);
message = string.Format("{0}: {1}", responseMsg.StatusCode,
    await responseMsg.Content.ReadAsStringAsync());
```

That's all there is to it! The same code can easily be implemented on a web server. You can use the source code for the toast and tile extensions to create similar classes on your web server. When the client registers the channel, instead of copying it to the clipboard, you would prepare a message to post the information to the host server. This is the perfect example of a scenario that makes a lot of sense to implement with Azure, which provides a fairly trivial way to stand up the necessary components to handle the notification registration and tracking. You can learn more about Azure and how well it works with Windows 8 through a special project called the Windows Azure Toolkit for Windows 8, available online at http://watwindows8.codeplex.com/.

Feel free to use the authentication helper or any other code from this sample in your own applications to simplify the process of generating toast notifications.

Summary

In this chapter, you learned how to keep your applications alive, fresh, and connected, even when they are not running. You can inform the user the new information is waiting for them through the use of badges. Tiles can be dynamically updated to provide previews of images and content in the application, and notifications provide timely "toasts" that overlay the user's current application and give him or her the ability to respond by launching your application. All of these services are available from within your application or from an external server using the Windows Notification Services (WNS).

In the next chapter, you learn how to give your application charm through the use of contracts. Each time you launch or debug an application, you are already using the **Launch** contract. You've been exposed to some other contracts including **Settings** and **Share** already. You will learn more about these contracts as well as how to integrate **Search** and even stream content using the **PlayTo** contract.

8

Giving Your Application Charm

IMAGINE TRYING TO BUILD AN APPLICATION THAT IS SO flexible it can predict how to interface with all other applications that will be written for the target platform. You would have the unprecedented ability to integrate seamlessly with those future applications. Whether sharing settings and preferences, sending over contact information, or embedding an image, the user would only have to perform a few simple actions to get the job done. As a developer, of course, you would have to analyze all of the potential future applications to write the appropriate interfaces and adapters to share information in a way those applications expect.

Windows 8 addresses this challenge at the operating system level and removes any guesswork out of developing applications that integrate well with each other. Instead of having to understand the interfaces that other applications use, as a developer you can learn a common set of agreements known as *contracts* that Windows 8 applications might function with. Contracts provide a way for your application to integrate data without knowing the details of how that data will be used by other applications. It is an incredibly powerful feature introduced with Windows 8.

In Windows 8, a contract is simply an agreement between one or more applications. It defines the set of requirements an application should meet in order to participate in a pre-defined set of interactions. Windows 8 also supports extensions that represent a unique agreement between your application and the operating system. For example, when Windows 8 requests the user to select a photo for his or her account profile, your application can appear in the list of available options if you decide to provide an extension in your application for that feature.

Windows 8 supports six contracts. The contract names and their brief explanations are provided in Table 8.1. You learn how to implement many of these contracts later in this chapter.

TABLE 8.1: **Windows 8 Contracts**

Contract Name	Description
Application to Application Picking	Allows users to pick files from one application directly from within another application. http://msdn.microsoft.com/en-us/library/windows/apps/hh465174.aspx
Cached File Updater	Provides a way for your application to provide updates for certain files so that users can use your application as a central repository; one example may be to synchronize files between a cloud provider and the local device. http://msdn.microsoft.com/en-us/library/windows/apps/hh465192.aspx
PlayTo	Enables the streaming of digital media to connected Digital Living Network Alliance (DLNA) devices such as projectors and televisions. See http://www.dnla.org/ for more information about the DLNA standard. http://msdn.microsoft.com/en-us/library/windows/apps/hh465176.aspx
Search	Creates integrated search functionality so that users can search your application's content from other locations and transfer searches from within your application to other providers like the file system. http://msdn.microsoft.com/en-us/library/windows/apps/hh465231.aspx
Settings	Provides a standard, contextual location for users to access settings specific to your application. http://msdn.microsoft.com/en-us/library/windows/apps/hh770540.aspx

Contract Name	Description
Share	Allows users to share content from your application to other applications and provides the ability for your application to receive shared content including text, hyperlinks, files, and bitmap images. http://msdn.microsoft.com/en-us/library/windows/apps/hh758314.aspx

There are ten extensions your Windows 8 application can implement. These extensions are listed in Table 8.2. Extensions are like agreements between your application and Windows 8.

TABLE 8.2: Windows 8 Extensions

Extension	Description
Account Picture Provider	Indicates your application can take or provide pictures for users to use as their account pictures. http://go.microsoft.com/fwlink/?LinkId=231579
AutoPlay	Allows your application to appear as a choice when the user connects a device to the computer. If selected, your application can be automatically launched when such a device is connected. http://msdn.microsoft.com/en-us/library/windows/apps/hh452731.aspx
Background Tasks	Used by applications to run code even when the application has been suspended or terminated; intended for small work items that don't require user interaction. http://www.microsoft.com/download/en/details.aspx?id=27411
Camera Settings	Indicates your application can provide a customer user interface for camera options and choosing effects when the camera is used to capture photos or video. http://msdn.microsoft.com/library/windows/hardware/hh454870
Contact Picker	Enables your application to provide contact data and includes it within the list of applications that Windows 8 displays when the user requests contacts. http://msdn.microsoft.com/en-us/library/windows/apps/hh464939.aspx

File Activation	Extends existing file types and defines new file types that your application can register to handle.
	http://msdn.microsoft.com/en-us/library/windows/apps/hh452684.aspx
Game Explorer	Specifies that your application is a game, allowing Windows 8 to limit access to the game if the user has enabled family safety features.
	http://msdn.microsoft.com/en-us/library/windows/apps/hh465153.aspx
Print Task Settings	Allows your application to display a custom print-related user interface that communicates directly with a printing device.
	http://msdn.microsoft.com/en-us/library/windows/hardware/br259129
Protocol Activation	Enables your application to handle existing and new protocols for communication.
	http://msdn.microsoft.com/en-us/library/windows/apps/hh452686.aspx
SSL Certificates	Provides the means to install a digital certification with your application.
	http://msdn.microsoft.com/en-us/library/windows/apps/hh465012.aspx

By now you are familiar with the Windows 8 **Charms Bar** that is invoked by swiping from the right edge of the screen or pressing **Windows Key+C**. These *charms* are each associated with a specific contract. The **Start** charm is a unique charm that opens the **Start** screen and allows you to activate applications by launching them when you tap or click a tile. The **Device** charm activates the **PlayTo** contract and displays any DLNA devices that are available as targets. The **Search**, **Share**, and **Settings** charms correspond to contracts with the same name and are the focus of this chapter.

Searching

The **Start** button for Windows was featured front and center when Bill Gates took the stage almost 20 years ago to announce Windows 95. This button has become almost synonymous with Windows, so it came as a surprise to many when they learned the **Start** button had been eliminated from Windows 8. There are numerous articles and blog entries that attempt to tackle the reasons why this button was eliminated and replaced with the combination of a new **Start** screen coupled with a powerful search mechanism. The primary reason, according to Microsoft, is that almost 70% of all searches in Windows 7 were used to find and launch programs.[1]

In Windows 8, search is featured front and center. I've been using Windows 8 as a primary operating system since it was first released as the Developer Preview in September of 2011. Although it took some retraining of my "muscle memory" to stop going for the **Start** button anytime I want to launch a new application, I've become used to the new way of getting around Windows, and I like it. I can open any program out of hundreds or thousands with a few simple taps on my keyboard.

To understand how this works, click the **Desktop** icon on your **Start** screen and imagine a scenario in which you want to launch Notepad. Now tap the **Windows** key followed by an **N** and an **O** and press **Enter.** That's a simple sequence of four presses in succession. Chances are, unless you have some other program installed with a similar name, you will be staring at a new instance of Notepad. This is because the default behavior for the **Start** screen (which is toggled by pressing the **Windows** key) is to begin searching applications. For partial matches, the most frequently and recently used applications will appear at the top of the list. Figure 8.1 shows the result of tapping the key and typing the two characters. Notice that all applications with "no" in the name are listed, and Notepad is highlighted as the default (resulting in it being launched when I press the **Enter** key).

Notice that there are three special search types listed in the right margin. The default is for applications on the system. You can tap the **Settings** option to see the 47 available matches related to app settings (the total count on your machine may be different), or **Files** to search for the same text on the file system. You can also see a long list of applications beneath these three built-in options. Those are all applications that support the **Search** contract.

---

[1] http://blogs.msdn.com/b/b8/archive/2011/10/18/designing-search-for-the-start-screen.aspx.

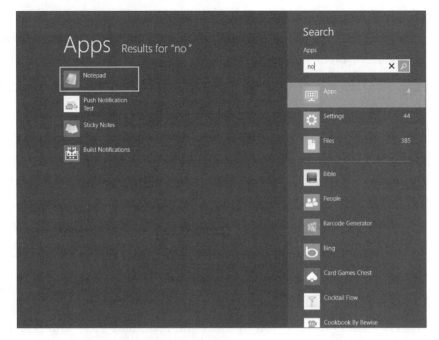

FIGURE 8.1: A quick search for Notepad

You can invoke the **Search** charm several ways. One is to swipe from the right side of the display to reveal the **Charms Bar** and then tap the **Search** charm icon. You also make the **Charms Bar** appear by holding down **Windows key+C**. Finally, you can launch **Search** directly by holding down the **Windows key+Q** (think "Q" for "Query"). When the bar appears, type the word **chicken** and tap the icon for Internet Explorer. The search is automatically passed to the web browser, as shown in Figure 8.2.

Keeping the same search text, you can tap the Dictionary.com option if you have it installed on your system and read the definition of chicken. This is shown in Figure 8.3.

The search integration makes it possible for you to conduct searches across applications. Applications that support the **Search** contract will allow you to search content while also providing the ability to search other sources. This makes it possible to start a search in one application and then refine it until you find the source that provides the information you need. Adding search capabilities to your application is supported by special Visual Studio 2012 templates.

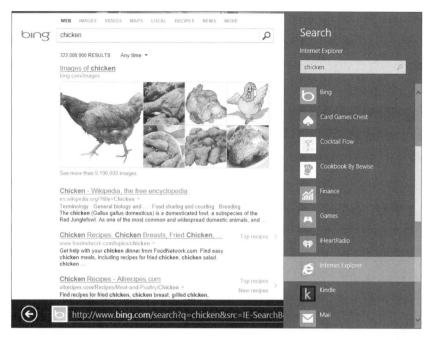

FIGURE 8.2: A search for chicken with Internet Explorer

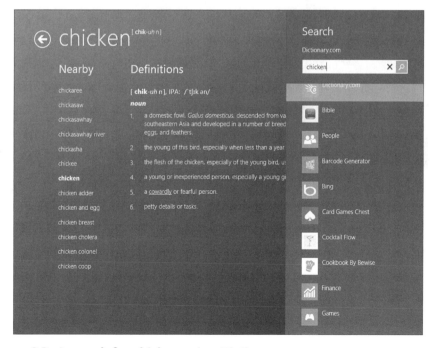

FIGURE 8.3: A search for chicken using Dictionary.com

The Wintellog3 application demonstrates integrated search capabilities. My first step to add search capabilities was to right-click the project in the Solution Explorer, choose **Add→New Item** from Visual Studio, and select the **Search Contract** option, as shown in Figure 8.4.

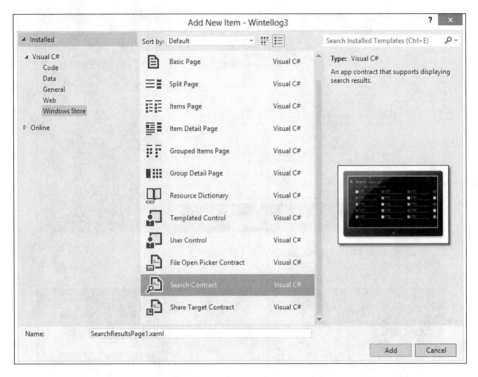

FIGURE 8.4: **The Search contract item type**

The template for the **Search** contract can perform several actions on your behalf. It will add search as a supported contract in the declarations section of your application's manifest. It creates a basic XAML page to host the search results and builds some of the plumbing necessary to respond to search requests. It also adds code to the App class to handle incoming search requests. These default settings may work fine for most applications, but because the Wintellog3 application uses an extended splash screen, the code was modified to support loading the blogs before launching the search.

I added a property called Extended to the App class to track whether or not the extended splash page was launched. If not, the page must load first in order to retrieve the list of blogs and items. When the extended splash page is loaded, subsequent search requests are passed straight to the search page as the necessary data is loaded and present. The code to check this flag is placed within the override that is called when search is activated:

```
protected override void OnSearchActivated(SearchActivatedEventArgs
args)
{
    if (Extended) { SearchResultsPage.Activate(args); }
    else { ExtendedSplash(args.SplashScreen, args); }
}
```

The splash page was modified to accept SearchActivatedEventArgs in addition to the existing LaunchedActivatedEventArgs. The logic to determine the first page to load was extended to activate the search page when search arguments are passed in. This allows the same extended splash page to handle a variety of scenarios ranging from search, initial activation, activation after termination, and launching from a secondary tile.

The search results page (**SearchResultsPage.xaml.cs**) contains all of the code necessarily to facilitate the search. The static Activate method checks for the existence of a Frame. If one does not exist, it creates one and then navigates to the search page. It passes in the search text and a reference to the previous content so the user can navigate back when they are done searching. This method is shown in Listing 8.1.

LISTING 8.1: **Method to Activate the Search Page**

```
public static void Activate(SearchActivatedEventArgs args)
{
    var previousContent = Window.Current.Content;
    var frame = previousContent as Frame;

    if (frame != null)
    {
        frame.Navigate(typeof (SearchResultsPage), args.QueryText);
    }
    else
    {
        var page = new SearchResultsPage
                    {
                            _previousContent = previousContent
                    };
        page.LoadState(args.QueryText, null);
```

```
        Window.Current.Content = page;
    }

    Window.Current.Activate();
}
```

When the state for the page is loaded, a set of filters is created. A filter provides a way to narrow down the search. It is up to you to determine what filters make the most sense for your application. In the **Wintellog3** example, the user is given the option to narrow their search to a specific blog. First, the total number of matches is computed:

```
var total = (from g in App.Instance.DataSource.GroupList
                from i in g.Items
                where i.Title.ToLower().Contains(query) ||
                    i.Description.ToLower().Contains(query)
                select i).Count();
```

Then a filter list is created with an entry for all matching items:

```
var filterList = new List<Filter>
    {
        new Filter(string.Empty, "All", total, true)
    };
```

The `Filter` class contains the identifier for each specific blog, the title of the blog, and the count of matches within that blog:

```
filterList.AddRange(from blogGroup in
    App.Instance.DataSource.GroupList
        let count = blogGroup.Items.Count(
            i => i.Title.ToLower().Contains(query) ||
            i.Description.ToLower().Contains(query))
        where count > 0
        select new Filter(blogGroup.Id, blogGroup.Title, count));
```

The filters and query text are stored in the base page, and data-binding handles creating the page. By default, all search results are shown. The user can choose a filter to narrow the search results. Any time the filter is changed, including the first time it is set, the `Filter_SelectionChanged` method is fired. This method takes the current filter and uses it to apply the query and create a list of results. This logic is shown in Listing 8.2.

LISTING 8.2: Filtering Individual Items Based on the Query Text

```
private void Filter_SelectionChanged(object sender,
    SelectionChangedEventArgs e)
{
    var query = _query.ToLower();

    var selectedFilter = e.AddedItems.FirstOrDefault() as Filter;
    if (selectedFilter != null)
    {
        selectedFilter.Active = true;

        if (selectedFilter.Name.Equals("All"))
        {
            DefaultViewModel["Results"] =
                (from g in App.Instance.DataSource.GroupList
                    from i in g.Items
                    where i.Title.ToLower().Contains(query)
                        || i.Description.ToLower().Contains(query)
                    select
                        new SearchResult
                        {
                            Image = i.DefaultImageUri,
                            Title = i.Title,
                            Id = i.Id,
                            Description = i.Description
                        }).ToList();
        }
        else
        {
            var blogGroup = App.Instance.DataSource.
➥GetGroup(selectedFilter.Id);
            DefaultViewModel["Results"] =
                (from i in blogGroup.Items
                    where i.Title.ToLower().Contains(query)
                        || i.Description.ToLower().Contains(query)
                    select
                        new SearchResult
                        {
                            Id = i.Id,
                            Image = i.DefaultImageUri,
                            Title = i.Title,
                            Description = i.Description
                        }).ToList();
        }
        object results;
        ICollection resultsCollection;
```

```
    if (DefaultViewModel.TryGetValue("Results", out results) &&
        (resultsCollection = results as ICollection) != null &&
        resultsCollection.Count != 0)
    {
        VisualStateManager.GoToState(this, "ResultsFound", true);
        return;
    }
}
VisualStateManager.GoToState(this, "NoResultsFound", true);
}
```

Note the use of the Visual State Manager (VSM) to change the state when no results are found. The result of applying the search term entered by the user is shown in Figure 8.5.

FIGURE 8.5: **Search results**

You can search from within the application at any time by pressing **Windows key+Q**. If the application is already loaded, you may notice that you receive search suggestions when you begin typing search text.

Suggestions are easy to implement; you simply register to an event that is fired when the user types in search text. For this application, the results are based on finding partial matches in the titles of blog post entries. First, the event is registered after the blog content is loaded:

```
Windows.ApplicationModel.Search.SearchPane.GetForCurrentView()
    .SuggestionsRequested += SplashPage_SuggestionsRequested;
```

The built-in search mechanism remembers previous search queries and will show those in the list of suggestions. When the event is fired, you can add other suggestions to this collection. Suggestions can either be query suggestions (search terms that may generate results the user is looking for) or result suggestions (potential matches based on the search term). The UI is capable of displaying up to five items of either type. The implementation of this is shown in Listing 8.3. The search text is ignored if it is less than three characters. A LINQ query filters out text from the titles, matches anything that starts with the characters the user has entered, and then cleans up the result, stripping white space and special characters to provide a distinct list of unique words that appear in titles.

LISTING 8.3: Providing Search Suggestions

```
void SplashPage_SuggestionsRequested(Windows.ApplicationModel.Search
        .SearchPane sender,
    Windows.ApplicationModel.Search
        .SearchPaneSuggestionsRequestedEventArgs args)
{
    var query = args.QueryText.ToLower();

    if (query.Length < 3) return;

    var suggestions = (from g in App.Instance.DataSource.GroupList
                       from i in g.Items
                       from keywords in i.Title.Split(' ')
                       let keyword = Regex.Replace(
                           keywords.ToLower(), @"[^\w\.@-]", "")
                       where i.Title.ToLower().Contains(query)
                       && keyword.StartsWith(query)
                       orderby keyword
                       select keyword).Distinct();

    args.Request.SearchSuggestionCollection
        .AppendQuerySuggestions(suggestions);
}
```

The last piece of functionality to implement is handling the selection of search items. You'll notice in the XAML for the search page that the grids support item selection through the following attribute:

```
IsItemClickEnabled="True"
```

This will allow an item to be selected by a click or tap. To handle the selection event, add a handler for the ItemClick event:

```
ItemClick="ResultsGridView_ItemClick_1"
```

The result simply navigates to the items detail page for the selected item:

```
private void ResultsGridView_ItemClick_1(object sender,
    ItemClickEventArgs e)
{
    Navigate(typeof (ItemDetailPage),
        ((SearchResult) e.ClickedItem).Id);
}
```

To recap, handling the **Search** contract involves a few steps. Although you must handle the search request and determine whether you will navigate to the search page directly or use an extended splash page to load data first, the template provides all of the necessary plumbing needed to implement the search. After the search is loaded, you implement the search filters and provide search results when a filter is selected. Finally, you handle search selection by navigating to the appropriate page within your application.

Sharing

Sharing content is now more popular than ever in today's Internet-connected social media landscape. In previous versions of Windows, the primary way to share data between applications was by using the Windows Clipboard. If you wanted to build an application that could post content to the Internet, you had to build the process yourself by creating a user interface for sharing content and building the right code to interact with the various APIs exposed by different social media providers. Windows 8 changed the game by providing a standard API for sharing different types of data that may range from lightweight text to bitmap images and even file system objects.

The **Share** contract enables applications to share data in a standard way without having to know the details of what other applications are installed on the system or how they might handle shared data. Your application can act as a Share Source by providing content the user may want to share. It may also act as a **Share Target** that consumes content. **Share** interactions are facilitated through the `DataTransferManager` WinRT component that exists in the `Windows.ApplicationModel.DataTransfer` namespace. Full documentation for this namespace is available online at http://msdn.microsoft.com/en-us/library/windows/apps/windows.applicationmodel.datatransfer.aspx.

Sourcing Content for Sharing

The Wintellog3 application acts as a Share Source and can share details about blogs, posts, and images. Before you can successfully share, you will need appropriate applications installed that can receive the content. The ImageHelper2 application from Chapter 3, *Extensible Application Markup Language (XAML)*, can receive images; the Mail client can receive links and text. I recommend you download, build, and deploy the Windows 8 Sample SDK application called "Sharing content target app sample" available online at http://code.msdn.microsoft.com/windowsapps/Sharing-Content-Target-App-e2689782/.

This application is specifically designed to receive all shared content types and is a great way to see how the process works. When the user chooses the **Share** charm, the `DataRequested` event is fired on the `DataTransferManager` component. The `App` class provides a method to register for this event:

```
public void RegisterForShare()
{
    var dataManager = DataTransferManager.GetForCurrentView();
    dataManager.DataRequested += DataManager_DataRequested;
}
```

The event is fired with a reference to the `DataTransferManager` and a parameter of type `DataRequestedEventArgs`. The parameter exposes a `Request` property of type `DataRequest` that in turn exposes a `DataPackage` object. This object is used to wrap any data you wish to share with other applications. Table 8.3 lists the types of data you can associate with the package.

TABLE 8.3: **Data Types Supported by the DataPackage Class**

Type	Description
Bitmap	A bitmap image
Data	A custom data format, stored as JSON based on a schema defined at http://schema.org/ or a custom schema that is published and available for other applications to consume
HTML	Hypertext Markup Language content
RTF	Rich Text Format content
Storage Items	A list of type `IStorageItem` used for sharing files between applications
Text	Plain text content
URI	Uniform Resource Identifier

The data package also provides support for asynchronous requests by setting a data provider. The provider indicates the type of information to provide along with a callback that is invoked when the target application is ready for the data. This approach is used when the data you have to share requires significant processing time to package and deliver.

Along with the actual data content, you may also provide a thumbnail image that represents the data, a title, and a description. To actually implement the sharing, a property is exposed on the main App class to allow each individual page to supply a handler for sharing so that the proper context can be provided:

```
public Action<DataTransferManager, DataRequestedEventArgs>
    Share { get; set; }
```

Pages that don't provide any sharing functionally will set this to `null` when they are navigated to like the main `GroupedItemsPage`:

```
protected override void LoadState(Object navigationParameter,
    Dictionary<String, Object> pageState)
{
    App.Instance.Share = null;
    DefaultViewModel["Groups"] = App.Instance.DataSource.GroupList;
    groupGridView.ItemsSource =
        groupedItemsViewSource.View.CollectionGroups;
}
```

The handler itself checks to see if a callback is registered, like this:

```
void DataManager_DataRequested(DataTransferManager sender,
    DataRequestedEventArgs args)
{
    if (Share != null)
    {
        Share(sender, args);
    }
}
```

If no data is supplied, a message will be provided to the user indicating there is nothing to share. You can provide additional information if necessary to indicate why the share operation failed. The following code is added after the check to see if a callback exists:

```
else
{
    args.Request
        .FailWithDisplayText(
        "Please choose a blog or item to enable sharing.");
}
```

The result of a share attempt is shown in Figure 8.6.

The pages that allow sharing register a method to handle the callback:

```
App.Instance.Share = Share;
```

If the user navigates to a blog entry, the share operation will provide the URL for the blog. First, a "reality check" ensures a current blog exists:

```
var group = DefaultViewModel["Group"] as BlogGroup;
if (group == null)
{
    return;
}
```

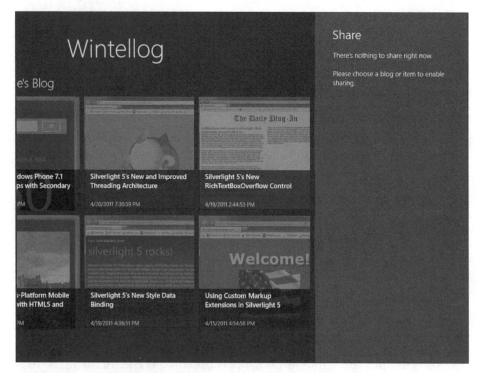

FIGURE 8.6: A failed share attempt with a custom message.

Next, a title and description are supplied along with the URL:

```
dataRequestedEventArgs.Request.Data.Properties.Title = group.Title;
dataRequestedEventArgs.Request.Data.SetUri(group.RssUri);
dataRequestedEventArgs.Request.Data.Properties.Description =
    "Wintellog RSS feed.";
```

The `ItemDetailPage` contains more complex logic for sharing. If the user simply invokes the **Share** charm without selecting any text, the application will provide a link to the blog post along with the entire contents:

```
dataRequestedEventArgs.Request.Data.SetText(item.Description);
```

If an image exists for the blog post, the image itself is packaged as a bitmap:

```
if (item.DefaultImageUri != null)
{
    dataRequestedEventArgs.Request.Data.SetBitmap(
```

```
        RandomAccessStreamReference
            .CreateFromUri(item.DefaultImageUri));
}
```

The information for the blog post is also packaged using the custom data format.

Custom Data

Custom data enables you to package data based on a well-known schema like one provided at http://schema.org/ or your own. A schema is provided for blog posts at http://schema.org/BlogPosting, so any application that recognizes that schema can parse the information that is shared.

Custom data is typically stored in a JSON format. Due to limitations in the built-in `DataContractJsonSerializer` class (it does not provide a standardized format and requires attributes to successfully serialize an instance), I chose to use the popular open source Json.NET serializer by James Newton-King. You can read about it at http://james.newtonking.com/projects/json-net.aspx.

The library is packaged using NuGet (http://nuget.org), so installing it is as simple as opening the package manager (**Tools→Library Package Manager→Package Manager Console**) and typing the following (note the package name is case sensitive):

```
install-package Newtonsoft.Json
```

This automatically pulls down all necessary files and inserts a reference into the current project. This has already been done for you in the sample application. With the Json.NET library, I can create an anonymous type to hold the blog information and serialize it to JSON with a single line of code, as shown in Listing 8.4.

LISTING 8.4: **Serializing a Dynamic Type with Json.NET**

```
private static async Task<string> CustomData(BlogItem item)
{
    var schema = new
        {
            type = "http://shema.org/BlogPosting",
            properties = new
                {
```

```
                        description = string.Format(
                        "Blog post from {0}.",
                        item.Group.Title),
                        image = item.DefaultImageUri,
                        name = item.Title,
                        url = item.PageUri,
                        audience = "Windows 8 Developers",
                        datePublished = item.PostDate,
                        headline = item.Title,
                        articleBody = item.Description
                   }
           };
      return await JsonConvert.SerializeObjectAsync(schema);
}
```

To package the custom data, the SetData method is called and passed the schema and the JSON content:

```
var data = await CustomData(item);
dataRequestedEventArgs.Request.Data.SetData(
    "http://schema.org/BlogPosting", data);
```

There are hundreds of existing schemas available for sharing rich data and content between applications. If you want to provide your own schema, you simply need to provide a unique URL that describes the schema format and then package the data using that schema. Any application that is aware of your schema can process the data by checking the schema type and handling the resulting data. You will learn how to receive and process shared data later in this chapter.

Text Selection

What if the user only desires to share a small excerpt from the blog post? Text selection is built into the existing text-based XAML controls. The content of the blog posts are hosted in a RichTextBlock control. The control exposes a SelectionChanged event:

```
<RichTextBlock x:Name="richTextBlock" Width="560"
    Style="{StaticResource ItemRichTextStyle}"
    SelectionChanged="RichTextBlock_SelectionChanged_1">
```

Whenever this event fires, the selected text is saved to a local variable:

```
private void RichTextBlock_SelectionChanged_1(object sender,
    RoutedEventArgs e)
{
    var richTextControl = sender as RichTextBlock;
    _selection = richTextControl != null ?
        richTextControl.SelectedText : string.Empty;
}
```

When the **Share** charm is invoked and a selection exists, it is provided like this:

```
dataRequestedEventArgs.Request.Data.Properties.Title =
    string.Format("Excerpt from {0}", item.Title);
dataRequestedEventArgs.Request.Data.Properties.Description =
    string.Format("An excerpt from the {0} blog at {1}.",
    item.Group.Title, item.PageUri);
dataRequestedEventArgs.Request.Data.SetText(
    string.Format("{0}\r\n\r\n{1}", _selection, item.Group.RssUri));
```

Figure 8.7 shows the result of selecting a single sentence from a blog post and then sharing it to the sample application referred to earlier in this chapter.

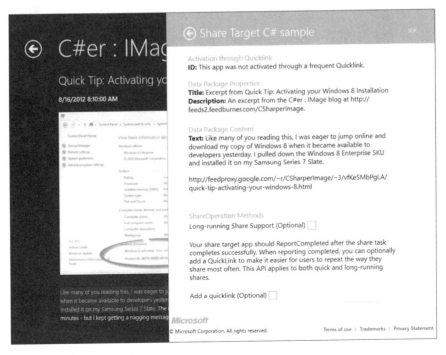

FIGURE 8.7: Sharing a simple excerpt

The decision to include the URL of the original post in the text instead of the package itself is an example of targeting the share for a specific purpose. It is the excerpt that is the focus when text is selected, not the source page. Sharing the source URL in the main package may cause other applications to pull the full page and lose the intent of simply sharing an excerpt. Therefore, the only content provided is in the text portion of the data package.

Receiving Content as a Share Target

The flipside to sharing is receiving content. The sample application referred to earlier in this chapter provides several examples of consuming shared content. To add support as a **Share Target**, simply right-click the project in the Solution Explorer, choose **Add→New Item,** and then select the **Share Target Contract** option. An example of this is shown in Figure 8.8.

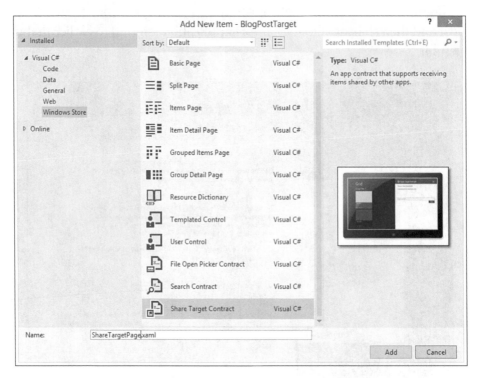

FIGURE 8.8: Adding the Share Target contract to your application

The template will perform several tasks. It will add a page that acts as the target for the share. You use this page to prompt the user for any necessary information needed to complete the sharing operation. For example, if you have the Puzzle Touch application installed (you can obtain this free application from the **Windows Store**) and you share an image, you will be prompted to pick the size and difficulty of the puzzle. This is shown in Figure 8.9.

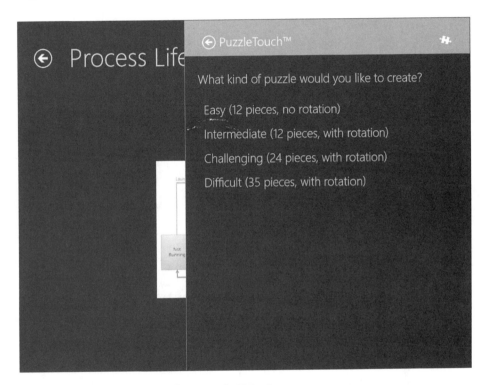

FIGURE 8.9: **Share prompt for Puzzle Touch**

The template will also update the manifest for your application. It adds a **Share Target** declaration and by default will support the text and uri data formats. It will display the title and description, prompt the user for a comment, and provide a button to complete the **Share** operation. You can see the result of this in Figure 8.10.

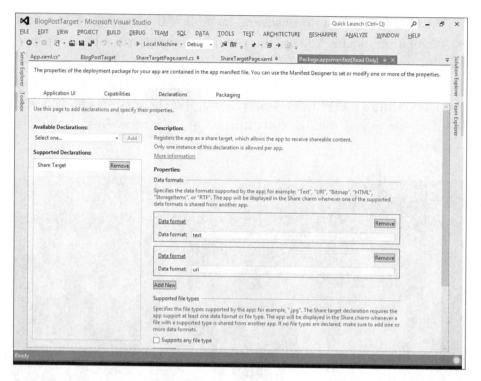

FIGURE 8.10: **The Share Target declarations**

The BlogPostTarget application for Chapter 8 demonstrates how to handle the receipt of custom data. When the **Share** operation begins, the application is activated from the **Share Target** contract. The code to handle this is automatically added to the App class by the template:

```
protected override void OnShareTargetActivated(
    ShareTargetActivatedEventArgs args)
{
    var shareTargetPage = new ShareTargetPage();
    shareTargetPage.Activate(args);
}
```

The Activate method on the ShareTargetPage control loads information from the data package. Listing 8.5 shows the default code to obtain various properties and set them for data-binding.

LISTING 8.5: Boilerplate Code to Load the Contents of a Share Operation

```
_shareOperation = args.ShareOperation;
DataPackagePropertySetView shareProperties =
    _shareOperation.Data.Properties;
var thumbnailImage = new BitmapImage();
DefaultViewModel["Title"] = shareProperties.Title;
DefaultViewModel["Description"] = shareProperties.Description;
DefaultViewModel["Image"] = thumbnailImage;
DefaultViewModel["Sharing"] = false;
DefaultViewModel["ShowImage"] = false;
DefaultViewModel["Comment"] = String.Empty;
DefaultViewModel["SupportsComment"] = true;
Window.Current.Content = this;
Window.Current.Activate();
if (shareProperties.Thumbnail != null)
{
    var stream = await shareProperties.Thumbnail.OpenReadAsync();
    thumbnailImage.SetSource(stream);
    DefaultViewModel["ShowImage"] = true;
}
```

To receive the custom data format that is shared by the Wintellog3 application, the code in **BlogPostTarget** checks to see if the data format exists in the package, using the same schema identifier that was used to save the data:

```
const string BLOG_POST = "http://schema.org/BlogPosting";
if (!_shareOperation.Data.Contains(BLOG_POST)) return;
```

If the format exists, the data is extracted and checked to ensure it is not empty:

```
var data = await _shareOperation.Data.GetDataAsync(BLOG_POST);
if (data == null) return;
```

Finally, the data is deserialized to the original format and saved. The same tool that was used to serialize the data (Json.NET) is used to perform the reverse operation. The example uses an anonymous type, so a template is passed to Json.NET for it to use. The template mirrors the data that is saved in the Wintellog3 application. Listing 8.6 shows the steps involved.

LISTING 8.6: **Loading Custom Data from the Share Operation**

```
DefaultViewModel["ShowBlog"] = true;
DefaultViewModel["BlogPost"] = Newtonsoft.Json.JsonConvert
    .DeserializeAnonymousType((string) data,
    new
    {
        type = "http://shema.org/BlogPosting",
        properties = new
        {
            description = string.Empty,
            image = new Uri("http://schema.org/"),
            name = string.Empty,
            url = new Uri("http://schema.org/"),
            audience = "Windows 8 Developers",
            datePublished = DateTime.Now,
            headline = string.Empty,
            articleBody = string.Empty
        }
    });
```

When the custom blog post information has been extracted, data-binding is used to display it to the end user. Listing 8.7 shows the XAML used to provide a clickable title (tapping the title will open the blog post in the default browser, typically Internet Explorer) and a scrollable section with the article content.

LISTING 8.7: **XAML to Show the Blog Post**

```
<StackPanel Visibility="{Binding ShowBlog,
➥Converter={StaticResource BooleanToVisibilityConverter}}"
        Orientation="Vertical">
    <HyperlinkButton NavigateUri="{Binding BlogPost.properties.url}"
        Content="{Binding BlogPost.properties.headline}"/>
    <ScrollViewer Height="200">
        <RichTextBlock Margin="20">
            <Paragraph>
                <Run FontWeight="SemiLight"
                    FontSize="13"
                    Text="{Binding
➥BlogPost.properties.articleBody}"/>
            </Paragraph>
        </RichTextBlock>
    </ScrollViewer>
</StackPanel>
```

You can see the result of a **Share** operation in Figure 8.11. Notice the title and description are displayed, followed by the title as a hyperlink and the content of the article. The application will successfully display this content from any other application that uses the same schema.

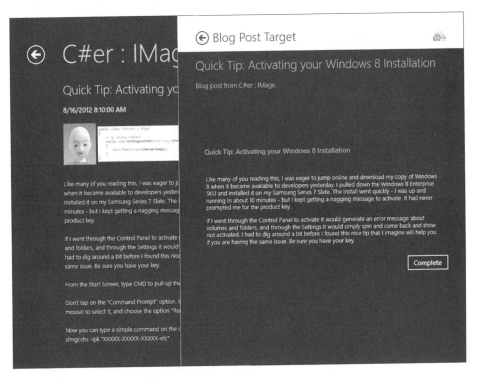

FIGURE 8.11: **Sharing a blog post**

The **Share** contract is a powerful feature that allows sharing of content between applications. Your application can expose information without knowing what other applications are installed. This enables you to support advanced scenarios such as posting content to Twitter or Facebook without having to implement the code yourself. When the user installs an application that supports social media as a **Share Target**, your application is only a few taps away from posting the content online.

Settings

The settings contract provides a consistent way to expose application information and settings. You learned how to wire settings in Chapter 4, *Windows 8 Applications*. That example used a custom control to handle the animation of the panel. In this chapter, you learn how to use an open source toolkit to make creating a settings panel even easier. The toolkit I'm referring to is by Microsoft employee Tim Heuer and is called Callisto:

http://timheuer.com/blog/archive/2012/05/31/introducing-callisto-a-xaml-toolkit-for-metro-apps.aspx

The first step is to install Callisto using NuGet. You learned how to use the Package Manager Console earlier in this chapter. There is also a graphical interface. You can navigate to **Tools→Manage NuGet Packages for Solution** to open the visual dialog. Select **Online** in the left pane and type **Callisto** in the search box. The package will display, and you can simply click the **Install** button to download and reference the package, as shown in Figure 8.12. An alternative location to download the package is from the online source repository at https://github.com/timheuer/callisto.

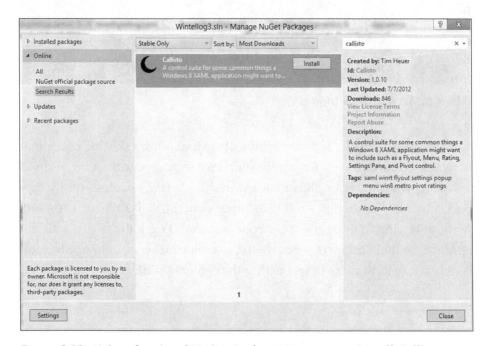

FIGURE 8.12: **Using the visual NuGet Package Manager to install Callisto**

After Callisto is installed, you can quickly and easily add a settings panel. First, a new item is added of type **User Control** called **WintellogSettings**. The XAML contains a simple list showing the name of the application, a hyperlink to access the source code website, and a button to get the URI for the channel (this will now be accessible in settings instead of through an application bar command as it was previously). The XAML for the settings panel is shown in Listing 8.8.

LISTING 8.8: Simple XAML for the Settings Panel

```
<Grid Style="{StaticResource LayoutRootStyle}">
    <StackPanel Orientation="Vertical">
        <TextBlock Style="{StaticResource BodyTextStyle}"
                    Text="Wintellog by Jeremy Likness"
                    TextWrapping="Wrap"/>
        <HyperlinkButton
            NavigateUri="http://windows8applications.codeplex.com/"
            Content="Click to Access Source Code"/>
        <Button Content="Tap to Copy Channel URI"
                Click="Button_Click_1"/>
    </StackPanel>
</Grid>
```

The code-behind will handle the button click to obtain the channel URI and display it as shown in Listing 8.9.

LISTING 8.9: Code to Display the Channel URI

```
private async void Button_Click_1(object sender, RoutedEventArgs e)
{
    var message = App.Instance.Channel != null
        ? "The channel has been copied to the clipboard."
        : string.Format("Error: {0}", App.Instance.ChannelError);
    var dataPackage = new DataPackage();
    if (App.Instance.Channel != null)
    {
        dataPackage.SetText(App.Instance.Channel.Uri);
    }
    Clipboard.SetContent(dataPackage);
    var dialog = new MessageDialog(message);
    await dialog.ShowAsync();
}
```

An event handler for CommandsRequested is registered in the App class when the application is first launched:

```
private void RegisterSettings()
{
    var pane = SettingsPane.GetForCurrentView();
    pane.CommandsRequested += Pane_CommandsRequested;
}
```

The event handler registers a menu item called "**About**":

```
void Pane_CommandsRequested(SettingsPane sender,
    SettingsPaneCommandsRequestedEventArgs args)
{
    var aboutCommand = new SettingsCommand("About", "About",
        SettingsHandler);
    args.Request.ApplicationCommands.Add(aboutCommand);
}
```

Finally, the handler itself uses the Callisto SettingsFlyout class to show the panel. The code is shown in Listing 8.10.

LISTING 8.10: **Using the SettingsFlyout Class from Callisto**

```
private SettingsFlyout _flyout;
private void SettingsHandler(IUICommand command)
{
    _flyout = new SettingsFlyout
        {
            HeaderText = "About",
            Content = new WintellogSettings(),
            IsOpen = true
        };
    _flyout.Closed += (o, e) => _flyout = null;
}
```

Notice how using the special control is as simple as specifying a header, assigning the content (in this case, a user control), and setting it to open. The code also clears any references to the control once the settings panel is dismissed. The result of accessing the new about page from the **Settings** charm is shown in Figure 8.13.

This simple example introduced a hyperlink and button, but you can use the same approach to capture multiple settings for your application. Simply build the user interface for the settings that are available and then persist them using the methods you learned in Chapter 6, *Data*.

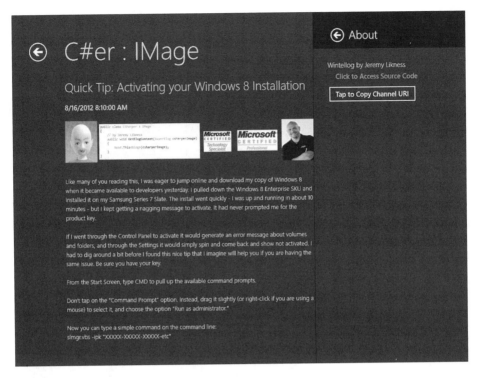

FIGURE 8.13: The "About" settings panel

Summary

In this chapter, you learned how to give your application some charm by using the built-in Windows 8 contracts. Contracts provide a consistent, standardized way for applications to interact with each other and the Windows 8 platform. You can provide integrated search, share rich text, images, and other data and provide a consistent experience to the end user for managing applications settings.

In the next chapter, *MVVM and Testing*, you will learn how to better organize your code using the MVVM pattern. One of the many benefits of this pattern is improved testing capabilities. I will explain why testing is important and show you how to build automated unit tests for Windows 8 applications. You will learn how MVVM can help you build applications using other technologies like WPF and Silverlight that can share code with your Windows 8 applications.

9
MVVM and Testing

MVVM IS THE ABBREVIATION FOR A USER INTERFACE DESIGN PATTERN called Model-View-View Model. This is a pattern (a reusable solution to a commonly occurring problem) that was introduced many years ago for Windows Presentation Foundation (WPF) development and was later adopted by Silverlight, web-based applications like knockout.js, Windows Phone, Xbox, and Windows 8 apps. The central idea behind MVVM is a separation of UI implementation from presentation and business logic that uses data-binding to connect the layers. This results in a number of benefits including making it easier to work on the design (look and feel) aspects of applications and to apply testing. You can use the Portable Class Library (PCL) with the MVVM pattern to write components and tests that are shared between WPF, Silverlight, and Windows 8 apps. You learn about the PCL later in this chapter.

You may have already noticed that the Visual Studio 2012 C# with XAML templates provide MVVM out of the box. The `LayoutAwarePage` contains a `DefaultViewModel` dictionary property. Data, including classes that implement property change notification, is bound to the dictionary and then referenced from code. MVVM is preferred for Windows 8 applications because it takes advantage of the data-binding features in XAML you learned about in Chapter 3, *Extensible Application Markup Language (XAML)*. Another advantage of the MVVM pattern is that it helps facilitate testing.

Testing is one of those topics that many developers seem to have a love/hate relationship with. In this chapter, I hope to show you that unit tests done correctly can save significant time during the development process and increase the maintainability and extensibility of the application. MVVM provides a good foundation to work from for tests because well-defined, decoupled code is also code that is easy to write tests for.

The proper use of MVVM with testing makes it easier to build applications, especially when you have larger teams or separate teams of designers and developers. The ability to incorporate unit tests also helps reduce the rate of customer-initiated incidents because bugs are caught earlier in the process. Unit tests make it easier to extend and refactor applications, and the MVVM pattern itself allows for what I call *refactoring isolation* or the ability to make modifications to areas of the application without having to visit and update every module as a side effect of changes.

UI Design Patterns

User interface (UI) design patterns are reusable solutions that have evolved to solve the problem of maintaining the presentation layer of your application independently of the underlying business logic, services, and data. Some of the problems being solved include the following:

- **Fluidity of the user interface**—Often there can be significant changes to look, feel, and interaction over time. A well-defined and properly implemented UI design pattern can help insulate those changes to minimize impact on the core business logic and data concerns. This is evident in the existing templates that can expose data in various views (snapped, landscape, and portrait) without having to change the underlying classes that provide the data.

- **Parallel development and design**—Often the design team is separate from the development team, with different skillsets and involving multiple designers. UI design patterns can maximize the efficiency of this workflow by providing the separation necessary to allow the developers and designers to work in parallel with minimal conflicts. Design-time data allows designers to work directly with the

XAML to create the desired look and feel without having to understand or interact directly with the underlying logic.

- **Decoupling of presentation logic**—There are common patterns in the presentation layer, such as providing a list of items and allowing the user to select a single item, that can be solved in multiple ways (combo box, grid, list box, and so on). UI design patterns help decouple data elements from the presentation implementation so the core functionality can remain the same regardless of how the pattern is presented.

- **View-logic testing**—Complex view logic is often the domain of developers. Testing the logic is made easier by not requiring a full-blown UI. An example is dependent or cascading lists: Selecting an item in the first list determines the content of the second list. Ideally, you should be able to implement this behavior and test it without having to draw a corresponding combo box control and process click events.

In 2005, a developer named John Gossman working on WPF—which at the time was code-named *Avalon*—published a blog post that would ultimately introduce the MVVM pattern to the world (http://blogs.msdn.com/b/johngossman/archive/2005/10/08/478683.aspx). In his post, he described "a variation of Model/View/Controller (MVC) that is tailored for modern UI development platforms where the View is the responsibility of a designer rather than a classic developer."

The introduction to his post provides valuable insight into one of the original motivations for the pattern: the designer/developer workflow. His post further explains that the view is defined declaratively (a reference to XAML) and is responsible for inputs, keyboard shortcuts, visual elements, and more. The view model is responsible for tasks that are too specific for the general model to handle (such as complex UI operations), for maintaining the view state, and for projecting the model to the view, especially when the model contains data types that won't map directly to controls.

MVVM uses data-binding and the Visual State Manager (VSM) to communicate between the UI implementation and your business and presentation logic. Instead of raising events, the view drives the view model through data-binding—whether it is by updating a value that in turn synchronizes to a property on the view model or by mapping an event to a command that fires on the view model. Presentation logic exists in the view model as code and takes the form of behaviors, triggers, visual states, and value converters in the view.

In applications based on the built-in Visual Studio 2012 templates, the LayoutAwarePage automatically detects changes to the view state (for example, going into snapped view or changing the orientation from portrait to landscape). The InvalidateVisualState method uses the VSM to set the new visual state:

```
string visualState = DetermineVisualState(ApplicationView.Value);
foreach (var layoutAwareControl in this._layoutAwareControls)
{
    VisualStateManager.GoToState(layoutAwareControl,
        visualState, false);
}
```

In XAML, the VSM enables you to define the appropriate templates for the various states. You've learned how to provide a snapped view or how to switch from using the GridView control to a ListView control when the orientation changes. The design is defined in the XAML independently of the underlying code, creating a clean separation of concerns.

You can see what this looks like for the Wintellog project in Figure 9.1. Note the LayoutAwarePage facilitates the view model dictionary, handles changes with the VSM, and is the base class that the XAML for the view is derived from. The BlogDataSource class coordinates with the application to gather data and then exposes this via the view model dictionary, starting with the GroupList property.

Like other patterns, MVVM is a solution to common problems. When implemented correctly, it should make the job of building your Windows 8 application easier. Unfortunately, the pattern can be abused and end up slowing down projects and making them more complex than necessary. I've built dozens of large enterprise applications using the MVVM pattern and am glad that Microsoft decided to make the pattern a part of their built-in templates for Windows 8 apps. The first use of MVVM in Visual Studio dates even earlier to the Panorama templates used for Windows

Phone development. Although the pattern has been used for years, there are many lingering misconceptions. Table 9.1 lists some of these misconceptions and the truth that addresses them.

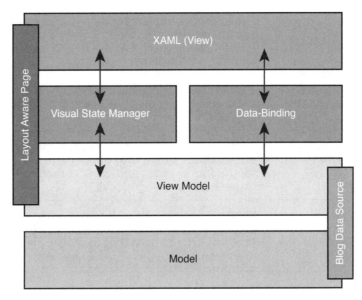

FIGURE 9.1: The MVVM pattern used by the Wintellog application

TABLE 9.1: Common MVVM Misconceptions

Misconception	Truth
MVVM is extremely complex.	MVVM can be incredibly simple when implemented correctly.
Code-behind isn't allowed in MVVM.	Code-behind is simply an extension of the declarative XAML for the view. The view is responsible for managing the user interface, including user inputs, and there is no reason the code-behind cannot deal with events and interactions.
MVVM is hard to implement.	Many frameworks exist (for example, MVVM Light and Caliburn.Micro) that can enable you to have your project up and running in minutes, including the built-in Visual Studio 2012 templates for C# with XAML.

MVVM eliminates the need for value converters.	Value converters are reusable, testable pieces of code that can map data from the model to the view, and there is no reason to eliminate them when using the MVVM pattern.
MVVM reduces the performance of the application.	The improper implementation of any pattern can create performance issues. Proper use of MVVM facilitates unit tests that can help tweak and improve performance.
MVVM is only good for very large projects.	A good MVVM framework coupled with solid understanding is just as suitable for small projects as it is big ones.
MVVM is about commands and messaging systems.	MVVM simply specifies the responsibilities of various modules within the code. Commands, messaging frameworks, and other constructs are just helpers and building blocks.
MVVM is hard to understand.	MVVM is no more difficult to understand than data-binding and the Visual State Manager because it really is just a pattern that describes how best to use these features.

In the rest of this chapter, you learn about the various parts of MVVM and how to apply it with a special focus on testing. If you've read the previous chapters in this book and followed the examples, you already have an understanding of MVVM because you've created specific classes that implement property-change notification to facilitate data-binding. Those classes can actually be thought of as your view models. You also learn more about view models later in this chapter.

Contrary to the misconceptions about MVVM, there are many advantages the pattern provides above and beyond the separation of design from development. In my experience, these are the top ten benefits you may receive by using MVVM in your applications:

1. **A clean separation of concerns (decoupling)**—MVVM follows best practices for software architecture.

2. **Designer/developer workflow**—MVVM enables parallel development and design by multiple team members working on the same project through its support of design-time data.

3. **Unit testing**—You learn more about testing later in this chapter.

4. **Use of data-binding**—MVVM takes direct advantage of the rich and powerful data-binding system in XAML for Windows 8 apps, which also allows for design-time data.

5. **Improved code reuse**—View models can be used to power multiple views, and various helpers and scaffolding can be reused throughout your project and across various products in your organization, even in different technologies including WPF and Silverlight.

6. **Modularity**—MVVM encourages a modular design that makes it easy to modify parts of the application independently of each other.

7. **Refactoring containment**—Through the clean separation of concerns, MVVM minimizes the impact to other areas of the application from refactoring.

8. **Extensibility**—A well-designed MVVM framework makes it easy to extend the application by adding new screens and modules.

9. **Tools support**—Various tools, such as Expression Blend and the designer, are built into Visual Studio that can take direct advantage of MVVM.

10. **Pattern vocabulary**.

The final item, pattern vocabulary, requires some additional explanation. When you are learning how to read, there is a strong correlation between the size of your vocabulary and your ability to comprehend what you are reading. This should not be surprising because vocabulary provides the building blocks for the text you are trying to comprehend, and not understanding those blocks can lead to confusing conclusions and misinterpretations of the text. Although there is a strong correlation, vocabulary certainly doesn't guarantee comprehension because you must be able to piece the words together and derive their meaning as a whole.

Developing software is an exercise that also involves a vocabulary. You start with the vocabulary of the language you are developing in. Programs have their own syntax and grammar, and comprehension relies on your ability to interpret the keywords correctly and understand them in context.

Patterns provide a higher-level vocabulary that can describe entire subroutines and components within the system. As with vocabulary, knowing a pattern isn't the same thing as comprehending how it best fits into a software application (or whether it belongs at all).

The more you are able to understand and integrate patterns, the more you will be able to build your vocabulary and better comprehend complex software systems. I've found the developers who are involved in the most successful projects and who have tackled the most complex systems also tend to have a strong pattern vocabulary. They are not only aware of many patterns that exist in software development, but also understand when and where they make sense.

I believe MVVM is popular because it has been so successful at providing the benefits listed earlier when implemented correctly. MVVM is an important pattern to learn and understand for Windows 8 applications especially because it is the default pattern provided by the built-in C# with XAML templates. Like all patterns, it is a tool and must be used for the right job. In the next few sections, I cover MVVM in more detail to help you learn the pattern and determine how to take advantage of it in your applications. Let's start by examining the components that make up MVVM.

The Model

The model is often confused with a "data model," which is far too specific. A better definition is the application's model of the world. It is the model that encompasses everything that must happen to solve the business problem *without* defining a specific user interface or presentation of data. Some like to call this the *domain model*, but a domain model is a conceptual representation, whereas the *model* in MVVM is an actual implementation.

To provide a simple example, a banking system might contain customers and accounts. The representations of customers and accounts are part of the model. The model describes how they are related: A customer has one or many accounts. It describes state (an account is open or closed) and provides behaviors (an account accrues interest). Making the model work requires implementations of classes with properties; a database to store the information; and loads of APIs to fetch data, transfer it, and apply various algorithms.

When built correctly, the model should expose only the parts needed by the application. For example, the presentation layer shouldn't have to worry about how the data is stored (is it in a database or in an XML file?) or how the data is retrieved (was it parsed and passed as a binary object over a TCP/IP socket or sent over a REST service?). A model that is too open will create unnecessary dependencies and overcomplicate the code.

The model for the Wintellog application encompasses the blogs and blog posts as well as the network and syndication APIs used to retrieve them. It includes the WinRT APIs used to send tiles and notifications. The code used to store the items in cache and retrieve them is also part of the model. All of these components work together to deliver the end user experience, without interacting directly with the user. When a blog item is displayed within the application, it's not the physical page on the Web that is shown, but a data bound representation of the `BlogItem` entity.

Your main goals should be to write flexible, extensible, testable, and maintainable code. When the model of your application follows these principles, the MVVM pattern can easily connect to the interfaces and classes that are needed without creating dependencies on parts of the system that have nothing to do with presentation logic. The model is the "application model" of the real world, but at some point that model must be presented to the end user. This is done through output, which in the case of Windows 8 applications is a rich and powerful user interface (UI). The screen that the user is presented with is referred to as the *view*.

The View

The view in Windows 8 apps is what interacts with the user. The view itself is the user interface. The user interface is almost always represented using the declarative XAML markup. The XAML participates in the dependency property system, and the view is able to present information to the user as well as respond to user inputs. Table 9.2 shows common parts of the views and their function.

TABLE 9.2: The View in MVVM

Component	Description
XAML	Declarative markup to provide layout, controls, and other components that make up a screen
Value converters	Special classes used to transform data to a user element type and back
Data templates	Templates that map data elements to controls
Visual state groups	Named states that impact the properties of various elements to provide a physical state based on the logical states of controls
Storyboards	Animations and transitions
Behaviors	Reusable algorithms that can be applied to various controls, typically by using attached properties
Triggers	Algorithms that can be applied to controls and invoked based on configured events, usually handled through attached properties
Code-behind	Extensions of the XAML markup to perform additional UI-specific tasks

It should be obvious from Table 9.2 that the view is not completely ignorant of presentation logic. Commands map controls to actions on the view model, and data-binding declarations require knowledge of the structure of the underlying data to bind to. Animations, visual states, templates, behaviors, and triggers all represent various components of business logic that relate to the view.

What may not be as obvious is that all of these components are stateless with regard to the model of the application. Storyboards maintain a state (started, stopped, playing, and so on), and visual state groups maintain a state, but all of these states are related to the UI. Behaviors and triggers also operate based on events or act on generic controls and should not be designed with dependencies on the underlying data and business logic. Even code-behind is typically written to facilitate certain aspects of the UI. More complex code should go somewhere else—not because there is a rule that code-behind is not allowed, but because more complicated algorithms

need to be tested, and having a separate and decoupled class makes it easier to test without having to wire up a full UI.

So where does the bulk of presentation logic go, and what is responsible
for maintaining the business state of the application? This state includes the
data that is being presented as well as the status of various commands and
processes that both drive the UI and respond to user inputs. The answer
is the essence of the MVVM pattern and the one element that makes it
unique: the view model.

The View Model

The *view model* is what makes MVVM unique. It is simply a class that holds
the responsibility of coordinating the interaction between the view and the
model. The view model is where the bulk of the presentation logic should
reside. In my opinion, a well-written view model can be tested without
creating any views and has three main methods for communication with
the view:

- Data-binding
- Visual states
- Commands and/or method calls

With this definition in mind, you've already created several view models. The BlogDataSource class exposes the GroupList, which in turn contains
instances of BlogGroup and BlogItem. View models typically implement the
property-change notification interface. They often include references to
APIs that enable the exchange of data and communication with the model.
The use of interfaces makes it easier to write portable code that can be
reused across your organization.

Those are all of the components of MVVM. The key to MVVM is the
view model, or a class that supports property change notification so that it
can participate in data-binding. A view model might be a simple domain
object like an instance of a BlogItem, or it may be a class that exposes collections, commands, and interacts with other interfaces more like the
BlogDataSource. Decoupling the view model from the UI enables not only
testing, but also code reuse. Combined with the Portable Class Library

(PCL), you can effectively write business logic that is shared between various platforms.

The Portable Class Library

The Portable Class Library (PCL) is a special project type in Visual Studio 2012 that enables you to write assemblies that work on multiple .NET platforms. It is the ideal way to create shared components with business logic that you can reuse in your desktop and Windows 8 applications. An assembly built with the PCL project template can run on those platforms without being recompiled.

The PCL works by providing a targeted subset of APIs that are common to all platforms. When you create a PCL project, you are prompted to choose the frameworks you would like your code to run on, as shown in Figure 9.2.

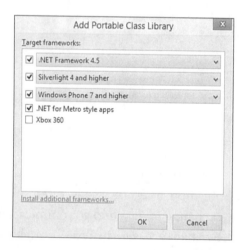

FIGURE 9.2: Choosing target frameworks for the Portable Class Library

The amount of portable code available will depend on how old the frameworks are that you target, the number of frameworks you target, and type of the target frameworks. For example, a project that targets Xbox will have far fewer APIs available than a project that targets Silverlight.

Likewise, the .NET Framework 4.0 will impose more limitations than a project that targets the .NET Framework 4.5. To see what APIs are available when you make a selection, expand the **References** for your project in the Solution Explorer. Right-click and choose **Properties**, and you will see a Path property. Copy the path and open it in Windows Explorer.

Figure 9.3 shows the folder available when you accept all of the defaults. Each combination of frameworks results in a new profile that contains the set of APIs that will work across those platforms. The reference actually uses a new feature known as Extension SDKs that allow references to include multiple files and configuration as opposed to a single project or assembly. You can read more about Extension SDKs online at http://msdn.microsoft.com/en-us/library/hh768146(v=vs.110).aspx.

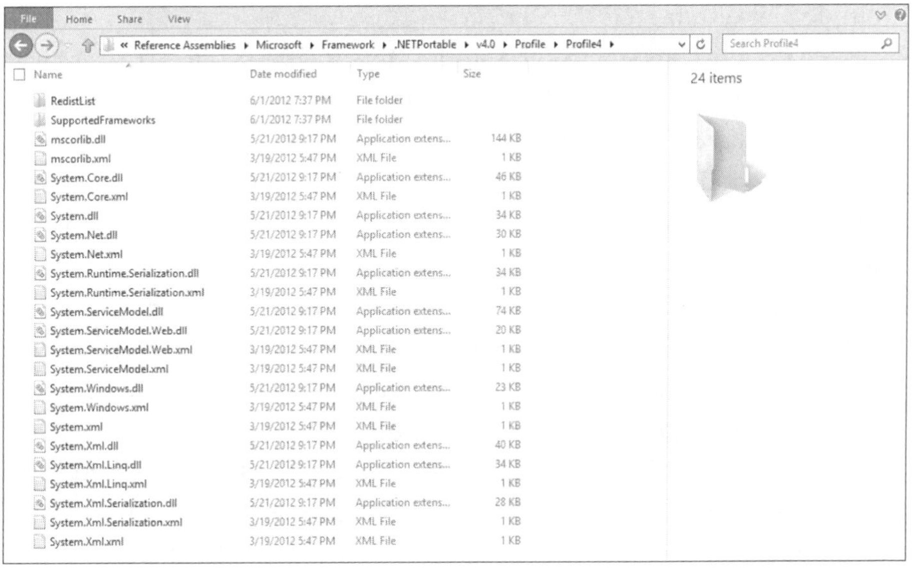

FIGURE 9.3: A Portable Class Library profile

As you can see, the example profile supports several libraries. In addition to core services, there is support for networking, serialization, and web services, as well as XML including LINQ. For any of the referenced assemblies, you can use the **ILDASM.exe** tool to inspect the APIs that are available. The assemblies are simply copies of the .NET Framework assemblies that are supported by the particular profile.

The **WintellogMvvm** project for Chapter 9 has been refactored to take advantage of the Portable Class Library. The **PortableWintellog** project was created to support both the .NET Framework 4.5 and Windows 8 applications. The project provides a number of classes and interfaces that can be shared without modification between Windows 8 and desktop apps.

The Contracts folder contains interfaces that are shared across the platforms. PCL projects are the perfect place to define interfaces and contracts that don't take strong dependencies on non-portable APIs. These interfaces can help you separate logic that is platform-specific from other logic through a concept called *Inversion of Control* or IoC for short. IoC helps you build classes that are easier to test and are more likely to be shared across multiple platform targets.

In the previous versions of the application, the StorageUtility class was a static class used to write and read from the local cache for the application. The BlogDataSource class controlled access to the StorageUtility. In a sense, it took on an additional responsibility to interface with the static methods exposed by the class. Although this was a straightforward way to access storage, it also created a strong dependency or coupling between the data source and the implementation of the storage logic. This prevented the BlogDataSource class from being shared by any environment other than the Windows 8 platform. It also made it tough to test the class because any test would require that appropriate storage exists.

In the PortableWintellog project, the control has been inverted. This simply means the BlogDataSource class no longer has the responsibility of determining how storage works. Instead, it works with the IStorageUtility interface. The interface provides the method signatures to save and restore items but does not impose any type of implementation. This makes the BlogDataSource more loosely coupled because it no longer has a direct dependency on the storage implementation.

There are numerous advantages to this approach. First, it is possible (and easy) to test the storage logic in the BlogDataSource class without relying on the presence of storage. You can easily create a helper class (as you see later in this chapter) to emulate storage for the purpose of testing. Second, you can implement the appropriate storage based on the target environment. The WintellogMvvm project contains an implementation for Windows 8 apps. The **WintellogWpf** project, a desktop app based on WPF, contains an implementation for desktop applications. Even though the implementations are different, the interface allows the same BlogDataSource class to be shared between both versions of the application.

Take a look at the WintellogWpf project. It references the portable class library and reuses all of the logic contained within the BlogDataSource class. This includes the logic to fetch individual blogs and items from the list, the interaction with the cache, and even some online functions. The HttpClient is shared between both desktop and Windows 8 applications, so it is used consistently to load the page for a post to parse related images.

The StorageUtility implementation uses the local file system to store the cache instead of isolated storage. An internal helper method computes a path to the application folder on the system:

```
private static string GetRootPath()
{
    return Path.Combine(
        Environment.GetFolderPath(
        Environment.SpecialFolder.LocalApplicationData),
        "Wintellog");
}
```

Here is the code to list files. It checks to see if the directory exists before querying for the file list. The code is wrapped in a Task to execute asynchronously:

```
var directory = Path.Combine(GetRootPath(), folderName);
return
    Directory.Exists(directory)
        ? Directory.GetFiles(directory)
        : new string[0];
```

Remember the earlier discussion about Inversion of Control? The application controls dependencies by injecting them at the start. In the

App.xaml.cs file, you'll find the following snippets that map the portable contracts to WPF-specific implementations:

```
Ioc = new TinyIoc();
Ioc.Register<IStorageUtility>(ioc => new StorageUtility());
Ioc.Register<IApplicationContext>(ioc => new ApplicationContext());
Ioc.Register<IDialog>(ioc => new WpfDialog());
Ioc.Register<ISyndicationHelper>(ioc => new SyndicationHelper());
```

After the dependencies are resolved, the IoC utility is used to inject them into the BlogDataSource class through its constructor:

```
Ioc.Register(ioc => new BlogDataSource(
    ioc.Resolve<IStorageUtility>(),
    ioc.Resolve<IApplicationContext>(),
    ioc.Resolve<IDialog>(),
    ioc.Resolve<ISyndicationHelper>()));
```

The technique of having an external helper inject the dependencies is referred to as Dependency Injection (DI) and is a common method for handling IoC. The small class for IoC included with the sample application only scratches the surface of scenarios available for IoC. There are many mature frameworks available, including one that I've used for several years, the Managed Extensibility Framework (MEF), that is available for use in Windows 8 through a NuGet package:

http://nuget.org/packages/Microsoft.Composition/

With all of the logic encapsulated in the various shared and local classes, it was straightforward to create some XAML in the **MainPage.xaml** for the blog. The functionality is far more basic than in the Windows 8 application, but it completely reuses the existing class. In fact, it demonstrates how you can have a significantly different look and feel while using the same business logic in your core classes, as evidenced by the screenshot in Figure 9.4.

Sharing the code between platforms and applications is powerful, but there is an even bigger benefit to using the Portable Class Library for common code: testing. With this approach, you'll only have to test the core components once even though they might be used by multiple applications. You might be asking, "What is the point of software testing?"

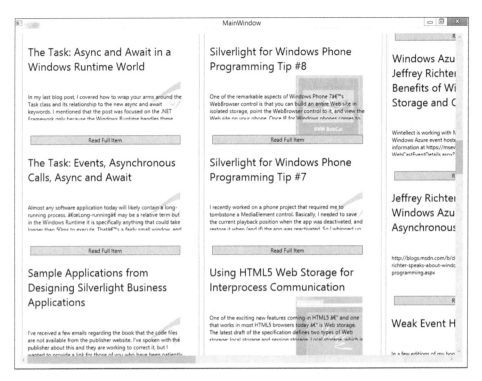

FIGURE 9.4: The WPF version of the application

Why Test?

The first question I'm often asked when I speak about testing is, "Why test?"

I've been writing enterprise software for well over a decade, so I tend to take testing for granted. In reality, however, it is a very valid question and one that is often asked when companies are allocating resources and building their teams. "If the product is well-written, does it really require tests?" "I understand we need to test it, but isn't that the responsibility of the developer?" "Unit tests just slow down the process—can't we just have a sales person review the builds when they are pushed out?"

There are dozens of valid reasons to perform testing—I'll share a few of the benefits I've encountered during my career. These are benefits I've seen regardless of the vertical, size of the project, or composition of the team doing it.

Testing Eliminates Assumptions

Developers are biased. There is no escaping the fact that when you set out to build an application, you have a notion of how it should work. When that notion is correct, it is easy to build the software the customer is looking for. That is usually not the case because most developers build for what they expect. You can test the "happy path" through an application all day long and not find a single bug. Turn it over to users, however, and things get ugly fast. They don't know they're not supposed to enter the text into the number field, that the date has to be in a special format, or that it's not fine to close the browser or undock the laptop halfway through a multi-step form.

Invariably the users will find a way to interact with the application that was completely unexpected and that results in errors. As developers, it is our duty to address those scenarios. It's not only about trapping and logging errors in code, but also working with the design team to provide a user interface that makes it clear what the intent is and how to use the software. There is a fine art to pulling this off, and as a visionary chairman liked to tell me, "It takes a lot of technology to create the illusion of simplicity."

The specification for a particular unit or module is often focused on what should happen and some simple data validations. Every step of the process introduces assumptions about layout, appropriate validation, business logic, and validation. Testing, especially testing by a team that is not technical and represents a valid user of the system, helps eliminate those assumptions early in the process so you can produce a higher–quality product.

Testing Kills Bugs at the Source

If someone asked you to help them find a watch he lost five years ago, how would you start? Imagine how many people might have crossed the same spot over time. Storms could have shifted its position. New construction could have paved over the very place it was resting for months, buried under a layer of mud. If that same person asked you to help only five minutes after losing the watch, you'd probably feel a lot more confident about your odds of success.

Bugs are easier to fix when they are found closer to the source. When you isolate a bug inside a specific component, you have a view of the component that makes it easier to comprehend the context the bug was discovered in and take steps to resolve the issue. Bugs that happen as the result of complex modules interacting across third-party boundaries are far more difficult to track down. Bugs that are found in the field are often the most frustrating because it can be difficult if not impossible to obtain the forensic evidence you need to properly troubleshoot the problem in the production environment.

Tests can contribute to finding bugs early in the software development lifecycle. The earlier you find the bug in the process of developing the application, the easier it is to fix. Unit tests ensure components behave as expected at a local level. Integration tests ensure that modules interact appropriately in spite of ongoing changes to underlying code and APIs. Coded UI tests validate the function of the user interface and help flag breaking changes to the application flow that are often side effects of changes to business and validation logic.

Testing Helps Document Code

My favorite open source projects are ones that ship with thousands of lines of well-written unit tests. For me, this is the easiest and fastest way to learn how to interface with a third-party API. The manual may be fine, but it's the tests that provide sample code, multiple examples of ways to call the API, and more importantly, expected conditions that will make things break. There have been a number of projects that I discovered a way of using the component that just wasn't obvious from the documentation but was addressed with a test.

Well-written unit tests with adequate code coverage help document the code and make it easier for developers to consume, maintain, and extend the code base. The unit tests give insight in the breadth and depth of the project. They demonstrate various ways to call the APIs. They show what some expected exception conditions are and how to handle them. They provide a baseline to work from when you are extending a code and serve as a template for additional tests as the code base evolves.

Integration tests and coded UI tests also require a specific script. That script involves knowledge of the system and how it is expected to behave. It is not uncommon for the test cases to be written at the start of the project as part of the specification process. As a developer, I always prefer having explicit and well-thought out test cases because it gives me a standard to measure my deliverables against. A story is fine, and I can write code to a story, but a set of explicit tests is a validation checklist I can use to verify that I wrote the code correctly and understood the story in the business context it was intended.

Testing Makes Extending and Maintaining Applications Easier

This point falls in line with the previous one. I still remember the project early in my career for which I was forced to start writing unit tests when I didn't fully appreciate their value. I gritted my teeth and wrote unit test after unit test while complaining that it was nothing but "busy work" and slowed down my progress. Fortunately, although some of the tests may have been poorly written, our architect provided great guidance, and the majority of the tests served their functions well.

I learned just how well when I was asked to perform a major change to one of the interfaces that would require significant refactoring. In the past, exercises like this would have been like writing code in the dark—I would have slammed in the changes and held my breath, hoping the code would compile, and then stepped through the final product with fingers crossed. I'd have held my breath again when it was pushed to production because that was always when the problem we didn't think of happened and resulted in those fun early morning support calls.

With unit tests in place, things were different. I was able to tweak parts of the interface and then run the unit tests to determine what areas were impacted. Instead of looking at the application as a whole and trying to figure out what broke, I could focus on the unit tests and determine what was required to make each one pass. This resulted in concise, precise, iterative changes that not only cut the time it took to refactor by half, but also left the product far more stable when it was pushed to production after.

Testing Improves Architecture and Design

One side effect of writing tests is that it forces you to think about how components are built and interact. This has the direct and positive side effect of improving both the architecture of the application as well as the approach to design. I witnessed this change personally when we took a large team and shifted from the haphazard "napkin specifications" to a process that included writing solid unit tests. It's not uncommon for developers to throw together classes and APIs only to discover they aren't appropriate and have to be rewritten. Tests help bring to the surface issues with the APIs early in the process so they are mature and tested by the time it is necessary to integrate with other components.

I ran into this early on in my own career. When building complex systems, I would often dive headfirst into a coding marathon and emerge on the other end with thousands of lines of code. The only problem was that I would flip the switch and find some small defect that would take time to discover and even longer to fix. When I started using tests, I began to approach those complex systems as smaller, simpler units. I'd focus entirely on the design, construction, and thorough testing of the component and then move to then next. It took a little more time to create the building blocks for the system, but they would quickly and easily integrate and save time overall due to a lower defect rate when complete.

Testing Makes Better Developers

The same effect tests have on the quality of the code base I believe positively impacts developers. This is another observation from personal experience. The same developers who grumbled at the notion of writing tests at the beginning of the project are often excited to share their modules and show the tests that validate them. The act of spending additional time thinking about components and authoring tests changes the entire approach to software design. Common patterns are quickly and easily discovered and readily applied in other areas where the solution makes sense, and approaches to error handling, API definition and organization of algorithms within code evolves based on the positive feedback of the tests themselves.

Conclusion: Write Those Unit Tests!

Hopefully you've come to the conclusion now that tests are important. Some developers reading this may be surprised it's even a topic of discussion, as there are many shops that include testing as a *de facto* part of the development lifecycle and many that follow full Test-Driven Development. My suggestion if you are new to testing is to take it one step at a time. A great place to start is by adding unit tests to your projects.

Unit Tests

Unit tests are a category of tests known as *white box* tests. The entire software system can be looked at in two ways. The end user sees a "black box" because she is not exposed to the source code, database definitions, and other processes that drive the application. Instead, she is aware of interactions (most often directly through the user interface) that go into a black box and results that come out of that black box. This is the realm of QA and automated UI tests.

White box tests would be better referred to as "clear box" tests because they imply exposure to the inner workings of the system. Unit tests require a fundamental knowledge of what's happening at the source code and stored procedure level. Integration tests require knowledge of the APIs and boundaries between systems. White box tests ensure the internal system is working and is the set of "checks and balances" that keeps the black box functioning correctly.

I've seen many tests that were called unit tests but really weren't. If you loathe running the tests for your project because they require an Internet connection, a specially configured directory, and they take hours to run, you are most likely running some form of integration tests and not a true unit test. Unit tests have common characteristics that are important to understand:

- Unit tests should focus on a specific function of a class. Classes should only have a single responsibility, so if you find you are spending hours writing the unit tests for a class, it's probably a sign that the class should be refactored.

- Unit tests should be completely isolated so they run "no matter what." You shouldn't have to create a special environment for them to run, and they should not have dependencies on classes outside of the one you are testing.

- Unit tests should be short and simple. They should not take too long to execute even when you have many in a project, and it should be extremely clear what the test is doing and what the success or failure conditions are.

- Unit tests should be easy to write. The simplest and most efficient way I've found to write unit tests is while I'm defining the target class. Test-Driven Development (TDD) takes this a step further by having you write the test *first* and then define the class and API to make the test succeed.

You can learn more about test-driven development online at http://www.agiledata.org/essays/tdd.html.

To help you understand unit tests, I've created a few for the Wintellog application. Had this been developed using a full Test-Driven Development cycle, there would literally be hundreds of tests. For the purposes of this chapter, however, I wanted to provide a few specific examples. All of the tests included in the Chapter 9 sample application can be run using the Windows Store Unit Testing Framework.

Windows Store Unit Testing Framework

Visual Studio 2012 has built-in support for writing unit tests. The default test system is known as the MSTest framework. Although Visual Studio 2012 does support plugging in other test frameworks including the popular NUnit (http://nunit.org/), I focus on the features that are available "out of the box" for the Professional-level SKU (unfortunately, unit tests are not available for the free Express version of Visual Studio 2012). This includes a test template for Windows 8 unit tests.

When you add a new Windows 8 style project to your solution, one of the options is to create a Unit Test Library for Windows Store apps. This template will create a project that references the assemblies and SDKs used for testing including MSTestFramework and TestPlatform. The project is similar to a full-blown Windows 8 app and even has its own application manifest. You can see an example of a project created using this technique in the Chapter 9 sample application. The project is named **WintellogTest**.

To run the tests, navigate to **Test→Run...→All Tests** or hold down **Ctrl+R** and then press **A**. The package will be compiled and executed. You should see results similar to what is shown in Figure 9.5.

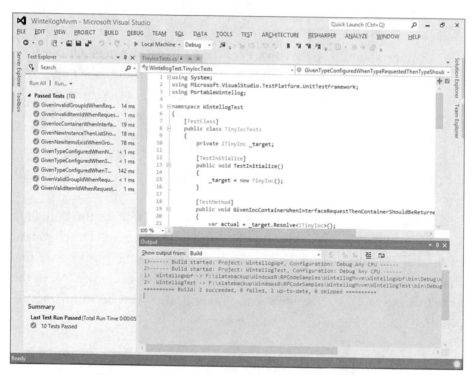

FIGURE 9.5: Unit test results in Visual Studio 2012

The individual tests are listed along with an indicator of whether or not they succeeded and how long they took to run. You can also filter this list by clicking the little drop-down icon next to the search icon. In addition to filtering by result, you can filter by test file name and fully qualified name. Figure 9.6 shows the filter applied for only those tests in the **TinyIocTests.cs** file.

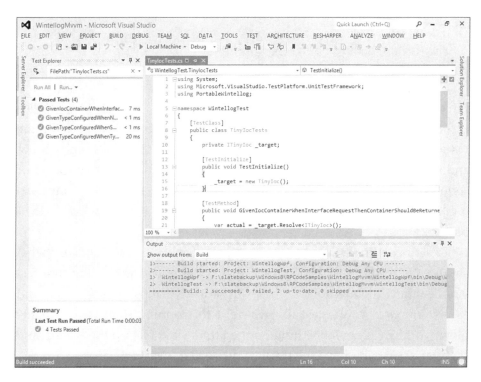

FIGURE 9.6: **Filtering by test file**

Setting up tests is relatively straightforward. You declare a class and tag it with the TestClass attribute, like this:

```
[TestClass]
public class TinyIocTests
```

There are a number of popular conventions for declaring tests. I prefer to have a file per target class type and create a test class with the target class name followed by "Tests." There is usually a specific target for the test that I track:

```
private ITinyIoc _target;
```

For any setup that must run before each individual test, you can declare a method and tag it with the TestInitialize attribute. This example simply spins up a new instance of the IoC helper:

```
[TestInitialize]
public void TestInitialize()
{
    _target = new TinyIoc();
}
```

Finally, tests are declared as methods that are decorated with the TestMethod attribute. There are many different methods for both naming and scoping tests. I try to have targeted tests that focus on one aspect or code block in the target method, but sometimes those will involve supporting tests as well. I like to name tests following the given … when … then pattern:

Given a certain set of pre-conditions, *when* an action is taken, *then* what should the result be? Although this helps name the test, within the test you'll almost always follow three prescriptive steps: arrange, act, and assert. You *arrange* the test to prepare it for running (that is, set up the given), *act* by calling something on the target class (set up the when), and then *assert* that you have the results you need (validate the then).

Let's take a look at a simple test to start with. The IoC container configures itself, so if you request the ITinyIoC interface, it should resolve to the instance of the IoC container you've created. This reads as:

"*Given* the IoC helper has been created, *when* the interface for the IoC helper is requested *then* the helper should return the instance of itself."

The test looks like this:

```
[TestMethod]
public void GivenIocContainerWhenInterfaceRequestThen
➥ContainerShouldBeReturned()
{
    var actual = _target.Resolve<ITinyIoc>();
    Assert.AreSame(_target, actual, "Test failed: instance
➥was not returned.");
}
```

The *arrange* happens in the TestInitialize method when the target is created. The *act* happens with the call to resolve the interface. The *assert* validates that what was expected (the instance itself) is what was actually returned from the class. If there is a mismatch, the test fails, and a specific message is provided. From this example, we can move to a slightly more complex one:

"*Given* a type is configured with the IoC helper, *when* the type is requested *then* an instance of the appropriate type should be returned."

This is really the true heart of what the IoC should do. The lightweight container that I wrote for this application allows you to pass in the type you are satisfying (usually an interface or abstract class, but it can be a regular class as well) and a function that returns a new instance of the type. By default, the IoC helper will hold onto the first type created. This is known as a shared instance. You can, however, request a new instance be returned, and this will execute the function again to generate a new, non-shared instance.

Here is the test that the mapping works—the base type is simply System. Object, and the mapped type is dynamic:

```
_target.Register<object>(tinyIoc => new {id = Guid.NewGuid()});
dynamic expected = _target.Resolve<object>();
Assert.IsInstanceOfType(expected.id, typeof (Guid),
    "Test failed: dynamic type was not returned.");
```

The *arrange* sets up the IoC helper to return a dynamic type when object is requested. The *act* calls the container to resolve the instance. Finally, the *assert* verifies that a dynamic type with a property called id of type Guid was indeed returned.

You can browse the remaining tests to see the check for subsequent calls returning the same instance (shared) while calls that request a new instance work the way they were expected to. These were fairly simple examples and tested a fairly self-contained component. What happens when you have components like BlogDataSource that rely on other components to work? This is where some good mocks and stubs can come into play.

Mocks and Stubs

In unit tests, you focus on one piece of code. The idea is to test the main responsibility for that code and not concern yourself with external components that may include other parts of the current application. In the case of the `BlogDataSource` class, you care about the logic it uses to read blogs, inspect the cache, and assemble a list of groups and items to expose to your application. It is not the responsibility of the class to understand how storage works or know how to create a dialog on the target platform. Those responsibilities are delegated to other components.

There is plenty of debate over the precise definition of what a mock or stub is, but I tend to follow the general guideline that a *stub* is simply a fake implementation of a class used as a placeholder so that another class that depends on it can run. A *mock* is slightly more. A *mock* is also a fake implementation (meaning it is created specifically for testing and is not part of the production system), but in addition to allowing another class to run, a mock may track some sort of state so it can be inspected as part of the *assert* portion of a test. This allows you to check that certain methods were called the right way to ensure the logic in the target component is behaving correctly.

There are several ways to create stubs and mocks. The first is by creating your own helper classes. You can see these in the **TestHelpers** folder of the **WintellogTest** project. The `DialogTest` class is an example of a mock because it emulates an asynchronous dialog but also records the message passed for later inspection. The full class is shown in Listing 9.1.

LISTING 9.1: Mocking the `IDialog` Interface

```
public class DialogTest : IDialog
{
    public string Message { get; set; }

    public Task ShowDialogAsync(string dialog)
    {
        return Task.Run(() =>
            {
                Message = dialog;
            });
    }
}
```

The mock does not involve any type of UI, so it can be easily run from within the test system. It stores the message passed so you can test that your dependent component used the dialog appropriately. The other classes provide similar functionality by either standing up fake data sources for the dependent classes to use or recording properties that can be inspected later on.

You can see the mocks being used in the BlogDataSourceTests class. There is one large test:

"Given new items exist, when the blog group is populated then the total and new items should reflect the correct totals."

The test will emulate existing items in cache and a new item from the Web. It also exposes a flaw in the current design of the BlogDataSource class. The class itself still tries to use the HttpClient to fetch a page from the test data, which will fail because the URL does not exist. Although the component handles this fine and the test checks that the dialog was called with an error message, ultimately the web call should be abstracted behind an interface as well. This will allow you to mock the call and control whether or not you want it to be successful and what it should return.

The first step defines a sample cached item, a sample blog, and provides the storage mock with a fake hash code to process:

```
var cached = new BlogItem {Id = Guid.NewGuid().ToString()};
var blog = new BlogGroup { Id = Guid.NewGuid().ToString() };
_storageUtilityTest.Items = new[] {"123"};
```

The mock for storage is then passed a function that will return the blog or cached item depending on what is requested:

```
_storageUtilityTest.Restore = (type, folder, hashCode) =>
        {
            if (type == typeof (BlogGroup))
            {
                return blog;
            }
            return cached;
        };
```

Finally, the simulated "new item" is added along with the blog to the mock for the syndication helper class that processes feeds:

```
var newItem = new BlogItem {Id = Guid.NewGuid().ToString()};
_syndicationHelperTest.BlogItems.Add(newItem);
_syndicationHelperTest.BlogGroups.Add(blog);
```

The first step is to load the groups. This is called, and the list is checked to ensure the appropriate number of blogs were processed:

```
await _target.LoadGroups();
Assert.AreEqual(1, _target.GroupList.Count,
    "Task failed: should have generated one group.");
```

Next, the groups are iterated to load individual posts. Note this step could easily just have involved a single call based on the single group because that is how the test was set up, but I preferred to write it this way to more closely match how it is implemented in the target applications:

```
foreach (var group in _target.GroupList)
{
    await _target.LoadAllItems(group);
}
```

Now the test has been *arranged* and *acted*, so it is time to *assert* the results. The item counts are checked, the lists are compared, and finally the dialog mock queried to see if it was called to show the error encountered when trying to download an empty URL. Just writing this exercise proved the value of testing—it turns out the previous versions of the application had a bug, and the total count wasn't being properly updated. The test found this out quickly, and I was able to apply the necessary fix. Listing 9.2 shows the final asserts.

LISTING 9.2: **Asserts for the BlogDataSource Test**

```
Assert.AreEqual(2, _target.GroupList[0].ItemCount,
    "Test failed: item count should have been 2.");
Assert.AreEqual(1, _target.GroupList[0].NewItemCount,
    "Test failed: new item count should have been 1.");
CollectionAssert.AreEquivalent(new[] {cached, newItem},
    _target.GroupList[0].Items,
    "Test failed: lists do not match.");
Assert.IsTrue(!string.IsNullOrEmpty(_dialogTest.Message),
    "Test failed: dialog was not called with error message.");
```

There are a number of available frameworks that make it easier to create stubs and mocks. Microsoft Fakes and MOQ are a few examples that allow you to dynamically configure a mock or stub to use in your unit tests. This keeps you from having to create complex mocks or stubs of your own, and you can tailor the behavior to fit the specific test you are writing. The examples in this chapter used the Windows Store unit test project. If you are using the PCL to share code for your project, you can just as easily create a traditional desktop unit test project and build your tests there as well using the testing and mocking frameworks of your choice.

Summary

In this chapter, you learned about the MVVM pattern and how it can benefit the applications you build. I showed you how to use the Portable Class Library (PCL) to create code that is shared between various platforms and built a WPF application using the same core classes that the Windows 8 apps use. You also learned some of the benefits of testing and several methods to write unit tests in Visual Studio 2012. For classes with dependencies, you learned how to mock the dependencies manually.

In the next chapter, you will learn how to prepare your application for the Windows Store. You will learn how to set pricing for your application and enable in-application purchases to activate features (referred to as "products") and how to test them. I'll show you how to use the Windows App Cert Kit to test your application for potential issues prior to submitting them to the store and show you a convenient way to create a distributable package for sharing code outside of the store.

10
Packaging and Deploying

WHEN YOUR APPLICATION IS COMPLETE, YOU MUST FIND A WAY TO GET it out to your potential customers. There are a number of options to do this, including a technique called side-loading that is explained later in this chapter. Many developers will want to leverage the partnership they can create with Microsoft through the Windows Store. The store is available both through a set of online pages that are created for your application and a local Windows 8 app called "Store" that is pre-installed on the Windows 8 machine.

The concept of an application store has been around for several years and was popularized through various smartphone platforms. The store provides a centralized location for managing, purchasing, downloading, and deploying applications. The concept of the centralized store ensures there is a single focal point for users to discover applications and provides enhanced security to the end user because the applications that are presented by the store have been screened and tested. You learn more about the screening process for applications submitted to the Windows Store later in this chapter.

The Windows Store

The Windows Store provides services for developers and companies to publish their applications (including Windows 8 apps as well as traditional desktop style applications) and users to discover, purchase, and install them. The store supplies the infrastructure for discovery of applications both through Windows 8 and online. It features significant reach, which means more potential profit for developers considering selling applications through the Windows Store. There are a variety of business models you can follow to monetize your application, including integration of ads through either Microsoft's owner advertising network or third-party services such as AdDuplex (www.adduplex.com).

Discovery

It is important to make it easy for potential customers to not only discover your application, but also be able to purchase and install it on their systems. Windows 8 and Internet Explorer 10 work together to provide the necessary features to create a seamless transition between the online experience and the locally installed Windows Store application. When you submit your application to the Windows Store, it will automatically be promoted both through the Windows Marketplace that you can view with a web browser and through the Windows Store application itself.

To see an example of how integration works, open Internet Explorer 10 from the **Start** screen (launch the Windows 8 version, not the desktop version). Navigate to the online Cut the Rope application at http://cuttherope.ie.

Swipe open the **Application Bar** and you'll notice the wrench icon has a plus (+) sign next to it indicating enhanced features. When you tap the wrench, you'll see a number of options including the ability to install the app for the website, as shown in Figure 10.1.

When you tap the option "Get app for this site," you are taken to the corresponding page in the Windows Store where you can easily download the application. When the application is installed, the enhanced menu in Internet Explorer will update to present you with the option to launch the local version of the application. Wondering how the site is able to integrate this way? Use the wrench to view the site on the desktop and view the source (right-click anywhere on the page and choose **View Source**). You'll find several HTML meta-tags, as shown in Listing 10.1.

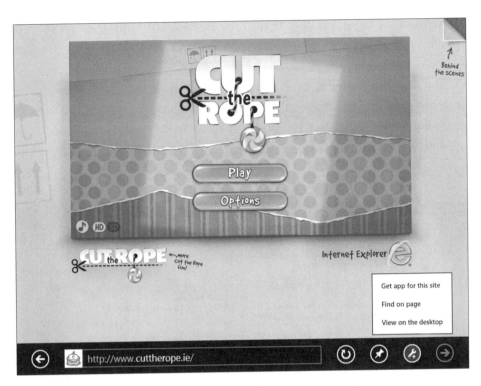

FIGURE 10.1: Example of integration between a website and the Windows Store

LISTING 10.1: HTML to Integrate the Cut the Rope Website with the Windows Store

```
<meta name="application-name" content="Cut the Rope" />
<meta name="msapplication-tooltip" content="Play Cut the Rope!
➥A mysterious package has arrived, and the little monster inside
➥Has only one request… CANDY!" />
<meta name="msapplication-navbutton-color" content="#659729" />
<meta name="msApplication-ID" content="App"/>
<meta name="msApplication-PackageFamilyName"
    content="ZeptoLabUKLimited.CutTheRope_sq9zxnwrk84pj"/>
<link rel="shortcut icon" href="/favicon.ico" type="image/x-icon" />
```

The tags provide context that Internet Explorer 10 can use to provide a link to the end user. The key tag is the msApplication-PackageFamilyName that can be found in the manifest for your application. Providing the name will allow Internet Explorer 10 to determine whether or not the application is currently installed and if not, pass the identifier to the Windows Store for you to download.

For another example of integration, open Bing from the Windows 8 Internet Explorer 10 and search for Rowi, the name of my favorite Twitter application. Scroll down. The listing for Rowi includes the store icon, overall reviews, and a link to download it, as you can see in Figure 10.2.

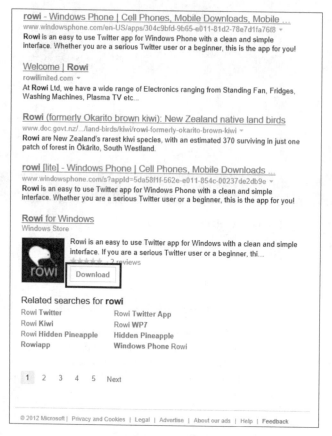

Source: Hidden Pineapple, LLC. Used with permission.

FIGURE 10.2: **The Bing listing for the Rowi Windows 8 Twitter application**

Clicking the link takes you right to the local Windows Store entry on your Windows 8 device. This is because the URL starts with ms-windows-store and provides a unique identifier that can be passed to the Windows

Store application to show the entry. That makes it easy to browse information about the application and tap the **Install** button to install it locally. The Windows Store page is shown in Figure 10.3.

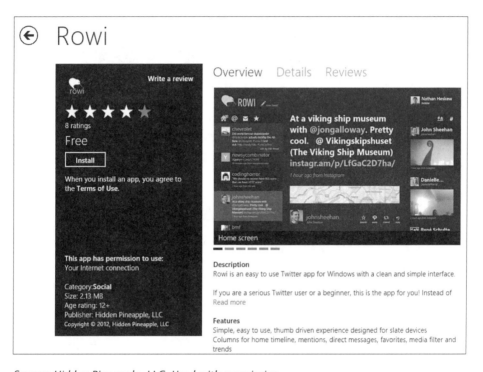

Source: Hidden Pineapple, LLC. Used with permission.

Figure 10.3: Windows Store page for Rowi

Of course, the easiest way to discover applications is to launch the Windows Store itself. The main page provides featured applications and allows you to browse various categories from highly rated applications to recently added ones. The Windows Store also uses semantic zoom to give you quick access to various categories, as shown in Figure 10.4.

You learn how to list your application in the Windows Store later in this chapter. First, you may be asking yourself, "Why would I want to list it through the store?" To answer that question, you should first learn more about the reach of the Windows Store and the cost to get involved.

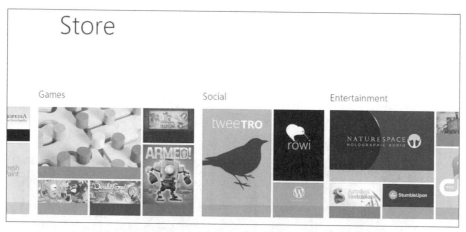

FIGURE 10.4: Semantic zoom in the Windows Store

Reach

According to Microsoft, the Windows Store enables developers to sell their apps in more than 200 markets, with currency support for 70 different markets, and localization options to 100 different markets. That's quite a reach—you can read the details of the announcement here at http://blogs.msdn.com/b/windowsstore/archive/2012/01/05/global-reach.aspx.

According to Apple, 365 million iOS devices were sold through March 2012.[1] Compare that to over 600 million Windows 7 licenses sold through June 2012.[2] This is a significant number of devices. Windows 8 will retain backwards compatibility with Windows 7 devices on all but the Windows RT (ARM) versions, so the potential market is extremely large for developers. A Windows 7 application targeting just 0.1% of the entire market would still reach 600,000 installs.

The Windows Store allows you to price your application anywhere between $1.49 to $999.99 for the application and any in-app purchases for specific features. You'll learn more about these options in the next section of this chapter. The revenue share model starts at 30% to Microsoft and 70% to the developer. When the developer reaches the $25,000 mark, the

---

[1] http://techcrunch.com/2012/06/11/apple-wwdc2012-iphones-ipads-sold/.

[2] http://www.engadget.com/2012/06/06/over-600-million-windows-7-licenses-sold/.

revenue to Microsoft decreases to 20%, and the developer keeps 80% of subsequent sales. Using the previous example of 600,000 installs, if you sold at the lowest tier ($1.49 per sale), you would generate over $700,000 in revenue *after* the split.

To earn money from your applications, you must invest in a developer account with Microsoft. This enables you to submit your applications to the Windows Store. There are currently two pricing models for submission: $49 for an individual developer registration and $99 for a business registration. Both allow you to submit multiple application entries to the Windows Store.

Business Models

There are a variety of business models you can choose from to sell your application. The first step is to determine the overall cost of the application. You can set a price for your application and specify whether or not a trial period exists. The trial can either be time limited (that is, the user receives full functionality but then must purchase after a period of time) or feature differentiated (certain features are disabled until the user makes a full purchase). An example selection is shown in Figure 10.5.

The API to convert from a trial to a full paid model is straightforward. First, visit the following link to download the SDK sample for trial conversions and in-app purchases—http://code.msdn.microsoft.com/windowsapps/Licensing-API-Sample-19712f1a.

In the sample, the user is in trial mode and can click a button to purchase the full product. The first step is to get the licensing information for the current application:

```
var licenseInformation = CurrentApp.LicenseInformation;
```

If the application is in trial mode, request the full application purchase. The Windows 8 store will take over and manage the rest of the transaction for you:

```
if (licenseInformation.IsTrial)
{
    await CurrentApp.RequestAppPurchaseAsync(false);
}
```

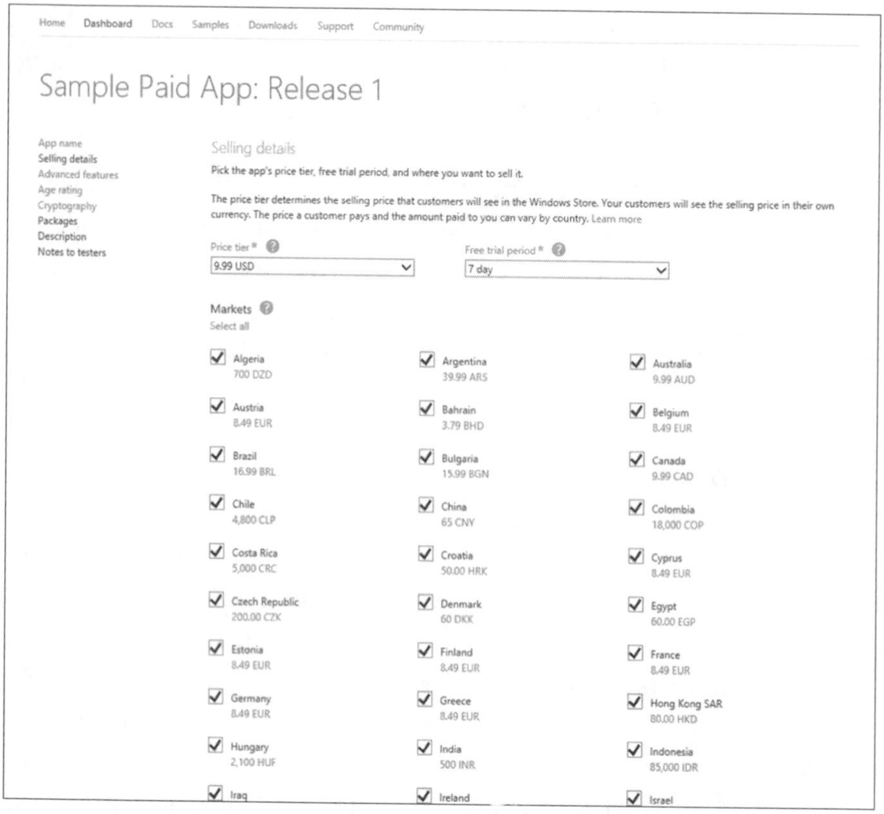

FIGURE 10.5: Choosing the initial pricing and trial model for your application

You will be unable to interact with the licensing server until your application is successfully submitted to the Windows Store. To test things like trial conversions and other in-app purchases, you can take advantage of a built-in simulator and replace all references to `CurrentApp` with `CurrentAppSimulator` (you'll see this in the downloaded example). The simulator allows you to load a special XML document to simulate the license state and purchase options for the application. Listing 10.2 shows the sample file for a trial-mode application that can be converted to a fully licensed version through a $4.99 purchase.

LISTING 10.2: Sample XML Document to Simulate Licensing Options

```xml
<?xml version="1.0" encoding="utf-16" ?>
<CurrentApp>
  <ListingInformation>
    <App>
      <AppId>2B14D306-D8F8-4066-A45B-0FB3464C67F2</AppId>
      <LinkUri>http://apps.microsoft.com/app/2B14D306-D8F8-4066
➥-A45B-0FB3464C67F2</LinkUri>
      <CurrentMarket>en-US</CurrentMarket>
      <AgeRating>3</AgeRating>
      <MarketData xml:lang="en-us">
        <Name>Trial management full license</Name>
        <Description>Sample app for demonstrating trial license
➥management</Description>
        <Price>4.99</Price>
        <CurrencySymbol>$</CurrencySymbol>
      </MarketData>
    </App>
  </ListingInformation>
  <LicenseInformation>
    <App>
      <IsActive>true</IsActive>
      <IsTrial>true</IsTrial>
      <ExpirationDate>2013-01-01T00:00:00.00Z</ExpirationDate>
    </App>
  </LicenseInformation>
</CurrentApp>
```

The file is loaded to the application simulator as shown in the **TrialMode. xaml.cs** file:

```
StorageFolder proxyDataFolder = await
    Package.Current.InstalledLocation.GetFolderAsync("data");
StorageFile proxyFile = await proxyDataFolder
    .GetFileAsync("trial-mode.xml");
await CurrentAppSimulator.ReloadSimulatorAsync(proxyFile);
```

You can reload the simulator as often as you like to test out different scenarios.

> **■. TIP**
>
> The simulator is an in-memory simulator. When you load a proxy file, you can make changes such as simulating in-app purchases. These changes are reflected in memory and do not change the licensing file itself. Anytime you restart the application, it will reset to the original state as indicated by the XML you provide. If you wish to test different scenarios, you can provide multiple files as shown in the SDK sample. The SDK sample loads the appropriate file for the scenario being tested and can reset the file by reloading the original. Be sure that when you are ready to make your final submission, you remove the test files and rename all references to the simulator.

The code also sets up an event handler to trigger any time the licensing information changes, such as through a simulated purchase (or real purchase when the application is in production):

```
licenseChangeHandler = new
    LicenseChangedEventHandler(TrialModeRefreshScenario);
CurrentAppSimulator.LicenseInformation.LicenseChanged +=
    licenseChangeHandler;
```

The simulator allows you to choose what the simulated result of a purchase is. For example, you can ask the simulator to indicate the purchase was not successful to test that your application appropriately manages the failure. Figure 10.6 shows the simulator. When the button is clicked to make a purchase, the Windows Store dialog pops up and provides a dropdown to choose the simulated result of the purchase.

The use of trial mode is very important. According to Microsoft's statistics, using the Windows Phone as an example, applications that provide a trial mode were downloaded 70 times more often than other applications. These trial downloads resulted in a 10% conversion rate and earned 10 times more revenue than applications that did not offer a trail mode. You can read the full blog post online at http://bit.ly/ekk9s5.

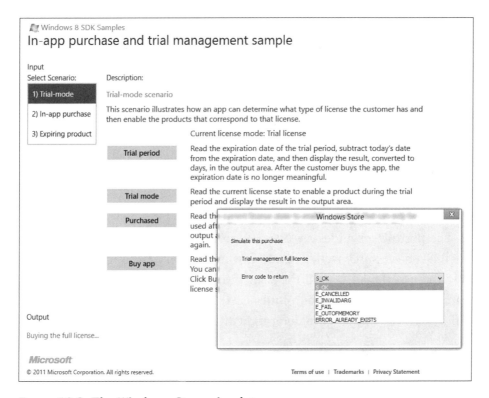

FIGURE 10.6: The Windows Store simulator

Your application can provide special "products" or features that are activated through separate purchases. This allows the user to customize his experience and purchase the features that make sense for his use of the application. For example, an image editor might provide a set of default formats out of the box but require an additional purchase to support more advanced formats more likely to be used by professional designers than hobbyists who are just "kicking the tires" of the tool. The products are set up online through your developer account but can be simulated with some simple XML using the proxy file:

```
<Product ProductId="product1">
  <MarketData xml:lang="en-us">
    <Name>Product 1</Name>
    <Price>1.99</Price>
    <CurrencySymbol>$</CurrencySymbol>
  </MarketData>
</Product>
```

Listing 10.3 demonstrates how to query the licensing information for production information to display to the user.

LISTING 10.3: **Querying for Product Information**

```
ListingInformation listing = await
    CurrentAppSimulator.LoadListingInformationAsync();
var product1 = listing.ProductListings["product1"];
var product2 = listing.ProductListings["product2"];
Product1SellMessage.Text = "You can buy " + product1.Name +
    " for: " + product1.FormattedPrice + ".";
Product2SellMessage.Text = "You can buy " + product2.Name +
    " for: " + product2.FormattedPrice + ".";
```

The product provides an IsActive property to inform you whether or not it has been purchased/activated. You can query that property and disable the functionality until the user purchases it. You request a product purchase the same way you requested the application purchase; the only difference is an added parameter indicating the specific product to buy:

```
await CurrentAppSimulator.RequestProductPurchaseAsync(
    "product1", false);
```

You may also provide an expiration date for products. This allows you to create recurring revenue by providing features that expire after a certain timeframe and require the user to make an additional purchase in order to continue using the feature. The product has an ExpirationDate property you can query to provide the user with information about when it will expire and which will prompt renewal.

Advertising

One option available to your applications is advertising. It is a common model to either support the application through ad revenue or provide a free version with advertising that can convert to a paid version that has no ads. Microsoft gives you two options for advertising in your Windows 8 applications. The first is through a third-party of your choice, and the second is with Microsoft's own service available online at www.windows-advertising.com.

To get started using Microsoft's advertising platform, first visit the link just listed and download the SDK. This provides you with the tools necessary to integrate advertising into your application. When you have the SDK, you can review the documentation for using it online at http://msdn.microsoft.com/en-us/library/hh506371(MSADS.10).aspx.

A full walkthrough for integrating an advertisement using XAML and C# can be found at http://msdn.microsoft.com/en-us/library/hh506359 (v=msads.10).aspx.

You also must sign up for an account to specify how to receive your revenue and track the success of your advertisements. If you choose to go with a third-party advertising provider such as AdDuplex, you will likely need to download their own SDK and follow their specific instructions for integrating advertisements into your applications. The Windows Store is flexible and allows applications that contain advertising from any provider as long as it meets the guidelines for store inclusion, which you learn about later in this chapter. The information about the application can be provided to the advertising provider to help tailor the ads shown, which will likely increase click-through rates and revenue.

Preparing Your App for the Store

There are several steps you must take to prepare your application for submission to the Windows Store. First, familiarize yourself with the app certification requirements that are listed online at http://msdn.microsoft.com/en-us/library/windows/apps/hh694083.aspx.

As of this writing, there are seven key things your application must do to be listed in the Windows Store. Six of them apply to Windows 8 apps and are summarized next.

Provide Value

The application should provide full value to the end user. There should not be any areas that are "under construction" or appear incomplete. If you offer a trial mode, that mode must reasonably resemble the full functionality either by providing full functionality for a limited time or by limiting certain features.

Offer More Than Just Ads or Websites

The application can contain advertising but must provide more value beyond the advertising—no application will be accepted that is nothing but a set of advertisements. You also cannot use the tiles, application title, description, notifications, or **Application Bar** to provide additional advertising. The experience for the application should take place within the application and not redirect the user to another location such as a website.

Behave Predictably

The application should adhere to the Windows 8 guidelines you've learned about throughout this book. This includes supporting the various orientations and modes (including snap). Your application should handle suspension and termination appropriately and not be coded in a way it is likely to freeze or stop responding if issues occur such as a loss of network connectivity. Application updates should increase or stabilize the application and never limit functionality in any way. It is important you only use WinRT APIs available to Windows 8 apps in your application.

Keep the Customer in Control

The application should adhere to all of the guidelines for notifying the user about use of features such as the Location API and enable them to disable notifications. If you collect personal information, you must provide a privacy policy that clearly states your intentions and complies with all relevant laws. If you intend to share personal information, you must allow the user to opt-in and provide explicit consent. Your application should not be malicious and should not instruct the user to perform actions that could harm his or her devices.

Cater to a Global Audience

Your application must not contain adult content. Metadata associated with the application should be appropriate to all age groups. The highest rating any content or metadata could potentially receive is Windows Store 12+ or content appropriate to consumers who are 12 years of age or older. Your application should also not contain content that advocates discrimination, hatred, or violence. It should not glamorize illegal activities nor contain content that would be considered obscene. You can read the full list of restrictions online at the URL provided earlier.

Be Easy to Identify and Understand

Your application should have a clear, unique title and an appropriate rating. You must provide technical support for your application. You also must be listed in at least one of the Windows Store's geographical markets and localize your application for all languages that it supports. Furthermore, when you provide updates to your application, you must fully describe the changes you are presenting. You must also provide at least one screen shot when submitting your application. You learn how in the next section.

The Process

The full process for application submission is outlined at http://msdn. microsoft.com/en-us/library/windows/apps/hh454036(v=vs.110).aspx.

The steps involved include the following:

1. Open a developer account. Remember you can purchase an indi-vidual account for $49 and a company account for $99.

2. Reserve the name for your app. You can reserve an app name for up to a year before you must submit the application. You can learn more about the guidelines for naming your app at http://msdn.microsoft. com/en-us/library/windows/apps/hh694077.aspx.

3. Acquire your developer license.

4. Edit the app manifest as appropriate.

5. Associate the app with the Windows Store. To do this, right-click the project in the Solution Explorer and then select **Store→Associate App with the Store**, as shown in Figure 10.7.

6. Copy screenshots. Simply right-click the project in the Solution Explorer and then select **Store→Capture Screenshots**. This will launch the simulator and allow you to take screenshots by clicking the camera icon in the toolbar on the right.

7. Create your App package. Right-click the project in the Solution Explorer and then select **Store→Create App Package**. You will be prompted to log into your developer account.

8. Upload your App package to the Windows Store online through your developer account.

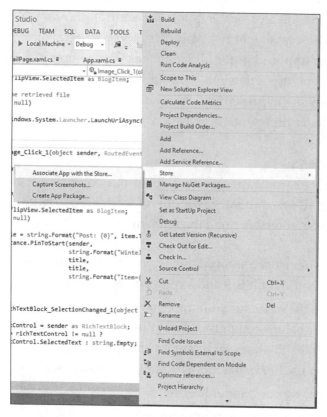

FIGURE 10.7: **Associating your app with the Windows Store**

The App Certification Kit

To help verify that your application is ready for submission to the Windows Store, you can run the Windows App Certification Kit. The Windows App Certification Kit will analyze your application and determine the following:

- Your manifest, including capabilities and declarations, is set up correctly.
- Your resources are all present and valid.
- Your app runs without crashing or hanging.
- Your app is built in Release and not Debug configuration.
- The files in your app use the correct encoding.
- Your app launches and suspends in the appropriate amount of time.
- Your app calls the appropriate WinRT APIs and doesn't attempt to call any unauthorized or non-Windows 8 APIs.
- Your app uses appropriate Windows security features.

To run the test, use the application search to find and launch "Windows App Cert Kit" or "appcertui." Choose the option to **Validate Windows Store App**, as shown in Figure 10.8 (you can also use this to validate other application types including desktop-style applications).

FIGURE 10.8: Associating your app with the Windows Store

When you select the option, the dialog will spin for a few minutes while it gathers system information and compiles a list of installed Windows 8 apps. You can select one or more applications to test. Figure 10.9 shows selection of the Wintellog MVVM application from Chapter 9.

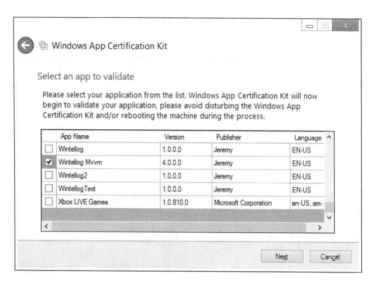

FIGURE 10.9: Choosing the application to test

Click the **Next** button, and the test will begin. It will take several minutes to run depending on your application and the device you are running it on. It is important that you allow it to run and not attempt to interact with the application. You will see it start and restart your app several times during testing. Simply allow it to run and wait for the final results.

When the test completes, you will be prompted for a location to save the results as an XML file. The test will also generate a local HTML file with the results. You can click a link at the end to view the results. If any tests did not pass, the results will provide the steps you need to take to fix the problem. You should ensure all checks pass before attempting to submit your application to the store. Figure 10.10 shows the results of running the test against the Wintellog MVVM application from Chapter 9.

You can learn more about the Windows App Certification Kit online at http://msdn.microsoft.com/en-us/library/windows/apps/hh694081. aspx.

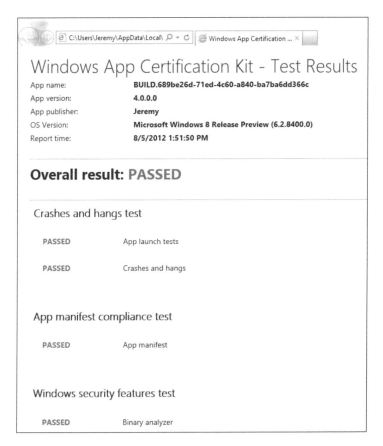

FIGURE 10.10: The Windows App Certification Kit test results

The article includes links to the individual tests that are run. The articles for each test explain what is tested and provide guidance for addressing tests that fail.

What to Expect

The developer center will provide you with an overview of the full submission process, along with an estimated time to receive a decision. You will be informed of every step within the process. Figure 10.11 shows an example dashboard that indicates where the app is in the certification process and what steps remain.

FIGURE 10.11: **The submission process**

When your application is approved, you will have access to additional dashboards that provide information about purchases and installations. You will be able to slice-and-dice information by region, age group, and other demographics to gain insights into how your app is being adopted. You will also be able to see your ratings and of course track revenue that is generated. Figure 10.12 shows an example dashboard.

Sometimes you may need to distribute your application without going through the Windows Store. This can happen when you have an early version of the application that you want to share with others for testing or beta use or when you are developing a Line of Business application for use within the company intranet. Fortunately there is a solution for this scenario called side-loading that allows you to create a package that you can distribute to other devices to install your package.

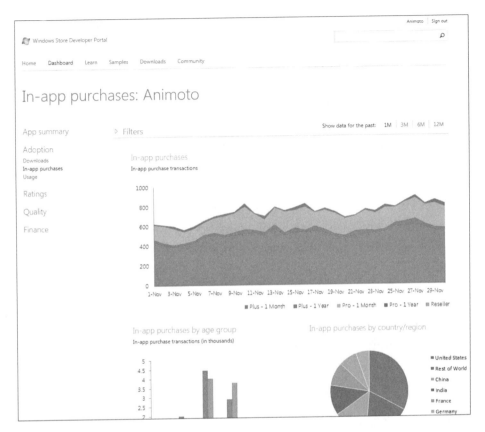

FIGURE 10.12: Windows Store dashboard for active apps

Side-Loading

You can add applications using Windows PowerShell. Although applications distributed in this fashion do not have to be installed or certified from within the Windows Store, they must be signed with a trusted certificate. They can only be installed on machines that trust the signing certificate.

You can learn more about managing certificates here:
http://msdn.microsoft.com/en-us/library/aa376553(v=vs.85).aspx

Learn about signing Windows 8 apps here:
http://msdn.microsoft.com/en-us/library/aa387764(v=vs.85).aspx

Finally, learn more about general side-loading guidelines here:
http://technet.microsoft.com/en-us/library/hh852635.aspx

The first step to side-loading your application is to generate a package that you can distribute. This is done by right-clicking the project in Solution Explorer and choosing the **Store→Create App Package** option. When the initial dialog appears to ask whether you wish to build a package to upload to the Windows Store, select the option **No** and click the **Next** button.

The next dialog shown in Figure 10.13 asks you to specify the location for the install, the version of the package, and how you wish to build the package (the default **Neutral** build will target all platforms). You can choose whether or not to include public symbol files. Including these will help users analyze any app crashes that may occur, but they can also expose proprietary information about your application that you may not want to include.

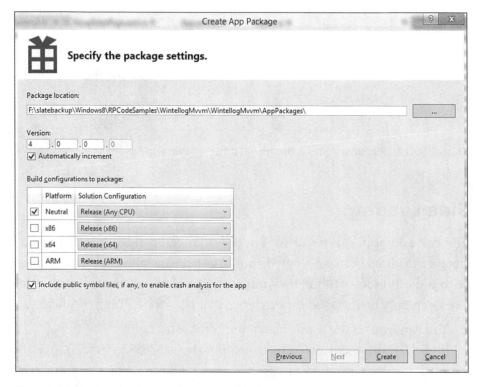

FIGURE 10.13: Packaging options for side-loading

Finally, click the **Create** button to create the package. The final dialog will give you a link to the location of the package and the option to launch the Windows App Certification Kit. Click or tap the file location and you will see a file and a folder. The easiest way to package these for distribution is to highlight both and choose **Send To→Compressed (zipped) folder**. That will provide you with a single file you can distribute. The target user will unzip the package on her machine.

To install the package on the target device, you must navigate into the folder and right-click the PowerShell script named **Add-AppDevPackage. ps1**. Chose the option **Run with PowerShell** (PowerShell is automatically distributed on every Windows 8 machine). The script will walk you through all necessary steps including updating any policies on the machine and installing the appropriate certificates. When these steps are complete, the application will be installed. You can see the results of an example installation session in Figure 10.14.

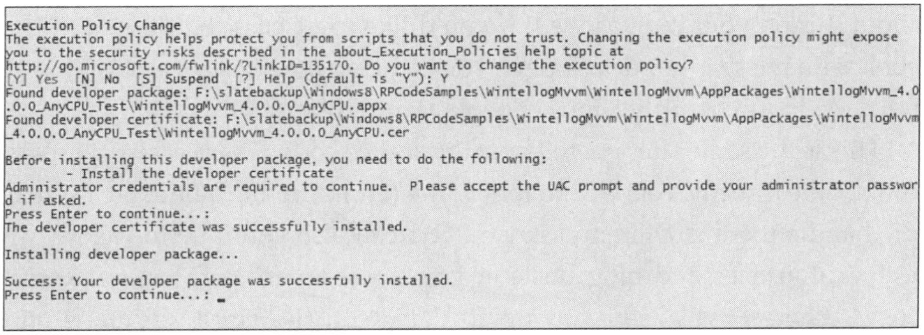

```
Execution Policy Change
The execution policy helps protect you from scripts that you do not trust. Changing the execution policy might expose
you to the security risks described in the about_Execution_Policies help topic at
http://go.microsoft.com/fwlink/?LinkID=135170. Do you want to change the execution policy?
[Y] Yes  [N] No  [S] Suspend  [?] Help (default is "Y"): Y
Found developer package: F:\slatebackup\windows8\RPCodeSamples\WintellogMvvm\WintellogMvvm\AppPackages\WintellogMvvm_4.0
.0.0_AnyCPU_Test\WintellogMvvm_4.0.0.0_AnyCPU.appx
Found developer certificate: F:\slatebackup\windows8\RPCodeSamples\WintellogMvvm\WintellogMvvm\AppPackages\WintellogMvvm
_4.0.0.0_AnyCPU_Test\WintellogMvvm_4.0.0.0_AnyCPU.cer

Before installing this developer package, you need to do the following:
            - Install the developer certificate
Administrator credentials are required to continue.  Please accept the UAC prompt and provide your administrator passwor
d if asked.
Press Enter to continue...:
The developer certificate was successfully installed.

Installing developer package...

Success: Your developer package was successfully installed.
Press Enter to continue...:
```

FIGURE 10.14: The result of running the installation PowerShell script

Using this method, you can deploy the package to multiple target machines without having to involve the Windows Store.

Summary

In this chapter, you learned about the Windows Store and various features it provides, including various models for selling your application and enabling in-app purchases for specific features. I shared the process for submitting an application to the Windows Store, including how to use the Windows App Certification Kit to test your application prior to submission. You also learned how to create a special package to side-load your application on target devices without going through the Windows Store.

I hope you have enjoyed this book! My intention was to provide you with all of the tools and information needed for you to build your application and submit it for sale in the Windows Store. Of course, the easy part is knowing the various parts that make up the app. The difficult part will be coming up with the idea for your application. I wish you every success with whatever you decide to build for the Windows 8 platform.

I welcome your comments and feedback. If you liked this book, I would ask that you please take some time to visit the Amazon.com website and leave your comments at http://bit.ly/win8design.

This will be a tremendous help when other developers are searching online for a solution because they can read honest reviews from their peers to help decide which book they are willing to invest in. Feel free to write about this on your blog as well! If you'd like to discuss the content of the book with me or other developers, you can visit the book forums online at http://windows8applications.codeplex.com/discussions.

This is the same site where I host the source code. There is also a link to contact me directly. Feel free to follow me (and drop me a line) on Twitter; my handle there is @JeremyLikness. You can also continue to follow my technical articles and blog posts at http://csharperimage.jeremylikness. com/ where I will keep you up to date with the latest additions and updates as well as any future book projects.

Thank you!

Index

A

ABI (Application Binary Interface), 25
About page, 145–147
accelerometer, 149
accessing and saving data, 183–189
  async keyword, 191–194
  await keyword, 191–193
  embedded resources, 197–198
  FileIO class, 195–196
  lambda expressions, 194
  PathIO class, 195–196
  threading, 189–191
activation, 161–163
actual target, 133
advertising, 328–329
animations, discrete, 83
application bar, 136–142
Application Data API, 172–176
application files, 172

application lifecycle, 157–160
  activation, 161–163
  Application Data API, 172–176
  connected, applications
    suspended/terminated
    remaining , 176–177
  custom splash screen, 177–178
  navigation, 168–171
  resume, 167–168
  suspension, 163–166
  termination, 166
application manifest, 43
  Application UI section, 43
  Capabilities section, 44
  Declaration section, 44
  Packaging section, 45
application settings, 172, 181–183
Application UI section of
  application manifest, 43

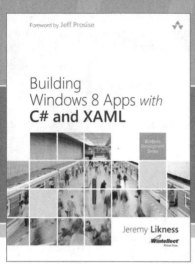

Foreword by Jeff Prosise

Building Windows 8 Apps *with* C# and XAML

Jeremy **Likness**

FREE
Online Edition

Safari Books Online

Your purchase of *Building Windows 8 Apps with C# and XAML* includes access to a free online edition for 45 days through the **Safari Books Online** subscription service. Nearly every Addison-Wesley Professional book is available online through **Safari Books Online**, along with thousands of books and videos from publishers such as Cisco Press, Exam Cram, IBM Press, O'Reilly Media, Prentice Hall, Que, Sams, and VMware Press.

Safari Books Online is a digital library providing searchable, on-demand access to thousands of technology, digital media, and professional development books and videos from leading publishers. With one monthly or yearly subscription price, you get unlimited access to learning tools and information on topics including mobile app and software development, tips and tricks on using your favorite gadgets, networking, project management, graphic design, and much more.

Activate your FREE Online Edition at
informit.com/safarifree

STEP 1:   Enter the coupon code: UYTQWBI.

STEP 2:   New Safari users, complete the brief registration form.
Safari subscribers, just log in.

If you have difficulty registering on Safari or accessing the online edition,
please e-mail customer-service@safaribooksonline.com